THE
DOUBT
LOOP

ADAM CRAWSHAW

TURNED SELF-DOUBT INTO A $1.4 BILLION EXIT

THE DOUBT LOOP

TURNING FOUNDER DOUBT INTO A COMPETITIVE ADVANTAGE

FIRST EDITION

THE DOUBT LOOP
Turning Founder Doubt into a Competitive Advantage

ISBN 978-1-5445-5112-8 *Hardcover*
    978-1-5445-5111-1 *Paperback*
    978-1-5445-5113-5 *Ebook*

This book is for the people who carried me
when I couldn't carry myself.

To my wife, who kept believing there was light
at the end of a tunnel I kept digging deeper—
and chose to walk beside me anyway.

To my mom, whose daily affirmations outshouted the
self-doubt voice long before I learned to wrestle it.

To my dad, who drilled into me that
reputations can vanish but education is forever,
so to always keep learning about whatever
I'm working on and about myself.

To Sandeep, who reminds me daily that
winning isn't measured only in business but in
the kind of husband, father, and friend you
show up as after the laptop shuts.

To my friends, who turned my vacant stares into the
running joke "The Mona Lisa Smile" instead of staging
an intervention—humor as unconditional love.

These pages are my overdue explanation
of what was happening inside my head, and a
thank-you note for never turning away.

CONTENTS

WHO THIS BOOK IS FOR

CURRENT AND FUTURE STARTUP FOUNDERS WHO DON'T HAVE IT ALL FIGURED OUT AND SECOND GUESS THEMSELVES

CURRENT AND FUTURE STARTUP FOUNDERS WHO HAVE IT ALL FIGURED OUT AND DON'T SECOND GUESS THEMSELVES

INTRODUCTION

I WAS FIVE the first time I watched a human fly.

It happened in Peru, Indiana—once the "Circus Capital of the World."[1] A pair of teenage acrobats climbed a rope ladder bolted to a metal pole, then stepped onto a wire stretched above the county-fair bleachers. They didn't wobble. They didn't even blink. They just…went.

Everyone craned their necks. I gripped the splintered bench, convinced someone was about to swan-dive into the popcorn machine. Inside that one heartbeat lived the entire paradox of self-doubt: terror you'll fall, followed by the thrilling suspicion… *but maybe I won't.*

Fast-forward six years.

Basketball had replaced my trapeze dreams. Every afternoon I rehearsed jump shots—left elbow in, right hand follow-through—until the cicadas quit for the night. By fall, I believed I could beat Reggie Miller in a game of P-I-G (basketball drill). The season opener said otherwise. Two minutes in, I racked five turnovers: errant passes, dribbles off my shoes, one panicked heave to nobody at all. The coach yanked me. *See? They've unmasked you,* the self-doubt hissed.

TEN YEARS OF BLUR

From my first day of college through most of my twenties, life compressed into a heat-warped reel of fluorescent lights and blinking spreadsheets. My self-doubt demanded horsepower, so I poured in hours no one should attempt.

I applied to exactly one school: Indiana University. Ivy-League packets never left my desk; my self-doubt had already vetoed them. I camped in the library, finished "group" projects alone, and chased a flawless 4.00. I graduated with a 3.96, undone by an A– in History of the Mafia. *Fuhgeddaboudit?* More like *Perseverate-on-it.*

Diploma still warm, I felt like a passenger randomly bumped to first class—one minute juggling shoes at TSA, the next seated beside corporate royalty.

First with Joe Perella,[2] the dealmaker who turned hostile take-overs into Wall Street's blood sport by interrogating every footnote and decimal. During an all-nighter, I brewed coffee, hustled back to my desk, and took a swig—of milk; the pot sat forgotten while I hit "Print" at 3:17 a.m. Next morning, Joe flipped through the deck, paused, and deadpanned, "Perilla?" *Nice work,* my self-doubt snickered. *You just put a hit on your credibility.*

Then with David Bonderman,[3] the contrarian who hauled Continental Airlines out of bankruptcy and believed money was hidden everywhere. My mandate was just as wide. One week I modeled freight yields for an African railroad; the next, I priced Turkish-betting kiosks, and even estimated stall fees at a Denver flea market. *They'll trust you only if you flip every stone on the planet,* the self-doubt reminded.

And finally with Michael Moritz,[4] the former *Time* reporter turned Sequoia (famous venture capital firm) legend who drilled a journalist's habit: Go panoramic, then zoom until you hit bed-rock. I dissected Chinese super apps, reverse-engineered Indian ed-tech cohorts, and, while single in my mid-twenties, built an oddly passionate thesis on funeral home rollups. *They'll respect you only if you can underwrite life, death, and everything in between,* the self-doubt decreed.

Ten years in other people's war rooms taught me work ethics, precision, breadth, and depth. The résumé looked airtight, yet the self-doubt voice still scoffed, *Nice apprenticeship, kid—now build something of your own.*

THE UNICORN THAT DIDN'T CURE

I first met Sandeep Kella in 2017, and the chemistry was instant. Every meetup flowed, there was no hidden agenda, and I always woke up the next morning more energized than I'd felt in years. Sandeep had already built and sold a successful technology company,[5] so he carried real scar tissue—along with a habit of questioning every bit of conventional wisdom and a disarming empathy that put people at ease. I knew we'd end up building something together.

That "something" was Assembly, which we launched in 2018, betting that the real gold rush lay in "picks and shovels" software vendors powering Amazon, Shopify, and Walmart first-party and third-party sellers. We were right, and we were right *fast*. In under three years, we sold half the company for $1.4 billion.[6]

Deal day looked nothing like the movies. I expected champagne to taste like arrival.

It tasted like battery acid.

We celebrated with a seafood tower, then tacos at the strip-mall joint where Assembly had been sketched on a napkin. For one sunset, I thought, *Finally—hill climbed.* At sunrise, the self-doubt returned: *Lucky timing. COVID-19 bump. Software-as-a-service (SaaS) multiples did the heavy lifting.*

So we kept lifting—tripling revenue, serving millions of customers, achieving record levels of profitability—and still the feeling perched on my shoulder.

That's when it clicked: The self-doubt voice isn't a phase you out-earn; it's a furnace you either feed or get scorched by. Smother it, and it fills the room with smoke. Pipe it into the engine, and it drives the machine.

FROM PANIC TO PROPELLANT

Think of adrenaline: The same molecule fuels a panic attack *or* a personal-best sprint. Chemistry doesn't change; context and choreography do. Self-doubt thoughts obey the same physics. Untamed, they shred confidence. Trained, they sharpen perception, demand preparation, and repel the Ego that sinks companies faster than anything else.

I still detour through airport convenience stores like a kid in a toy shop, gawking at the self-help shelf where every spine promises a one-word miracle—Do Less, Do More, Spend Less, Spend More, Why, What, Who, F*ck, Sh#t, Sleep, Don't Sleep, Eat, Rave, Repeat—as if success hides behind whichever verb you adopt today.

This book isn't a one-word solve; it's a field guide to the self-doubt hurdles you will hit, and to the frameworks, tools, and mindset rewires that turn each jolt of doubt into forward thrust. I've talked with thousands of entrepreneurs, managed hundreds of employees, and made more mistakes than any keynote bio admits. What follows isn't a victory lap—it's the playbook I wish someone had handed me before fear made me hang up my basketball shoes, before anxiety knotted my stomach every workday morning, and before impatience pushed me to chase the next milestone instead of savoring the one in front of me.

THE DOUBT LOOP

The Doubt Loop is a pocket-sized cycle for turning the gut-punch of self-doubt into forward motion. It starts with a pause: Notice the moment your stomach knots. Next, name the hidden fear, and say it out loud: I'll miss the wave, I'll waste their money, I'll flop on stage. Finally, convert the fear into a concrete action: a metric to track, an experiment to run, or a conversation to schedule this week. Loop through those three moves whenever your self-doubt pipes up, and doubt becomes fuel instead of friction.

Early chapters push doubt toward **curiosity**. "Catch the Wave" makes you interrogate timing; "Choose Your Fuel" forces a motive check; "Question Yourself" challenges identity. Each section invites the question "What don't I know yet?" before you waste your time on the wrong thing.

Mid-book, the loop shifts doubt into **discipline**. "Throw Spaghetti" narrows anxiety to testable experiments, "Feel the Burn" turns financial jitters into dashboards, and "Pick Your Poison" channels funding fear into deliberate capital choices. Throughout, self-doubt powers structure not paralysis.

Later, when wins stack up, the loop redirects doubt toward **durability**. "Build a Bear" uses humility to prevent cultural rot, "Don't Trust Data" keep data honest when success tempts shortcuts, and "Smell the Roses" installs Ego checks before confidence curdles into hubris.

Keep this loop handy. Each time the self-doubt voice flares, notice, name, convert, and then flip to the chapter built to turn that specific fear into progress.

LOOK BEFORE YOU LEAP

CHOOSE YOUR FUEL

DOUBT VOICE: Did I just torch a good career for a pipe dream?

ATLAS CAFÉ, SWEATING cold brew, 48 percent battery.

Forty-eight hours earlier, I'd handed in my Sequoia badge. Forty-eight minutes in, I faced a harsh reality. I thought being at a coffee shop starting a new company was supposed to be a euphoric moment where your "aha" moment came to life. Reality was quite different: no outlets, perpetually tempted to people watch, and somehow promoted by fellow coffee patrons to the "Can you watch my stuff while I go to the restroom?" guy. Oh, and an empty pitch deck.

"WHY THE F*CK AM I DOING THIS?"

That is the first hidden fear gate every founder walks through. That moment—whether it's at a coffee shop, on your couch, or reading an email from your boss: "pls fix. thx"—will come sooner or later. The answer to this question has more downstream effects than you'll realize. Get the motive wrong, and you'll create a life you secretly hate.

THE FOUR DOMINANT MOTIVES

We can strip most origin stories down to four mutually exclusive, basic human desires: Wealth, Control, Passion, and Ego. No route is wrong. No route is right. But choosing one is the first step when planning your future.

THE MOTIVE MATRIX

MOTIVE	DOMINANT HUNGER	HIDDEN COST
WEALTH	Build outsized financial freedom	More is never enough cycle
CONTROL	Call every shot, own the timetable	Unable to unplug, solo-founder stress
PASSION	Work on a problem you'd chase for free	Tainting your love if the idea goes sideways
EGO	Prove doubters or incumbents wrong	Tunnel vision; grudge can outlive the goal

Don't say, "I choose all of them." I once tried to convince myself there was a tidy ikigai (the tidy Venn-diagram sweet spot—work you love, are good at, the world needs, and that you will be paid for) overlap where my deepest Passion, my sharpest skill, and a nine-figure exit would live in perfect harmony. Building a company is more buffet line than bull's-eye—you pile one motive on the plate, another slides off, and a third gets left behind.

Why? Because each motive taxes the others. Chase Wealth and you'll court investors who dilute Control. Guard Control and you may sacrifice the rocket fuel that maximizes Wealth. Follow Passion and cash flow behaves like a moody teenager. Feed Ego and you risk burning bridges you'll need for anything else.

A startup is already juggling market shifts, team dynamics, product ups and downs, and consistent cash needs. Letting four primal hungers wrestle for the steering wheel is like handing car keys to quadruplets mid-food-fight: the outcome is going to be messy. One motive must drive you forward; the rest can ride shotgun, occasionally yelling directions but never grabbing the wheel.

SO WHAT'S YOUR MOTIVE?

Before we sprint into playbooks, it helps to know which engine is already revving under your hood. The following microquiz is designed to corner you into one dominant answer—no hedging, no "all of the above." Read each prompt, circle the first option that feels true, and then count which letter shows up most often.

1. Your idea just landed funding. You envision…
   a. Paying off your mortgage
   b. How it impacts your daily schedule
   c. Building version one of your product ASAP
   d. What the headline is going to say
2. Imagine failure. The nightmare headline reads…
   a. Sold for pennies on the dollar
   b. Founder forced out by the board
   c. Lost interest, customers are still in pain
   d. Rival startup wins the market
3. You get one free hour a day. You'd rather…
   a. Model exit scenarios and look at homes

    b. Rewrite the product launch blog yourself

    c. Talk to customers with no set agenda

    d. Stalk a competitor's release notes

4. Losing ownership percentage in your company feels like…

    a. Somebody is stealing money from you

    b. Somebody is stealing the steering wheel

    c. Oxygen, if it grows the mission

    d. Selling ammo to the enemy

5. Five years from now, you want friends to say…

    a. They never have to work again

    b. They're still calling every shot

    c. We've built something that matters

    d. We proved everyone wrong

Mostly (a)? Wealth. Mostly (b)? Control. Mostly (c)? Passion. Mostly (d)? Ego. If you've got multiple motives with two, then see what resonates most in the upcoming pages.

With your motive circled, lock onto the J-curve[7]: your company's flight path. Point A is ignition: the day you quit, incorporate, and hit "launch." Point B is the trough: every dollar and hour you pour in before the climb begins. Point C marks the breakeven point, when revenue finally repays the sacrifice. Point D is the payoff: the profit or exit check that lands in your account. Which point keeps you up at night?

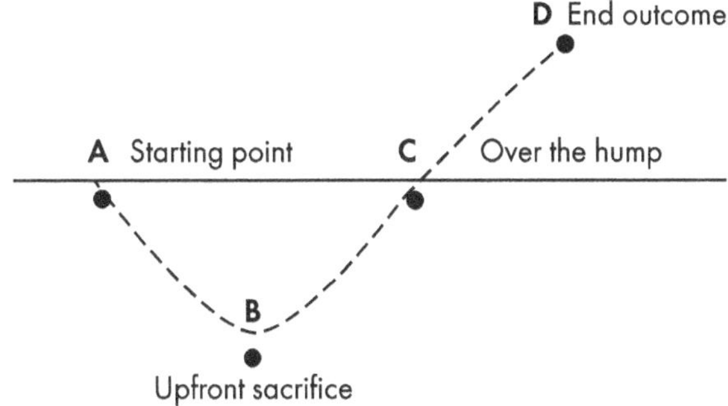

In the fantasy version of the J-curve, your up-front sacrifice is tiny (A ➜ billion is a blip), breakeven happens fast (A ➜ C is a sprint), and the eventual payout soars without limit (D rockets sky high). Real life won't give you that trifecta. Pick the one dimension that matters most right now and aim every decision at improving it.

SHOW ME THE MONEY

Two friends duck into a corner booth for Friday-night beers. Your friend asks, "How was the week?" Before the head even settles on your pint, regardless of what you say, your mind will immediately gravitate to numbers. "Another 10 percent growth gets us to $1 million in revenue."

When Wealth is your motive, every update instantly converts into the same bottom-line question: *Does this move me closer or further away from the bank account I want?*

The only metric that truly counts is Point D—the after-tax payoff you pocket. That single figure converts years of sacrifice, dilution, and salary trade-offs into the freedom number. Everything else along the path is just an investment or noise; if a decision doesn't enlarge that final check, it's reducing it.

Name your freedom number, set a clear deadline, and iterate on proven strategies that will get you closer to that number in a way that works for you.

First, pin down your number—the after-tax cash that makes work optional. Remember, startup Wealth is back-loaded. While you wait for that payday, you'll live on an average founder salary of much less than $150,000[8]—often lower than you'd earn at a regular company—and that figure ignores every personal dollar you pour in.

Next, set your time horizon. Exits routinely stretch seven to ten years, and 75 percent of startups never get there at all.[9] "Shots on goal" (keep launching ideas; the more kicks you take, the better the odds that one will score) is the survival mantra: If one idea stalls, fire up the next idea, so your Wealth motive stays alive. Note the maximum lean years you can stomach. If progress slips beyond that, pivot or reload, because your clock, not your Ego, should dictate when to jump ship.

While there are millions of ways to make millions of dollars, below are proven strategies that well-known founders have used to bend the J-curve in their favor:

→ *The Manifester* (Sara Blakely, SPANX) wrote "$10 million by 40" on a Post-it, rejected every investor, bootstrapped on her own, grew SPANX on profits, and turned a single product into a billion-dollar enterprise.

→ *The Lightning Exiter* (Michael Dubin, Dollar Shave Club) raised two skinny rounds, torched the cash on viral advertising, and worked backward from the exit, engineering a sale to Unilever just four years after starting the company.

→ *The Hungry Hoarder* (Ben Chestnut, Mailchimp) hoarded everything—equity, profits, decisions, even his own pay (capped his salary at $50,000)— plowing cash back into the business until Intuit's $12 billion buyout.

→ *The Clone-and-Flip Crew* (Samwer brothers) re-created proven US internet business models in underserved regions, scaled quickly, and then sold each venture to strategic buyers within twenty-four months before starting the next one.

→ *The Permanent-Capital Collector* (Andrew Wilkinson, Tiny) buys boring, profitable software businesses at bargain purchase prices, uses cash flow to buy more, creating the "Berkshire Hathaway of startup investing."

MY SANDBOX, MY RULES

Two friends claim their usual booth for Friday-night beers. Your friend opens with the ritual, "How was the week?" and you barely touch your glass before blurting the only update that matters to you: "…at least I'm not answering to anyone."

When Control is your fuel, conversations tilt toward levers and vetoes, not valuations; the winner is simply the one who pushes the launch button.

On the J-curve, the only thing that counts is the real estate you surrender below the line: how deep the dip goes at Point B and how long it drags before you clear Point C. Every outside dollar poured in at B widens that trough and hands levers to someone else, but nights, weekends, and grit don't cost equity. The faster you climb into self-funded territory, the sooner every decision belongs solely to you.

Start by spelling out exactly how much sway you refuse to surrender, draw the red lines that guard it, and then craft every financing, hiring, and governance choice to keep those levers firmly in your grasp.

First, define what Control means to you. Explicit Control is math—owning the majority of voting shares, installing a dual-class stock (a stock structure that gives founders extra voting power), keeping your board seats. Lose the numbers and you've legally ceded the throne. Implicit Control is the daily reality: who approves budgets, who can overrule product changes, and how freely you set your calendar. You can hold a technical majority on paper yet still feel like an employee if these softer levers slip.

Keep this data point in mind: By the time most startups reach *Series C*, founding teams typically own only *15–25 percent* of the company.[10] Dilution isn't personal—it's math. Investors tighten their grip with every round, and unless you articulate early what you need to feel aligned, you'll wake up one day holding far less than you expected.

Finally, accept the trade-offs. Maximizing Control often means slower growth, smaller rounds, or a narrower product scope. That's not a bug. It's the cost of keeping the launch button under your thumb. If the vision can't survive on founder-friendly capital or patient profits, either widen the circle of trust or choose a different motive, because dilution without clarity will gut the company.

You're in good company. Most founders crave Control. Sometimes it's hard equity; other times, it's as simple as who gets to have the final say. Here are several examples.

> → *The Platform Gatekeeper* (Jeff Bezos, Amazon) forced teams to pitch major ideas with six-page memos and guarded the customer experience obsessively. Even as

Amazon scaled, one rule held: customer obsession first, everything else second.

→ *The Human Checkmate* (Mark Zuckerberg, Meta) issued super-voting shares on day one and still outvotes Wall Street by 10x. Even as a trillion-dollar company, Mark can still hypothetically rename Meta whenever he wants.

→ *The Steward Owner* (Ingvar Kamprad, IKEA) placed voting shares in a nonprofit foundation, barring any future sale or strategy pivot not aligned with his mission, including keeping Swedish meatballs on the menu on the way out.

→ *The Audience Protector* (Jimmy Donaldson, MrBeast) self-funds content, picks sponsors selectively, and controls every brand extension from chocolates to burgers; by owning distribution, he answers to viewers, not networks.

→ *The Megalomanic Micromanager* (Elon Musk, Tesla) broadcasts audacious "Master Plan" milestones; impossible deadlines plus personal code reviews let him set the tempo and makes sure nothing drifts off course to his vision.

CAFFEINATED BY PURPOSE

Back to the booth. "How was the week?" your friend asks.

You don't mention valuation or board politics. You gush about finally nailing the feature that made an early user cry happy tears and how you impacted their life. When Passion is your fuel, the only key performance indicator (KPI) that matters is whether tomorrow's work still lights up you and the customer you are serving.

When Passion is the engine, the J-curve is just a line you're willing to surf for as long as it takes. Point A sparks the journey, Point B can plunge into sleepless years and maxed credit cards, Point C may arrive late—or never—but none of it rattles you. The only pulse check is whether every step, sacrifice, and detour keeps nudging the product closer to the end vision etched in your head. Outcome, timelines, even personal payouts are secondary fuel; progress toward the mission is the only metric that registers.

Start by pinning down what Passion means to you. Is it solving a pain you know personally, serving a community you love, or chasing aesthetic perfection? Distill it into one sentence that still excites you at 2:00 a.m. If it takes a paragraph to explain, you're chasing a trend, not a calling.

Next, sanity-check the feeling. Many early-stage founders say passion is their driving force, yet plenty still struggle to articulate their mission in a single clear sentence. Ask yourself: "Would I still do this with zero applause, no funding, and an invisible job title?" If that answer wavers, call it curiosity and keep your day job.

Then face the downside. Passion can sour. Picture the chef who opens a dream restaurant, grinds through eighteen-hour days, shutters after two brutal years, and can't enjoy dining out without tasting failure in every bite. Decide whether you're willing to risk turning love into regret.

Passion is the motive most founders list on slide one, and the first they abandon when the grind sets in; only a handful stay lit for the long haul. Here are a few who did:

→ *The Mission Monk* (Yvon Chouinard, Patagonia) built
  gear he wanted to climb in, committed 1 percent of sales

to the planet, then handed ownership to a purpose trust, which invests every dollar into fighting climate change.

→ *The Open-Source Purist* (Linus Torvalds, Linux) began building Linux as a personal project, sharing the code freely and rallying a global developer community long before commercial backing. He chased elegance and performance—and that obsession became the backbone of modern computing.

→ *The Craft Obsessive* (James Dyson) spent five years refining 5,126 vacuum prototypes, licensed in Japan, then used royalties to bankroll a UK manufacturing plant, never ceding design control and turning it into a billion-dollar brand.

→ *The Community Catalyzer* (Tristan Walker, Bevel) solved razor bumps for Black men, built a culture-first brand, and let users cowrite the product roadmap. This ultimately led to Procter & Gamble buying the movement.

→ *The Scholar-Operator* (Bren Smith, GreenWave) fell for regenerative ocean farming, proved kelp-plus-shellfish plots could revive ecosystems, and then built the company into a nonprofit that trains farmers and open-sources designs.

VENDETTA VENTURES

One more time—same booth. Your friend asks, "How was the week?" and before the words settle, you're practically grinning: "We launched, and my old employer looked at my press release!"

When Ego fuels the engine, updates are scored by the humiliation dealt with and incumbents embarrassed, not by revenue or retention.

Only two J-curve snapshots spark emotion: the plunge and the summit. A supersized dip at Point B is proof you "went big" — blazing through capital, headlines ablaze with round size, never mind the dilution. A skyscraper Point D crowns the narrative; the exit figure trumps every scorched bridge, lost share, or abandoned Passion project. If the numbers you can flaunt beat the ones you surrendered, the mission feels complete.

You'll need more than swagger. You'll need a playbook for turning rivalry into results. Before you sprint off to flaunt round sizes or headline exits, pause long enough to codify the target, the finish line, and the guardrails. That focus will keep the instinct to "win big and fast" from blowing past the milestones that prove you did.

First, decide who you're out to beat. Is it the ex-boss who never believed in you, the lumbering market Goliath, or a snarky comment section? Name the antagonist in one clear sentence. Vagueness scatters your focus. Specificity sharpens it.

Second, spell out what winning looks like. Poach 20 percent of their customers? Out-feature them by Q3? Ring the opening bell while they're still filing paperwork? Brace yourself: The haters will probably never send a thank-you card or cry on camera. Your scoreboard must satisfy you. External validation is a mirage that usually never comes to fruition.

Third, keep a ruthless eye on collateral damage. Studies of rivalry show enemy-chasing startups burn 30 percent more capital preprofit and are 1.5 times likelier to overexpand.[11] If your revenge run starts bruising runway, morale, or product quality, channel your spite into precision, not friendly fire.

Of all the motives, Ego is the most binary fuel. It's capable of propelling and flaming founders in spectacular fashion. Here are a few who rode that razor's edge:

→ *The Late-Fee Avenger* (Reed Hastings, Netflix) paid forty dollars to Blockbuster, vowed revenge, mailed DVDs, and then streamed them. Blockbuster filed Chapter 11 and Netflix is now an effective monopoly in the online streaming space.

→ *The Second-at-Bat* (Palmer Luckey, Anduril), ousted from Oculus by Mark Zuckerberg, set out to out-innovate defense contractors, winning massive Pentagon contracts on autonomous drones and AI border towers.

→ *The Shunned Founder* (Whitney Wolfe Herd, Bumble) exited Tinder in turmoil, flipped dating so women send the first message. An eight-billion-dollar IPO occurred on International Women's Day, flipping the proverbial middle finger.[12]

→ *The Snubbed Visionary* (Jack Ma, Alibaba) was rejected from dozens of jobs—even KFC—and failed university entrance exams twice. Dismissed from traditional paths, he built Alibaba to prove Chinese entrepreneurs could outbuild Silicon Valley, eventually eclipsing eBay in China.

→ *The Regulator's Nightmare* (Brian Armstrong, Coinbase) irked by banks blocking crypto, built an on-ramp and dared regulators to keep up. He took the company public before policy caught up and became the industry staple.

WHAT YOU CAN DO WITH A MOTIVE

Picking a dominant motive is like snapping a lens onto a camera—suddenly everything becomes clear. With your motive, every decision can be rephrased to: Which choice propels my goal the furthest, on my terms?

Co-founder search? Swipe left on brilliant people whose hunger clashes with yours; a Wealth-driven founder and a Passion-driven copilot will knife-fight over every pivot.

Team and culture follow the same script. Wealth founders dangle aggressive option grants and quarterly targets (often called OKRs in tech). Control founders keep head count lean and build generalists who relish autonomy. Passion founders screen for missionaries, not mercenaries, and tattoo the mission on sprint boards. Ego founders hire snipers—people who crave market domination and celebrate each competitive takedown. Your motive is the magnet.

Strategy choices shrink too. Wealth points you to market-maximizing plays and fundraising that spikes valuation. Control nudges you toward minimal funding and profitable niches. Passion pushes for craftsmanship and patient capital that respects product soul. Ego steers you to head-to-head positioning and public relation theatrics.

You can even wield this lens outward. Spot a rival's or customer's dominant motive and you'll see why they choose certain hires, launches, or price moves. Know that, and you can tailor your product, positioning, and negotiations to play directly to (or against) that hunger.

SO WHAT WAS MY VICE?

Picture me back at Atlas Café, caffeine sweating through my T-shirt, laptop cursor blinking like a taunt. I'd quit the pedigree job and assumed Passion would stage-dive from the rafters: instant brainstorm, strategy pouring onto the page. Instead, I felt the opposite of flow: Every idea contradicted the last, timelines morphed, and my grand "next slide" stayed blank. I was drowning in option paralysis.

That's the tax of motive ambivalence. Without a ruling fuel, every new data point yanks the wheel. A podcast says, "Bootstrap or die" and you swear off investors. Ten minutes later, a VC blog drops, "Raise early, raise big" and you reopen the deck. Your roadmap bloats, head-count decisions stall, and Monday stand-ups become philosophy debates.

The spiral only stopped when I forced the confession: Ego, not Passion, was my phantom driver.

After six years of critiquing founders from a cushy diligence perch, the self-doubt voice taunted: *Nice slide reviews, kid—can you actually build?* Assembly became my rebuttal. Every term sheet I declined, every 3:00 a.m. spreadsheet, every "Sure, let's buy that company" was really me sending a silent memo to my old self: *I can build; watch me.*

The punchline of this chapter is simple: When you question your path, choose one dominant motive and fence it. Whether you're chasing commas, control levers, midnight joy, or righteous payback, set your limits.

QUESTION THE INSIGHT

DOUBT VOICE: What if I just haven't spotted the land mine yet?

TWELVE MONTHS BEFORE Assembly had a logo, Sandeep and I were juggling half a dozen startup ideas like flaming pins. Each Monday, we'd swear the next concept was the keeper. Each Friday, we boomeranged to one stubborn hunch: Third-party software around Amazon and Shopify was a gold vein nobody was drilling.

The hidden fear that stalked every whiteboard session was maybe the only reason this idea was still available was because everyone else already spotted the land mine, and we're about to look like idiots.

To smoke-test that nightmare, we lived in conference rooms and café corners with bootstrapped founders, private-label sellers, private equity (PE) rollups, and VCs, asking the same question in a thousand dialects:

"WHAT ARE WE MISSING?"

They shrugged; we scribbled. They yawned; we obsessed. By month ten, pattern recognition beat paranoia: If a dozen smart people couldn't kill the idea, maybe the idea deserved to live. That's when we wrote the bet in plain English—five rungs, no buzzwords—so we could see exactly what had to be true and what you can begin testing.

THE BELIEF LADDER—ASSEMBLY

RUNG	CORE ASSUMPTION	WORLD VIEW AT THE TIME
1	E-commerce will keep compounding worldwide	Obvious
2	It's easy to launch, so store count will explode	Less obvious
3	Brands will prefer a bundled solution over time	Debatable
4	Value will leak from platforms to third-party apps	Controversial
5	Value will be distributed across small and big brands	Very controversial

Lower rungs (1–2) equals macro factors outside your control.
Higher rungs (3–5) equals micro factors inside your control.

To believe our macro, we had to accept two forces entirely outside our control: e-commerce would keep compounding worldwide, and because spinning up an online store was getting easier by the month, the number of potential customers would mushroom over the next five to ten years. If either of those tectonic plates slipped, Assembly would slide with them. We didn't steer them; we simply decided whether we wanted to join for the ride.

Below that sat our micro insights—the contrarian hunches

we could steer. We believed brands would migrate from single-point tools to an all-in-one solution, that sellers would rely on third-party software rather than platform dashboards (e.g., Amazon), and that scrappy up-and-comers, not just global giants, would win the shelf war. The higher each of those rungs turned out to be "right," the stronger our position, and the larger our slice of the growing pie.

BUILDING YOUR LADDER

Think of the ladder as a snapshot of your conviction on launch day. It's a handful of rungs that explain, in plain English, why your company should exist, and what needs to be true for you to be successful. Getting this right is the difference between six months of rabbit-holing and immediately testing what matters.

Start with an assumption dump. Open a blank document, set a ten-minute timer, and pour out every belief circling in your head. Don't polish; write fragments, half sentences, napkin numbers—anything that starts with "this has to be true." When the timer buzzes, you should have a messy page. Perfect. Now the sorting begins.

First, find the market. Read your scribbles and ask, "What outside force must keep moving in our favor?" Maybe smartphone penetration has to rise, or regulators must loosen a rule, or consumer behavior globally needs to change in some direction. Note why that shift is happening, how long it needs to last, and what would derail it. If the market dies, it's extremely difficult to succeed.

Next, look for every line that starts with a human pain point. What exactly has to change in a customer's daily routine for them to pay you? Is the problem getting more acute or merely annoying? Why now? Is it a new habit, new cost, or a new peer pressure? A crisp customer rung names the job (find dinner faster), the frequency (daily scroll), and the reason current tools fail (too many sponsored reviews).

Finally, point out the competition. Circle the lines about rivals and substitutes. Why haven't incumbents fixed the pain already? Maybe channel conflict, internal politics, or brand baggage slows them down. Spell out what you will do differently—cheaper, faster, or bundled in a way their org chart can't copy without a civil war.

With the raw material grouped, zoom out and tag each rung for control. If the outcome lives in Washington, the app store, or is occupied by an incumbent who virtually owns the entire market, call it *outside*. If you can move the needle with a line of code, a product design, or a couple of phone calls, call it *inside*. This distinction matters: Outside bets must be trusted; inside bets must be proven.

Now layer on the worldview. Ask how widely each belief is held today. Obvious truths already have crowds rushing toward them. Contrarian hunches are lonely and therefore valuable, if you're right. Mark whether each rung is mainstream, debatable, or borderline crazy. A balanced ladder usually features two solid mainstream waves to ride and a few sharper, less-crowded edges to shape.

For safe measure, let's look at a classic unicorn:

THE BELIEF LADDER—UBER

RUNG	CORE ASSUMPTION	WORLDVIEW AT THE TIME
1	Smartphones plus mobile will keep exploding worldwide	Obvious
2	GPS accuracy will become good enough for riding	Less obvious

RUNG	CORE ASSUMPTION	WORLDVIEW AT THE TIME
3	Riders will tap an app instead of raising their arm	Debatable
4	Brand helps riders feel safe jumping in a stranger's car	Controversial
5	Regulators and taxi medallion can be out-executed	Very controversial

Uber launched just as three forces aligned: Smartphone penetration rocketed past 40 percent in the US, putting GPS and app stores in every pocket;[13] Google Maps and card-on-file payments finally worked well enough for real-time routing and billing; and the post-2008 labor slump left a huge pool of underemployed drivers hungry for a flexible income. Uber didn't create these trends. It simply caught the wave before anyone else noticed its crest.

What Uber shaped were the contrarian moves: a one-tap pickup experience that beat flagging a cab, a two-way rating system plus one-million-dollar insurance to tame "stranger danger," surge pricing to keep cars circulating, and a "launch first, lobby later" stance that relied on happy riders to out-shout taxi regulators. Each gamble compounded the network effect, turning a niche luxury app into the default way to get across town.

LEAN ON THE MACRO, CONTROL THE MICRO

That choreography—stand on an unmoving tectonic plate, then stomp a pedal no one else can reach—it shows up in every breakout story. The macro wave is mandatory, but it's useless unless the founder bolts on a proprietary fin to steer the surge where only they can go.

Stripe rode an incontestable macro. Every shop, blog, and side hustle was racing online, yet draconian bank integrations still scared founders off. The Collison brothers reduced that pain to seven pasted characters: stripe.checkout(). Two lines of code turned a weeklong payment-card security rules slog into an afternoon task, so the entire e-commerce surge flowed through their tollbooth.

Airbnb recognized that big-city hotel capacity chronically ran short during conferences and holidays. Spare bedrooms already existed as dormant inventory; what people lacked was psychological safety. By layering identity checks, reviews, and host guarantees onto a slick listing flow, the company transformed "sleeping in a stranger's house" from sketchy gamble to adventurous bargain—unlocking millions of beds without pouring a single yard of concrete.

Coinbase wagered that Bitcoin would outlast volatility and regulatory side-eye. Early on, buying crypto meant wire transfers to opaque exchanges and praying your USB wallet didn't corrupt. Brian Armstrong replaced that ritual with a brokerage interface as friendly as Venmo: Link a card, tap "Buy," and watch sats (Satoshis, the penny of Bitcoin) appear. Friction fell, liquidity spiked, and Coinbase became the on-ramp for Main Street's first crypto mile.

Zoom out and the pattern repeats in thousands of other cases —small teams latching onto a rising tide and then yanking one lever only they could move. You don't need another dozen anecdotes; you need the mantra "Surf the force you can't change, then pour every ounce of ingenuity into the variable you can." Obsess over the part outside your grasp, and you'll burn cash and sanity. Master the slice you can bend, and the macro will do the heavy lifting for free.

PUT YOUR GOGGLES ON

Before you start swinging at assumptions, choose the goggles you'll be wearing.

Your belief ladder isn't abstract truth-seeking—it's a machine. And the output of that machine should directly feed your motive. If the assumptions are right and the ladder holds, the result shouldn't be confusing. It should feel inevitable.

With Ego, correct assumptions produce volume. The company is visible, talked about, compared, and contested. Wins are public. Losses sting but clarify position. If your ladder is sound yet the outcome is quiet, you didn't miss execution—you aimed at the wrong target.

With Wealth, the test is simple. If the assumptions are right, money shows up at scale. Margins expand. Leverage appears. Optionality increases. If your motive is wealth but the ladder resolves into a "nice business," that's not patience—it's misalignment.

With Control, accuracy buys freedom. The right assumptions reduce dependencies, surprises, and permission slips. You own the clock and the downside. But if your ladder requires constant capital, platform mercy, or external approval, control will always leak—no matter how disciplined you are.

With Passion, the payoff is energy. When the ladder fits, the work sustains you. You'd do it even if the scoreboard froze. If you're only excited by outcomes and drained by the work itself, your assumptions are pointing somewhere else.

None of these failures announce themselves. They show up as almost: almost loud, almost rich, almost free, almost fulfilling.

The worst-case scenario isn't that your idea fails. It's that you're crystal clear on your motive—and you design a business that doesn't feed it.

YOUR MARKET ISN'T $200 BILLION

Jab every data point you can find.

Most early-stage evidence is either outdated, cherry-picked, or straight-up wishful math. Back when I was an investor, I'd watch founders defend a critical slide with religious fervor, only to debunk the source after ten minutes on Google. Those encounters taught me to treat every round number as innocent until proven guilty.

Nowhere is the optimism gap wider than in the total addressable market. If a deck trumpets a "$200 billion TAM," run the citation to ground. Call the analyst, ask how they built it, and carve out everything you'll never touch. In practice, most early-stage TAM numbers turn out to be wildly inflated, often by multiples once you trace them back to reality.

Treat those shaky numbers like spoiled milk; if the carton date is fuzzy, throw it out. Garbage in, garbage out is more than a slogan. It's the quickest route to a blown cap table and a late-night board call.

This happens often. J.C. Penney's 2012 "Fair and Square" made a pricing bet on survey data that said shoppers hated coupons; reality wiped out a quarter of sales in twelve months.[14] Target Canada trusted glossy inventory models, opened 124 stores with empty shelves, and torched $2 billion before retreating.[15] Zillow Offers leaned on an overconfident pricing algorithm and swallowed nearly a billion in write-downs. Same pattern: unquestioned inputs.

Instead, build the model yourself. Start bottoms-up: Count only the customers you can realistically reach in the next five years, multiply by the price they've already paid for comparable solutions, and adjust for likely adoption, not perfect penetration.

If you need a stretch scenario to break $30 million in annual revenue, admit you're running a solid lifestyle business and fund it like one. There's honor and profit in that lane.

If you're aiming for venture speed, widen the funnel only after the core math clears the $100 million revenue or $1 billion exit hurdle on paper. Layer in adjacent segments you can unlock with new products, price expansions you can justify with clear return on investment, and geographies you can serve without crippling logistics. Every line should tie back to a testable assumption—something you can validate in a pilot or a paid proof of concept—so when skeptics poke holes, you've got receipts instead of rhetoric.

THE BABY IS UGLY

Close the deck, leave the office, and wade into the watering holes your users already haunt: Discords, sub-Reddits, factory breakrooms, conference lobby bars. Show up empty-handed. No demo to pitch, no hypothesis to defend, just honest curiosity: "What's the worst part of your day?" Then dig where it hurts. Ask the questions that make you squirm: "Why hasn't anyone paid for this?" "What would make you dump my tool tomorrow?" If the room goes quiet, good. It's cheaper to apologize to a stranger at a trade show than to your board after you've built a solution in search of a problem.

That discomfort is where assumptions snap. We thought our buyers were seasoned e-commerce veterans. A month of staying out late at industry conferences revealed the truth: Most sellers were teachers, nurses, and college kids running midnight side hustles. Their North Star wasn't "optimize ad spend." It was "grow the store enough to quit my day job." Different dream, different pain.

"I DON'T MEAN TO SH*T ON YOUR BABY."

I said that.

I accidentally mashed two clichés—"I don't mean to shit on your idea" and "throw the baby out with the bathwater"—and blurted, "I don't mean to sh*t on your baby."

Freudian slip, yes, but the result was surprisingly epic. The moment you imply someone's "baby" is ugly, "That seems like a pretty small business," "Surprised you don't have any staff yet," "Can't believe you spend nights on this," they'll either leap to defend its beauty or confess the scar tissue. The first reaction hands you the polished origin story; the second spills the raw, unvarnished pain they've been hiding. Either way, you exit with intel you'd never get from polite nods and survey checkboxes, and that's the ammo you need to build something worth bragging about.

STALK THE COMPETITIVE LANDSCAPE

"Obsess over the customer; ignore the competition" makes a great poster, but it leaves free intel on the table. Every dollar your rivals pour into ads, content, or failed features is a live experiment you can analyze for pennies. Study them hard enough, and they'll hand you a roadmap for what not to build, where the white space sits, and which tricks already resonate with paying users.

Channeling our inner Michael Moritz—the reporter-turned-investor famous for zooming from panorama to pixel—we treated every Shopify and Amazon-app listing like a crime-scene grid. We scraped the catalog and overfilled a spreadsheet: product DNA, pricing tiers, review keywords, growth levers, respect matrix (who praises or trashes whom on podcasts), and one O.J.–inspired prompt: If we stole this exact playbook, where would we break in, pivot, or outrun ourselves? Competitors had basically published their diaries. All we had to do was highlight the blind spots.

If you are looking for a basic cheat code guide, here it is:

THE PIRATE PLAYBOOK

TACTIC	WHAT TO TRACK	STEAL WITH PRIDE
WEDGE	First-use case they attack	Can we pick a narrower pain with faster payback?
CHANNEL	How customers find them today	Are there underpriced channels they ignore?
MONETIZATION	Freemium, flat fee, revenue share	Can we undercut them and capture the market?
WEAKNESS	Slow feature, bad support, high churn	Can we solve that flaw on Day One and market?

The first move is your **wedge**—a slice of the market so specific the incumbent leaves it undefended. Calendly grabbed meeting scheduling with one "pick-a-time" link; Notion slipped into teams as a single doc that could morph into anything. A wedge this sharp proves value within minutes, earns trust on a shoestring, and quietly positions you to expand once usage snowballs.

After planting that flag, sprint to a forgotten **channel**. While the giant pours millions into Google ads and trade-show booths, you haunt a niche sub-Reddit or ride a TikTok microtrend for pennies. Low-cost channels buy you time to build brand memory while bigger players are still stuck in budget meetings.

Next, weaponize **monetization** instead of copy-pasting the status quo. Flip the model: usage-based so dabblers start free, and power users celebrate bigger invoices; outcome-based so clients cheer when higher revenue means paying you more; or a bundled tier that makes canceling feel pricier than staying. The goal isn't always to be cheaper—just to make the old model feel awkward.

Finally, spotlight a competitor's glaring **weakness** and turn it into your billboard. Every heavyweight limps somewhere—maybe their onboarding takes twenty clicks, support emails vanish for days, or their mobile app feels like a 2010 relic. Patch that crack in your product and promote the fix right in your hero copy. When prospects see a side-by-side and realize you solved the gripe they complain about most, switching becomes a relief, not a risk.

Fill the table for every player in your space. Patterns pop fast: same wedge, same ad channel, same blind spot. Your job isn't to outspend them; it's to pivot one square in the grid where they're asleep.

Think this isn't playing by the rules? It is. It's the script of every incumbent dismantling in the last twenty years.

Dropbox versus Box—Drew Houston watched Box chase enterprises; he focused on viral consumer adoption, then marched into the enterprise later. Users were already in tow.

Instagram versus Snapchat Stories—Instagram copied Snapchat's Stories format, integrated it into an existing network, and scaled it dramatically. Snapchat pioneered the feature; Instagram leveraged distribution.

Microsoft Teams versus Slack—Slack proved workplace chat demand; Microsoft bundled Teams into Office 365, leveraging existing enterprise distribution to overtake usage in many large organizations.

Play the tape forward: If a competitor is educating customers or lobbying regulators, let them. Save your ammo for the gap they're leaving. In almost all cases, the market favors learners, not originators.

ASSUMPTIONS AREN'T FOREVER

Your ladder is a living document, not a stone tablet. Markets stall, laws change, channels saturate, and yesterday's edge can become tomorrow's cost of entry. That isn't evidence that you were naive; it's how the game works. Stripe launched assuming card-not-present fees would stay high enough to mask a healthy margin. Then interchange caps tightened in Europe, and the company rewrote half its pricing model. Airbnb once banked on cities ignoring short-term rentals; today it employs an army of policy specialists and collects hotel-style taxes in hundreds of jurisdictions. Assumptions moved, companies adapted, and life went on.

Treat your ladder like quarterly maintenance. Every three months, or after any shock (funding round, regulatory headline, supply-chain crunch), reread each rung and ask two questions: Has the fact pattern changed? Does this still have to be true for us to win? If a macro wave flattens, decide whether to wait it out or paddle toward a new one. If a micro lever dulls—acquisition costs double or a competitor copies your killer feature—draft a fresh rung and repeat.

Updating the ladder isn't losing conviction; it's proof you're steering with live instruments instead of last year's forecast. Expect to rewrite at least one rung a year. Companies that survive a decade will cycle through half a dozen ladders, each a snapshot of what mattered most then, and each a reason they're still alive to climb the next.

SO WHAT?

The quiet dread that your idea is whack isn't a buggy feature—it's the suspicion that your worldview is wrong. Name that fear, then flip it into what you believe for the company to work.

Ideas are napkin sketches; insights are the laws that make them inevitable. At Assembly, ours boiled down to two: (1) value would leak from big marketplaces to third-party apps; and (2) even night-shift sellers would pay for a bundle. Price tags, UI, and even brand could bend if those held.

Test every assumption on a ladder, bruise the rungs with actual conversations, and shore up weak steps while it's cheap. Borrow proof from rivals, map blind spots, and run your numbers. Test every aspect, including customers, competitors, and regulators, until the weak stories fail. Do the homework early to spot mirages before they drain your runway without walking away from a gold vein just because the first shovel hits rock.

CATCH THE WAVE

DOUBT VOICE: What if I paddle like
hell only to find the ocean flat?

IN 2017, the Shopify and Amazon-seller app stores looked like
a flea market run by code freelancers. Most founders called their
creations "lifestyle projects," sold them based on cash-flow multiples, and answered support tickets between beach volleyball sets.

In our hearts, we knew this was only temporary. A market
opportunity of this magnitude and a casual, low-key ecosystem
were unprecedented.

When we started, we expected a rush of investor interest—
smart money eager to bankroll the gold rush we saw so clearly.
But the phones stayed quiet. Pitch decks went out; polite "circle
back next quarter" replies trickled in. We trusted the thesis, yet
nobody acted like this was the next big thing. The hidden fear
wasn't *if* we were right but *when*: Would we spend the next decade
mumbling "just you wait" while our bank accounts and morale
ran dry?

"ARE WE TOO EARLY TO THE PARTY?"

That single doubt—timing, not insight—haunted us at the end of every day until the tide finally turned.

Fast-forward just three years: Those same lifestyle founders were giving away Teslas for taking an intro call, selling their companies for 15-times revenue to PE firms willing to skip due diligence, and hiring two executive assistants while working remotely from Joshua Tree.[16]

What changed? Not the insight—we'd bet that value would leak from the core platforms to nimble third-party apps, and that customers would want a bundled solution.

What changed was the timing.

In 2020, COVID-19 rocketed e-commerce penetration a decade forward, VC term sheets flooded in, and the multiple arbitrage we'd banked on went from bargain-bin to bidding war. If Assembly had launched a year later, someone would have priced us out, tinkering in a WeWork while someone else banked the $1.4 billion outcome.

But the same clock can just as easily run against you: One policy tweak, platform-fee change, or supply-chain hiccup, and the tide that promised to lift you can vanish, stranding even the strongest thesis on dry sand.

Michael Moritz's whiplash from Web 1.0's Webvan to Web 2.0's Instacart proves the extremes: ideas don't change—tides do.[17] After the dot-com crash, every rung on Webvan's ladder still could have been right, but too many were unproven at once. By 2012, four rungs—smartphones, broadband, gig labor, Amazon-trained shoppers—were solid enough for Instacart to skate across. Same grocery insight, different surf conditions.

If Webvan drowned in a rip current, and Instacart surfed the very same beach, the lesson is clear: before you grab a board, look at the water. Are investors napping or elbow-fighting for deals? Are customers squinting at your demo or lining up with credit cards? The answers decide how much cash you raise, how fast you hire, and how long you can stay sane if nothing clicks for a while. To make that gut check easier, let's name the four shoreline moods you'll encounter, and what each one means for money, manpower, and mindset.

THE TIDE FRAMEWORK

TIDE STATE	MARKET SIGNALS	FOUNDER STANCE
LOW TIDE	Analysts yawn, capital cheap, press indifferent	Prototype in silence; build relationships
RISING TIDE	Early adopters rave; incumbents shrug	Paddle hardest —speed beats polish
HIGH TIDE	Big tech explores the space; conferences created	Differentiate or niche; avoid talent wars
RECEDING TIDE	PR cools; valuations contract; tourists exit	Consolidate; acquire distressed; lock the hatches

The dream scenario, of course, is to wade in during Low Tide, when attention is scarce, talent and ads are cheap, and you can prototype without the glare. Then ride the wave out at High Tide, when budgets balloon, headlines multiply, and multiples reward even modest tractions. There's no single right entry or exit point, but knowing exactly which tide you're in lets you tune every move: stealth-mode relationship-building when the beach is empty, all-out speed when the swell arrives, sharp positioning once giants join the lineup, and disciplined consolidation when the water pulls back. Awareness, not perfection, is the edge.

WHY AREN'T THERE ANY WAVES?

Low Tide is the awkward silence at a cocktail party. Analysts haven't coined a name for your space, venture blogs can't find a comparable company, and customer inboxes echo with "Interesting, but not a priority." According to PitchBook, only 11 percent of US seed rounds close when total category funding sits below $250 million,[18] and venture math says the opportunity cost is too high. Counterintuitively, that vacuum is your discount window. Talent is cheaper, ads are pennies, and incumbents are busy elsewhere.

Take Max Levchin: In 2012, while Silicon Valley chased social apps, he launched Affirm to rebuild consumer credit in the shadow of the financial crisis. Banks were cautious and installment lending unfashionable. Levchin kept the team lean, focused on underwriting, and signed merchants one by one until "buy now, pay later" became a category.

Your playbook is learn, not earn. You should funnel cash into direct conversations—thirty-minute Zooms, small-scale pilots, landing-page tests—until you can reduce the roadmap to a single use that case customers will pay for immediately. Keep the team tiny (five to seven people max), ship weekly, and measure traction in qualitative heat: referrals, unsolicited testimonials, or one customer doubling seats.

The enemy here is morale. So manufacture momentum: Publish transparent metrics, celebrate each beta signup, and share customer quotes with your team. Treat Low Tide as paid graduate school—one you exit with a product nobody else had the patience to build.

IS THAT A TSUNAMI COMING?

A Rising Tide is that sweet spot when early users rave about you on social media, but the big incumbents still look the other way. Money starts pouring in: Seed rounds typically triple in size, on average. But competition hasn't turned cutthroat yet. In this window, speed beats finesse. Every month you wait is a month the next-fastest team grabs your beachhead.

Take Substack. Creator-economy chatter spiked in 2017 (newsletters-as-business searches were up 70 percent YoY), just as Apple loosened App-Store rules on in-app subscriptions. Chris Best bet big on paid, writer-owned mailing lists, lured marquee journalists with instant monetization, and doubled GMV in one quarter. It locked in mindshare before old-guard media had digested the shift to direct reader revenue.

Your playbook now is capacity first, polish later. Pre-buy extra server credits, overstaff support, and lock in long-term ad deals while rates are still reasonable. Once a market heats up, acquisition costs climb fast and early channels lose their efficiency. These are the cheapest customers you'll ever land.

Stress-test your budget assuming acquisition costs double next year and churn (customer turnover) ticks up a few points. If that breaks your model, narrow your focus to a stickier niche or add usage-based pricing to protect margins. Whatever you choose, ship faster than the news cycle. People remember the first mover, not version 3.0.

THE BEACH IS FULLY RESERVED

High Tide is shoulder-to-shoulder umbrellas—the category has its own Gartner Quadrant, and a New York Times trend piece just ran. Money is easy but vicious: company valuations look princely, yet so do hiring costs, ad auctions, and customer expectations. In markets like this, every input becomes more expensive, and the price of staying competitive rises just as fast as the capital flowing in.

Snowflake's cloud data play shows how an architectural wedge survives High Tide. When it emerged in 2012, enterprise warehousing was dominated by Oracle, Teradata, and Amazon Redshift. Snowflake separated compute from storage, letting customers scale each independently. Once workloads migrated, switching became painful, giving Snowflake room to grow even as capital flooded the data space.

If you're here, differentiate or niche down—lean on unique data sets, regulatory advantages, or embedded workflows that create real switching friction. As the market crowds, salaries climb, ads get noisier, and new features are copied faster than you can ship them. Fortify the parts of your business others overlook. Turn users into evangelists, build in network effects, or leverage a cost advantage that lets you outlast the opportunists.

Finally, preach patience to the team. High Tide feels like you're winning, but it's also when founders slip into spending habits that become fatal as soon as the water recedes. Budget for Plan-B burn: What if revenue flattens for twelve months? Who do you keep, what do you cut, and what strategic chip can you cash in if needed?

WHERE'S THE WATER?

Funding rounds evaporate, trade-show booths shrink, and Medium think pieces call the category "over." Data shows median SaaS multiples fall 60 percent within two quarters of a macro pullback.[19] It feels brutal, but for founders with dry powder (cash), it's clearance season, and a lot of money can be made.

Adobe offers the playbook: In 2009, while the Great Recession gutted marketing budgets and ad-tech valuations collapsed, Adobe scooped up web-analytics upstart Omniture for about $1.8 billion—roughly a fourfold revenue, which is a steal compared with the double-digit multiples that space commands today. That clearance-rack buy became the backbone of Adobe Experience Cloud, now a multibillion-dollar pillar of the company and proof that consolidation bargains can define the next growth chapter.

Start with triage: cut the fat, lean into upsells, and renegotiate anything with a signature line. Then go deal-hunting. Hard times shake loose everything—codebases, customers, even whole teams—from companies that can't keep pace. Talent costs drop, and you can trade stock instead of cash to conserve runway while giving partners upside when the cycle turns.

Above all, communicate. A founder who explains the plan can keep A-players engaged even through pay-freeze winters. Promise reality, not spin: "We have twenty months of cash, acquisition targets in play, and a path to break even at 70 percent of our current spend." Recessions don't kill prepared companies; opacity and panic do.

CAN YOUR MOTIVE SURF?

Motive and tide are dance partners: The first sets your rhythm, the second decides the waves you'll surf. Pick a motive that clashes with the current, and you'll feel every paddle stroke. Match them and the ocean does half the work. Below is how each motive plays out against Low, Rising, High, and Receding Tide.

Money-first founders thrive from late-Rising into High Tide, when capital is loose, multiples expand and secondary markets hum. Get in as signals pop, before acquisition costs triple, and lock liquidity targets early so greed doesn't keep you on the board when the swell crests. In Receding Tide, flip instinct from growth to bargains: distressed rollups can turn one more Wealth cycle.

Autonomy lovers are happiest at Low Tide when few are watching, and bootstrapping buys years of quiet runway. You can pace hiring, choose investors (or none), and hard-bake culture before outsiders crowd the lineup. Come High Tide, resist board seats and dual-class term-sheet sirens unless you're willing to share the rudder.

Mission die-hards ignore forecast apps and paddle out anytime, but reality says Low-to-Rising Tide works best. Early calm lets you iterate without hype; a fresh swell gives free amplification, once product-market love appears. Guard stamina in Receding waters—purpose fuels grit, yet payroll still needs dollars, not vision decks.

Spotlight seekers crave High Tide's camera flashes: Gartner quadrants, conference keynotes, Blitz-scale headlines. The upside is rapid-brand gravity; the hazard is wipeout speed when sentiment flips. Build rock-solid delivery cadences and cash buffers before the applause peaks, or the first current shift will rip the mic away.

Tides change and so can motives. Wealth converts to control after a payout, and Passion slides toward Ego when the press hits. Recheck every funding round or macro shock. The right pairing won't guarantee victory, but it will make every stroke intentional instead of reactive.

SINK OR SWIM

Remember the early Bitcoin die-hards—the ones every grandma likened to the "Nigerian prince" email scam? For nearly a decade, they were Thanksgiving punch lines, absorbing eye rolls about "magic internet money." Today, those same weird uncles are auctioning CryptoPunks from their yachts. The coin never changed—only its place on the adoption S-curve did. Some founders are wired to thrive in that long stretch of ridicule; others aren't, and that's perfectly fine. If you haven't already asked yourself, do it now.

"HOW LONG CAN I STOMACH FEELING WRONG?"

If the candid answer is, "I can't tread that long," don't muscle through denial—redesign the plan. You can lower the ladder (tackle a niche segment where a few rungs are already proven), borrow another swimmer's oxygen tank (raise enough capital to stretch your personal runway), or pause on the pier (consult, teach, or freelance while the market matures).

What you must not do is sprint into deep surf, hoping resolve will substitute for physics. Exhausted founders sink companies more often than bad ideas do. Give yourself permission to delay the leap, shorten the climb, or share the burden. Anything beats drowning unexpectedly.

SEIZE THE WAVE, DUDE

Surf reports tell you where the water stands. They don't dictate where it has to stay. Markets work the same way. While most founders wait for the swell, the boldest learn how to nudge the moon, lobbying regulators, educating customers, or bundling products in ways that yank demand forward and literally shift the tide beneath their boards. Here are a few examples.

→ Tesla refused to sit idle until battery prices dropped. By campaigning for zero-emission credits and state rebates, it sliced thousands off sticker prices, turned a niche curiosity into a mainstream option, and created a fresh revenue stream to bankroll faster production.

→ HubSpot changed the current by coining "inbound marketing," releasing the playbook for free, and certifying legions of practitioners. Those newly minted experts suddenly needed HubSpot's tools to practice what they'd just learned, tilting the entire market toward its software.

→ Peloton spent years weaving hardware, live video, and social competition into one seamless experience, manufacturing demand for at-home fitness long before gyms locked down. When the pandemic hit, the tide Peloton had been stoking surged overnight, and back orders piled in.

They didn't wait for High Tide. They engineered it.

We felt our own swell building: App multiples were climbing, and the best assets wouldn't stay unloved for long. Instead of coding a rival from scratch, we sprinted to the cashier, raised a $50 million growth-equity round, and bought the category's top tool outright. Overnight, we leapt from zero users to a foothold in half a million seller accounts, riding the wave while it gathered speed.

How do you spot a tide you can shift on your own? Look for markets where: (1) a policy lever, jargon, or workflow bottleneck keeps adoption pent up; (2) a small but vocal group of users already aches for a fix; and (3) there's an underpriced resource, whether tax credits, ad inventory, or legacy equipment, waiting to be revalued. If you can move even one of those three choke points, you're not just forecasting the waves; you're building the break.

BE A PARANOID LIFEGUARD

The core insight—people want groceries at their door; sellers need apps the platforms ignore; photos will live on phones, not film—rarely changes. What whipsaws founders and kills blue-chip companies is the timing: Infrastructure arrives, costs collapse, tastes pivot, and the same ladder of assumptions snaps from contrarian to consensus overnight.

I learned that the messy way on my first assignment at my first job (Perella Weinberg): the Kodak bankruptcy. I sat in a Midtown Manhattan hotel ballroom turned emergency shareholder meeting while Kodak's brass tried to explain why a onetime blue chip was begging for rescue financing. As they spoke, I flashed back to sweating in our family Chrysler Town & Country van outside a CVS, waiting for Mom to collect that yellow envelope of one-hour photos—proof, back then, that Kodak owned magic. The instinct to preserve memories never vanished. When smartphones squeezed a darkroom into every pocket, the wave shifted overnight, and Kodak never stood a chance.

This tidal "snap"—the moment the market shifts faster than a company can pivot—has wrecked ventures in young, midlife, and mature alike. The examples follow.

→ Quibi, barely out of the cradle, raised nearly $1.8 billion to stream seven-minute shows to commuters' phones. It launched in April 2020 just as lockdowns erased commuting and TikTok owned every spare scroll. Without an audience on the move, Quibi burned through cash and shuttered in six months.

→ Jawbone, a seasoned scale-up, rode high on Bluetooth speakers before pivoting to fitness bands. It correctly sensed the wearable boom, yet component prices plunged, and the Apple Watch set a new polish bar Jawbone's supply chain couldn't match. Years of inventory write-offs, lawsuits, and capital drains ended in a 2017 liquidation.

→ BlackBerry, once a category titan, perfected mobile email for suit-and-tie executives, betting the tide would stay corporate and keyboard-centric. The 2007 iPhone unveiled a touch-first, consumer-driven future; within twenty-four months, BlackBerry's share collapsed, and by 2016, the company had exited hardware entirely.

Different ages, same fate: Ignore the tide and the wave snaps the board—no matter how long you've been surfing.

IGNORE THE OCEAN COLOR

Strategy books split seas into two colors. Blue oceans are wide-open, competition-free waters—new categories where you write the rules and price points. Red oceans are sharky battle zones crowded with rivals, bloodied by price wars and feature parity. Founders lose months debating which sea is right, and how they plan to tackle it.

Here's the twist: Whichever color you pick, the tide will still decide whether you float or flail. A calm blue ocean at Low Tide can leave you marooned without capital or customers to prove you exist. A swelling red ocean at Rising Tide can lift even a scrappy entrant.

So revive the hidden fear that kicked off this chapter: "What if I paddle like hell only to find the ocean flat?" The antidote isn't swapping seas; it's reading the swell and matching your moves. Before you jump, run a three-part check: (1) know the tide you're in, (2) be honest about how long you can keep swimming, and (3) decide whether you can whip up your own current if the forecast looks calm. Get those right, and the water's color is just scenery.

SPOT YOUR SWANS

DOUBT VOICE: What if the headline writes itself, and it's my eulogy?

"WHAT KEEPS YOU up at night?"

People love to ask questions with the same grin a dentist has when brandishing the drill. You're expected to smile and purr something mature—"scaling culture," maybe "hiring A-players" —and accept the approving nod. The first time it hit me cold, I gave the textbook answer and felt like I fit in with the management elites—then lay awake wondering why I'd served them a line I didn't even believe.

In real life the boogeyman is far weirder: how many filler words I used in an all-hands company meeting; if my management team respected me or just thought I was a young, naive, first-time operator; an AWS bill that looked like a phone number; and a nightmare that TechCrunch writes:

"MARKETPLACE STARTUP CLOSES DOORS IMMEDIATELY AFTER CO-FOUNDER'S DISASTROUS STRATEGY SHIFT."

Now picture that dread on live TV. Emily Chang leans forward, red light blinking, and says, "Some call this one of the dumbest moves in modern tech. How do you respond, Adam?" My throat locks. And then I wake up.

Why does that script feel so real and vivid? Because reputational death is permanent. Money burns, employees churn, but a public flameout headline is forever searchable, forever memed, and spoken behind closed doors as "Isn't that the guy who..." That permanence is the hidden fear that hijacks REM and turns 3:00 a.m. into a crisis.

Earlier in my career, I learned a memo template that drags these dreams into daylight: two stark paragraphs—preparade and postmortem. One sketches the ticker-tape headline if everything clicks; the other writes the autopsy if everything burns. Together they fence the field of play—you've read the water; now it's time to find the Loch Ness Monster.

FIELD OF PLAY

VIEW	CORE QUESTION	OUTPUT
PREPARADE	If everything clicks, what appears on the front page?	Root cause of what caused the confetti
POSTMORTEM	If everything burns, what does the headline say?	Root cause of what caused the disaster

Your first instinct might be to treat the field of play as nothing more than the Belief Ladder from Chapter 2—if every assumption holds, you get the preparade, and if they all collapse, you're staring at the postmortem.

Sort of. The ladder shows which assumptions must remain standing. The parade/postmortem drill digs a layer deeper.

What if a black-swan event—an unpredictable, low-probability shock with an outsized impact—drop-kicks the ladder itself? By forcing your inner heckler to shout every lurid scenario in a safe room, you can grade each one as: (a) plausible, (b) fatal, and (c) avoidable.

What if it's not all doom and gloom? Just as a black swan can crater the entire business, its counterpart—the white-swan event, a low-probability windfall with outsize upside—can rocket the ladder sky high in a single flap. Give your inner dreamer the floor to sketch every out-of-nowhere jackpot, then run each through the similar lenses: (a) plausible, (b) game-changing, and (c) achievable.

Here's two swan events that happened:

SWANS IN REAL LIFE

COMPANY	WHITE-SWAN EVENT	BLACK-SWAN EVENT
ZOOM	Work from home jolts and spikes video demand	Zoom sessions breached, turning off enterprises
PELOTON	Health insurers subsidize and memberships soar	A child was killed, causing a nationwide recall

Zoom's white swan arrived in March 2020: a planetwide work-from-home shock that made "hop on a Zoom" the default verb for meetings. Plausible? A remote-work uptick was always on the cards; a pandemic-scale spike was low-odds but not impossible. Game-changing? Daily meeting minutes jumped more than thirty times, vaulting Zoom into critical-infrastructure status. Achievable? The company was cloud-native and freemium-friendly, so the usage surge could be absorbed without retailoring its stack (RIP Webex)—a checkmark on all three fronts, and it actually happened.

Peloton's disaster case happened in 2021: A child's death triggered a Tread+ recall. Plausible? Any home-gym maker faces safety risk. Fatal? Unit sales collapsed, the market cap halved, and the founder CEO stepped down—so a near-fatal hit. Avoidable? Better guard design and child-lock software might have prevented it. Peloton's response—full refunds, redesigned hardware, and safety-first marketing—aims to rebuild trust while diversifying into lower-price hardware to cushion future shocks.

Hindsight paints every swan in familiar colors. Before March 2020, a globe-halting pandemic sounded like a Hollywood pitch, and Peloton's Tread+ seemed as safe as any living-room bike. Afterward, both outcomes felt glaringly obvious: Of course a respiratory virus would shove offices online; of course a 450-pound tread could hurt the curious toddler it was never designed for. That whiplash—from "far-fetched" to "inevitable" in a single headline—is why the drill matters: the only moment you can price in tail risk or upside is before the sh*t hits the fan.

Look at the calendar, and the pattern jumps out: 2001 (dot-com crash plus 9/11 ripple), 2008 (global financial crisis), 2020 (COVID-19 shock). Three global tail events inside two decades —roughly a one-in-ten-year drumbeat. The corporate world follows the same rhythm. BCG's analysis of large public companies shows that major value collapses and sharp performance swings aren't rare anomalies but a recurring feature of every decade. In other words, black-swan shocks hit corporations with far more regularity than most leaders expect.[20]

Whether it's a pandemic, a regulatory whiplash like GDPR, or a viral breakout hit (think Pokémon GO), a swan—black or white—shows up on average once per business generation. Treat it as an inevitability, not a lightning strike; price it into your strategy before it prices you out of the game.

SPOTTING A SWAN

Swans glide overhead every decade or so. Your job is to coax the next one to land on your lawn, not crash through your roof. Begin by yanking your ambition past the comfort zone. Whatever motive you set in Chapter 1—Wealth, Control, Passion, Ego—double it. A $50 million exit doubles to $100 million; full autonomy turns into "Answer to no one, ever." The instant the target feels borderline impossible by ordinary means, your radar starts searching for an extraordinary lift-off (white swan) and, in equal measure, the absolutely worst-case scenario (black swan).

Why does this stretch trick work? Because business outcomes follow fat-tailed power laws: A sliver of events delivers the bulk of gains and losses. Zoom out—literally widen the lens—and those tails snap into view. Instead of asking, "What's most likely?" flip the script to, "What could double my value, or vaporize it overnight?" That inversion counters our habit of down-weighting extremes and forces every candidate swan to pass three filters: plausibility, magnitude, and your readiness to pounce—or to duck.

With the mindset in place, draft a long list. Scan nearby industries for shocks that blindsided peers; flip key variables: "What if demand increases ten times? What if our top supplier ghosts us?" Then tune in to regulators whose pen strokes can shred your margin. Demographic swells, meme storms, policy pivots—anything the market undervalues belongs on the page. Log the gleaming optimist possibilities in one column and the pessimist realities in another.

Then run triage. For each entry, ask: Is it plausible in the next five years? Is it game-changing or fatal relative to my doubled motive? Achievable (white) or avoidable (black) if it hit tomorrow? The few that clear all three gates earn a coveted spot on your short list; the rest get struck.

Now that you've spotted the swans, pressure-test your list. Hand it to your investors if you have them—people paid to poke holes. Pass it to people who know the business, and to the blunt friend who will leave you needing a cigarette and an apology afterward. The survivors of that gauntlet anchor your next move, because identifying swans is only half the job. Next, you'll build a strategy that courts the upside and cages the downside.

THE IMPOSTER'S PLAYGROUND

Voicing your darkest what-ifs isn't masochism; it's insurance. If a single lurid scenario snaps one of the core assumptions of your business, you've found the weak link. Identifying it is the reality of running a business: Bad things will still happen, but you can prepare for them.

So how do you pad the fall before Day One?

Start by spotting future single-point dependencies. As you sketch your business idea on a napkin, underline every assumption that hinges on one platform, supplier, or regulation. Then pencil a parallel path for each. You're not building backups yet. You're just making sure the roadmap never dead-ends at a single domino, especially if that domino has a history of taking out competitors overnight.

Second, keep cash as an optionality, not an ornamentation. In your first forecast, carve out a volatility fund large enough to bankroll a pivot or bridge a dry spell. Reserves planned proactively on Day Zero are easier to defend than lifelines begged for reactively when you are caught off guard.

Third, engineer relationship gravity from the outset. Bake loyalty loops—memberships, communities, usage streaks—into version one so customers become socially expensive to abandon. A tribe that earns perks or status by sticking around will weather price wars, clones, and copycats alongside you.

Assembly's worst-case scenario headline began with a single sentence: "Amazon clones our dashboard, cuts off the partner APIs, and we become the prettiest paperweight in e-commerce." The threat wasn't paranoia. Amazon had kneecapped partners before. That fear forced three hedges: building marketplace integrations outside of Amazon, enriching our platform with seller-owned data rather than Amazon pipes, and holding enough cash to spin up our infrastructure if the gate slammed shut.

Three other founders have played the same game—quietly future-proofing against the nightmare scenario:

→ Instacart looked doomed when Amazon swallowed Whole Foods in 2017, and pundits called "game over" for grocery delivery. Apoorva Mehta's counter was to stop competing and start arming the opposition: white-label picking tech, retailer-branded apps, and an ad platform that let Kroger, Publix, and Wegmans monetize their own shelves. By turning grocers into clients, Instacart won exclusives, jolted revenue, and transformed into a massive company.

→ Trader Joe's began as a minnow circling supermarket sharks. Its worst case was a race-to-the-bottom price

war that would vaporize margins. Joe Coulombe's
hedge was a radical focus: slash the assortment to
4,000 private-label SKUs, source opportunistic surplus
from growers, and wrap the haul in a quirky, vacation-
postcard brand. When big-box grocers later weaponized
discounts, Trader Joe's shoppers barely noticed—
the chain's moat was novelty.

→ REI feared becoming Amazon's fitting room:
Customers would test jackets in-store and then click
"Buy Now" online for less. The co-op defused the threat
by doubling down on membership dividends, used-gear
buybacks, and members-only events. Shoppers who
earned a rebate stuck around even when a cheaper cart
was two taps away.

The pattern is clear: Each founder weaponized doubt early,
then bought cheap options—data, communities, back-pocket
strategies, and cash cushions that paid out when the storm finally
broke and a "tail scenario" became real.

DO YOU WANT YOUR YACHT
GIFT WRAPPED?

If Imposer's Playground is about padding the fall, this playground
is about rolling out the red carpet for a white-swan windfall—the
"holy smokes" upside that can buy a yacht (if that's your thing)
and still leave change for the bow. The trick is to make sure you
are ready for the upside before the tide lifts.

Here are three setup moves you can sketch:

First, learn the difference between a "shiny object" distraction and a planted seed. A seed takes minimal lift, sits behind a

two-way door (meaning you can change your mind at any point), and keeps optionality alive: a provisional trademark, a skeleton partnership agreement, and a dormant API endpoint. If the upside never materializes, you shut the door and walk away; if lightning strikes, you're already holding the metal rod.

Second, sketch a plan to handle ten times the volume whether or not you can afford to build it yet. Map the servers you would spin up, the contract manufacturers you would activate, and the recruiters you would call. Scaling on paper is cheap insurance; scaling in real time is the chaos that kills momentum faster than any competitor.

Third, court serendipity, especially the stuff that makes you say, "That's weird." Weird is only weird until it's a billion-dollar business. Accept the quirky sponsorship, the obscure conference slot, the midnight podcast cameo. Each oddball collision widens the funnel of upside surprises.

At Assembly, we worked backward from a press release: "Independent 'Commerce OS' Powers the Long Tail—Assembly Hits $50 Billion Valuation."

With that headline in hand, we reverse-engineered a fresh Belief Ladder. Hitting a $50 billion valuation would require $3 billion to $5 billion in annual revenue—roughly 250,000 customers, each paying about $1,000 per month. Ambitious but not impossible. The next question naturally became, "What offering could command that price?" The answer pointed to features that truly move the needle for brands—automated ad buying, seamless multichannel selling, and predictive intelligence on which product to launch next. Those pillars went onto the long-term roadmap.

Other founders set up similar call options:

→ Long before *Iron Man* grossed a dime, Kevin Feige of Marvel Studios locked key actors into multipicture deals, wove post-credit Easter eggs, and storyboarded a decade of crossovers. When the first film landed big, the interlocking universe snapped into place and turned a comic archive into a $29 billion franchise machine.

→ LEGO once looked boxed into selling plastic bricks while iPads stole playtime. Years earlier, CEO Jørgen Vig Knudstorp had planted a quiet call option—low-royalty licensing deals, an in-house CGI crew, and legal room for builders to remix pop culture. When Warner Bros. green-lit *The LEGO Movie* in 2014, that seed detonated: Blockbuster ticket sales, tie-in games, and merch lifts recast LEGO as an entertainment brand.

→ And finally, years before the first moisturizer shipped, Emily Weiss of Glossier treated Into the Gloss as an always-on focus group, harvesting tens of thousands of comments for product briefs. The moment she dropped Phase 1, a preinstalled fan base crashed the server with orders—proof that community-as-R&D can hand-deliver a white swan with zero ad spend.

These stories look like luck in the rearview mirror, but they were engineered wagers. Spot your own yacht moment, line up the call options, and test your capacity to catch a surge for when, not if, it happens.

QUOTE INSPIRED BY MARGARITAS

My co-founder and I first inked Assembly's outline at La Cabaña, a tiny, no-frills Mexican hideaway in Los Angeles. Between crunchy —slightly stale—tortilla chips and one margarita too many, we scrawled a two-line constitution on a napkin: "Protect the house; build the empire." It rolled off the tongue and instantly became our decision lens, shaping every priority from that night forward.

Protect the house was our black-swan shield. From Day One, we vowed to buy companies or tools only at prices that survived a recession model. Amazon might have been the launchpad, but we stitched data pipes to Walmart, Instacart, Shopify, and eBay so one slammed-shut API could never cut off the oxygen. We maintained healthy profitability margins so when "growth at all costs" went out of vogue in 2022, we were in a position of strength. In short, we treated every "what if" as a blueprint for insulation.

Build the empire was our lottery ticket—the white-swan preparation. Those very hedges that we considered "insurance" doubled as launchpads. By wiring into every marketplace early, we became the neutral switchboard sellers craved once multichannel demand exploded. Our rails already served garage merchants in search of velocity, and Fortune 500 brands hunting margin, so whichever side of the market caught fire, we benefited.

What we learned was that protecting our house and building our empire weren't separate agendas; they were two ends of the same circuit. Alpha shows up during spike events—when markets rocket or crater—and the winners are the firms built to profit in either direction. Design a model that milks the melt-up and feasts on the fire sale and volatility becomes a feature, not a flaw.

READY FOR TAKEOFF

Remember that nagging voice: *"What if the worst-case scenario isn't just a dream?"* Instead of silencing it, let it lead the drill. Map every black-swan threat and build cushions; or, if it's real enough, weave it into your Belief Ladder. Then flip the script. Picture the headline that would make your jaw drop, plant low-effort seeds, and sketch a plan that can swallow ten-times growth.

"TO BAD MEMORIES AND GOOD MISTAKES!"

I first blurted that toast fifteen years ago; my friends stared the way the NBA stars do in *Space Jam* when the monsters hijack their talent, wondering what had just possessed me. Since then the line has aged like good bourbon because it captures the play you've just run: honor the inevitable stumbles in advance, lock in the lessons before they hurt, and keep the runway clear for the lucky breaks.

5

QUESTION YOURSELF

 What if I'm the
bottleneck to success?

I WAS STANDING at a Nashville wedding bar when the small-talk bomb dropped: "So what do you do?"

Easy question, messy answer. At that point in 2018, I was speed-dating ideas—vinyl-record marketplaces, vertical-community ad networks, and my latest crush: rolling up mom-and-pop fire-extinguisher-maintenance shops.

I launched into the thesis: Quarterly inspections are mandated everywhere, California's about to tighten reporting, the industry's fragmented—buy, bundle, print money.

My new acquaintance nodded, then grinned.

"Ever installed a suppression system yourself?"

"No, but—"

"Know who's liable when a tank misfires?"

"Uh…"

He flashed his fire-department badge. Reality check delivered. I backpedaled with my tail between my legs.

The insight was solid; the timing was fine, but a colder dread kicked in: What if I am the hidden flaw—the founder-shaped hole that sinks a perfectly good opportunity? The sniff test snapped on the first rung: credibility in an industry where lives and lawsuits hang on competence. That night I finally admitted the obvious: Ideas, timing, and motive aren't enough if the person in the mirror doesn't know how to carry the hose or drive the fire truck.

Which brings us to the final discipline of curiosity and the last checkpoint before you commit to your idea. The Mirror Test is often the hardest part: Before you hire, raise, or even wire-frame, stare down four practical questions about yourself—superpower, style, 2:00 p.m. energy, and credibility—and score them with the same honesty you apply to your market research.

THE MIRROR TEST

METRIC	KILLER QUESTION	GREEN-LIGHT ANSWER
SUPERPOWER	Which task makes me faster than five hires?	A skill that bends on the core rung in the ladder
STYLE	Chameleon or peacock?	Fits the culture of the market you'll sell to
2:00 P.M. ENERGY	What am I doing when caffeine is optional?	The activity you drift to when no one's watching
CREDIBILITY	Can I talk about this for three hours unprompted?	Yes, or a plan to acquire the stripes fast

After I shelved the fire-extinguisher roll-up and leaned into our e-commerce thesis, I felt that guardrail snap into place. The venture demanded speed, depth, and endless curiosity. Together, my co-founder and I had the full kit. My superpower? It was sheer horsepower, which was needed in this fast-moving category. Credibility gap? Covered by my co-founder's decade of operator scars. Style? I could hang with the twenty-something founders in the morning and brief private equity suits in the evening. And the 2:00 p.m. Joy? Mapping ecosystems until the icons blurred, I saw that Assembly wasn't just a better idea—it was a venture where my skills could materially tip our key assumptions in the right direction and give us a fighting chance at success.

The ideal state is simple to describe yet brutal to achieve: every critical task the business demands sits squarely inside either your sweet spot or a teammate's. When that alignment clicks, motion feels frictionless, and hours compound into momentum instead of dripping into frustration. The Mirror Test forces you to map that overlap (or lack of it) before investors, customers, or employees point it out in harsher terms. If a metric flashes red, you have only three levers: level up, partner up, or pivot the idea to something that matches your wiring.

DEFINE YOUR SUPERPOWER

A superpower is the task where your personal effort-to-impact ratio is absurdly lopsided—minutes of your time move the scoreboard like hours of anyone else's. As I mentioned, mine was sheer horsepower, or as I like to call it: Kool-Aid Man energy Give me a half-baked concept at breakfast, and by lunch, I'm elbows-deep in a launch plan with all the edge cases identified.

CUE	HOW TO SPOT	BUILT-IN TAX
FLOW STATE	Work that makes you lose track of time	Fires smolder while you're "in the zone"
COMPLIMENTS	Colleagues thank you twice a month for	People over-delegate that task to you
DELEGATION	Tasks land on your desk even when unassigned	Bottleneck risk— your inbox piles up

Flow, feedback, and delegation are the three flares that reveal that unfair edge. Work that drops you into timeless focus—that's flow. Colleagues who keep thanking you for the same help—that's external validation. Projects that boomerang to your desk even when unassigned—that's the market voting with its feet. Catch all three signals in the same activity and you've found the lever you'll still pull on day 700, long after adrenaline fades.

Consider how a superpower can bend an entire market:

→ Sara Blakely's storytelling magnetism transformed Spanx from a bootstrapped side hustle into a billion-dollar staple. She could distill an awkward, intimate problem into a thirty-second QVC pitch that made viewers laugh, nod, and reach for their wallets. That talent let her bypass traditional retail gatekeepers, drive word-of-mouth, and keep ownership while competitors fought for shelf space.

→ Jensen Huang's conviction turned NVIDIA from a niche chipmaker into the backbone of the AI boom. While rivals chased incremental CPU gains, Huang doubled down on programmable GPUs and CUDA,

arming developers with parallel computing tools. His
edge wasn't diversification—it was the discipline to ride
one thesis until the market caught up.

→ Whitney Wolfe Herd's cultural reframing turned
Bumble from another dating app into a category
challenger. By making women send the first message,
she turned a simple product rule into a stance on
agency and safety. That shift drew a distinct audience
and carved space in a crowded market.

Three founders, three different capes—each one the lever that
moved the world while the rest of the company built itself around
the tax column. Identify yours, cover the toll, and the unfairness
compounds in your favor.

DO YOU BLEND IN, WALDO?

Style is your public posture—the accent you adopt, the metaphors
you reach for, the clothes you wear when you pitch. Founders
usually fall into one of two camps: (1) a chameleon who dissolves into the market's native tongue until customers forget
they're outsiders; or (2) a peacock that broadcasts contrast so
loudly that nobody can ignore the new thing they're selling. Both
approaches work.

Katrina Lake shows the quiet power of chameleon mode.
Appearing on CNBC in head-to-toe Stitch Fix outfits and sprin-
kling retail-buyer jargon through investor decks, she spoke to
merchandisers in their own dialect while slipping data science into
an industry that still swore by gut feel. The entry was frictionless, but the trade-off was anonymity—people loved the service
yet often overlooked the founder behind it. Lake countered by

carving out thought-leadership channels where she could step out of camouflage without spooking her core buyers.

Peacock mode thrives when attention is scarce, and the incumbent story feels tired. Elon Musk's novelty flamethrowers said more about SpaceX's rebellion than any press release, while Drew Houston's first Dropbox demo—"Sync Your Stuff"—ditched enterprise lingo and won millions of everyday users before IT departments even noticed. The upside is viral lift; the downside is polarity—haters arrive as fast as fans, and rivals attack sooner. Founders who strut must pair spectacle with Swiss-clock execution or risk flaming out under the spotlights they built.

Neither posture is inherently superior; the trick is matching the costume to the crowd. Selling compliance software to hospital CFOs? Better practice the chameleon handshake. Disrupting legacy razors with irreverent humor? Unfurl the peacock tail. And if your natural style fights the market's immune system, enlist a partner who speaks the local dialect. The goal isn't to win a fashion contest. It's to make sure you can resonate and land with your customers.

SCRAP THE AFTERNOON NAP

Most first-time founders imagine they'll sprint from sunrise to midnight on pure zeal. Six months in, the 2:00 p.m. energy wall arrives, and what you still gravitate toward when your brain feels like sludge is a brutally honest readout of your wiring. That "slump magnet" isn't just a personal quirk; it's a litmus test for founder–company fit.

> → Howard Schultz hit the lull and wandered store
>   neighborhoods, chatting with baristas about bean

aroma and cup feel—tiny details that defined Starbucks's in-store ritual.

→ Anita Roddick used her slump to gather fair-trade tales from coconut and shea farmers, stories she printed on every Body Shop bottle to turn ingredients into activism.

→ Danny Meyer spent mid-afternoons pacing empty dining rooms, tweaking table angles and greeting scripts—the backbone of Union Square's "enlightened hospitality."

In each case, the task they instinctively tackled during the dip was exactly what their businesses needed most. That's the Mirror Test in action: if your 2:00 p.m. instinct fuels the company's core engine, you've found leverage. If it fixes something peripheral, or nothing at all, you've located a structural gap. Close it by reshaping your role, recruiting a co-founder, or if the misalignment is fundamental, rescope the venture.

The goal isn't to conquer fatigue; it's to confirm that the work you default to when energy is scarce drives the metric that matters. When those two lines overlap, the afternoon trough becomes proof you're paddling in the right ocean.

WHEN YOU MIGHT BE AN IMPOSTER

A founder should be able to talk about their domain for three hours with no slides, no notes, and before asking anyone for money. If you can't riff on the economics, the jargon, and the hidden landmines, you haven't lived in the problem long enough. Credibility isn't borrowed authority; it's confidence earned through immersion.

The Nashville firefighter popped my fire-extinguisher dream in thirty seconds. That sting was a gift. Either dive back into the trenches and learn, or partner with someone who already wears the stripes. Until you pass the "three-hour riff," you're asking investors to fund tuition, not execution.

I watched the same lesson replay midway through Assembly's rise. Freshly minted MBA teams stormed in as brand aggregators, buying Amazon sellers by the dozen with Excel bravado and zero operator muscle. On paper, they were building empires. In reality, they were juggling supply-chain snafus, suspended listings, and customer-support meltdowns they'd never seen before. Eighteen months later, half of those roll-ups had imploded or fire-sold at pennies on the dollar. Insight and timing matter, but so does knowing deeply what business you are in.

If your credibility gap is glaring, you have three moves: immerse (shadow customers until their pain becomes second nature), partner (find a co-founder with scars in the space), or niche down (start with a subset you already understand). Anything else is hoping the market won't notice, and markets always notice.

That's the Mirror Test at its harshest: are you the person the business needs today, or are you still auditioning? The quicker you answer, the faster you can address the gap, or discard the idea before it discards you.

THE CO-FOUNDER QUESTION

Going solo is possible, but it's lonely and stress-amplifying. A true co-founder adds a second superpower, a built-in pressure valve, and a real-time lie detector. You'll often find them where curiosity clusters: ex-teams, friend-of-friends, customer forums, at a bar, in an alley, anywhere really. Chemistry matters, but alignment matters more. Compare ladders, motives, and superpowers. If you both see the same contrarian rung and agree on how long you can tread water, you've cleared the hardest hurdle.

Reality is that gaps in your mirror metrics announce themselves quickly, and the fastest way to close one is to hand the missing stripe to someone who already wears it.

If I'd truly wanted the fire-extinguisher roll-up, the smartest next move would have been to hand that firefighter half the cap table. My investing muscle plus his domain expertise would have plugged the credibility hole in a single handshake. That's the litmus test: The sum of the parts must bend at least one key assumption on your Belief Ladder—faster trust, cheaper distribution, and deeper product insight. If adding a partner doesn't materially derisk a rung, you're collecting company, not compounding value.

The upside isn't just strategic; it's emotional. Stress that stays bottled pops at the worst time. A co-founder dissipates pressure in real time. Some days you're the buoy, and some days they are. Investors obsess over "founder–market fit," but "founder–founder fit" keeps you afloat when the tide flips.

WHEN THE FRAMEWORK DOESN'T APPLY

Sometimes the mirror shouts, "You're not qualified!" and you do it anyway. When the tide is still Low or just turning Rising, the ocean grants slack for outsiders who are willing to outlearn everyone else. In those early stages, customers are patient, press coverage is scarce, and mistakes cost less. If you combine that runway with irrational exuberance and grit, you can train yourself before the water gets choppy.

Data backs it up. An NBER study found that only about 11 percent of entrepreneurs start firms in the same two-digit industry where their fathers worked[21]—meaning nearly nine out of ten founders dive into waters they didn't grow up in. Outsiders are the rule, not the exception.

Take Michael Dubin. He wasn't a razor engineer; he was an improv comic and ad-sales guy. Yet during the DTC Low-to-Rising tide of 2012, he filmed a $4,500 warehouse video that went viral, crashed his servers with 12,000 orders, and sold Dollar Shave Club to Unilever for $1 billion just four years later.

Or Ben Cohen and Jerry Greenfield: two college dropouts armed with a five-dollar correspondence course in ice-cream making who opened a gas-station scoop shop in 1978—long before "craft" or "locavore" was cool. Their Low-Tide tinkering time birthed Ben & Jerry's, now a global brand that still markets those same homespun stories.

The pattern is clear: If the tide grants breathing room, and your conviction is volcanic, you can earn the missing stripes while the market is still forgiving. Budget trench time, recruit blunt advisors, and update your Belief Ladder as you climb. Once the water hits High Tide, you'll need the skills in place, but during Low and Rising, ignorance plus obsession can be a perfectly rational bet.

WHO'S THE FAIREST OF THEM ALL?

The mirror's taunt never quits: Someone out there is smarter, richer, better connected—why even paddle? Good. Let that comparison sharpen your focus, not dull it. Your job isn't to top every leaderboard; it's to tip a single belief-ladder rung from doubt to proof. If your skills or the cocktail you and a co-founder mix can shift that one assumption, you're already ahead of the tide.

Remember the hidden fear that opened this chapter: What if I'm the bottleneck? The honest answer is yes; at some point, in some dimension, you absolutely will be. So will every other founder. The difference is whether you recognize the gap early enough to patch it with learning, talent, or partnership before the water rises.

The mirror doesn't demand flawlessness. If your mix of super-powers, style, 2:00 p.m. energy, and credibility bends even one key assumption in your favor, that's enough to light the fuse.

You've got one last thing to do before taking the leap: Prepare yourself physically and mentally for what could potentially be the hardest period of your life.

BRACE FOR IMPACT

EXHAUSTION DOESN'T ANNOUNCE itself; it ambushes you in baggage claim.

My wife's San Francisco to Orange County flight landed at 6:00 p.m. I woke at 6:40 p.m. to six missed calls and a phone in low-power mode—on my screen and in my veins. I sped to the curb, apologized on loop, and took her straight to dinner, determined to salvage the evening.

Halfway through the entrées, she stopped mid-sentence and said with a sigh, "Hey, Mona Lisa." That's my friends' nickname for the deadpan stare I wear when my body is physically present but my brain is benchmarking churn (tracking how many users quit this month). I was right there across from her, yet I was galaxies away.

"IT IS NOT THE CRITIC WHO COUNTS... THE CREDIT BELONGS TO THE MAN WHO IS ACTUALLY IN THE ARENA, WHOSE FACE IS MARRED BY DUST AND SWEAT..."[22]

This is the stealth fear that ambushes almost every founder: If I don't throw every ounce of myself into this company, I'll fail. That all-or-nothing script sounds heroic, but it's the fastest route to burnout, not brilliance.

Too many business books tack burnout to the back as an afterthought. By then, you're running triage on a life that's already scorched. Addressing balance on Day 0 flips the script. You wire healthy defaults before the first all-nighter, so product sprints don't cost you your partner's trust, your kid's recital, or your own mental uptime. Front-loading the practice makes you a sharper founder in the boardroom and a safer bet as a spouse, parent, friend, and teammate, because nothing scales if the pilot burns out before takeoff.

The hidden entry fee for the arena isn't just dust and sweat. It's forfeiting the moments that remind you why you're alive—birthday candles, gate hugs, even a full-night's sleep—because startup lore screams 24/7 devotion or bust. Everywhere you turn, founders brag about back-to-back all-nighters as if exhaustion were a merit badge, and Twitter threads frame "I haven't taken a day off in three years" as the new monkhood. It's a seductive script, but it doesn't show the receipts: frayed marriages, stalled hobbies, friendships ghosted into voicemail purgatory.

In reality, the winners play a subtler game: devotion plus balance. Yes, they sprint, but they also build pit stops including hard-coded dinners, ten-minute meditations, and Saturday mornings offline, because they understand that a burnt circuit board can't ship products. Balance isn't laziness; it's preventative maintenance, the refuel that lets you hit the throttle again tomorrow at the same pace.

Seasoned venture capitalists quietly know this. They prize second-time founders not just for refined playbooks but for visible scar tissue. These operators have already maxed out the stress meter, learned work-life triage, and crucially discovered how to stitch themselves back together. A résumé packed with pivots, layoffs, and missed soccer games tells investors, "I've been punched, I'm still standing, and I know when to duck."

The sharpest founders go even further. They build dashboards for the invisible: sleep hours, skipped workouts, spouse-request backlogs. They spot the early fog, know when to reset, and course-correct before the arena's next haymaker lands. That habit of tracking warning signs and adapting in real time is the real moat, because a company only scales as far as its founder can stay on their feet.

ARENA WARNING SIGNS

IMPACT	EARLY WARNING	LONG-TERM DAMAGE
TIME	"Rain check?" texts, skipped workouts	Decision fog, chronic fatigue
RELATIONSHIPS	Missed birthdays, date-night phone checks	Trust erosion, isolation
MINDSPACE	Mona Lisa smile, 3:00 a.m. Slack scroll	Burnout, anxiety loop

Your **time** is the first domino. A slipped workout here, a "rain check?" text there—harmless in isolation. Pile up a week of them and you start swapping REM (deep sleep) cycles for caffeine and to-do list roulette. Cognitive science is ruthless: Even modest sleep debt tanks creativity, emotional regulation, and strategic thinking.[23] Sacrificing time is sometimes unavoidable—fundraise week, product launch—but smart founders treat it like a short-term loan, paid back with interest the moment the crunch passes.

The second domino is **relationships**: the birthday you half-Zoom through, the dinner you attend but scroll past. Early warnings arrive as sighs and side-eyes; let them stack, and you're suddenly the absentee protagonist in someone else's life. Relationships can absorb brief shocks (your partner will forgive a late night or two), but a sustained deficit converts into trust erosion and eventually isolation.

Domino three is internal **mindspace**—the invisible cycles that stitch ideas together. The telltale signs are that blank Mona Lisa stare, the 3:00 a.m. doomscroll because your brain can't power down. Lose mindspace and you don't just move slower; you start making worse calls, amplifying the stress loop that stole you in the first place. Recovery here is the slowest, which is why letting mindspace go dark while the other two pillars wobble is a writing on the wall.

You can afford to mortgage one of these pillars for a quick sprint; on rare, all-hands-on-deck weeks, you might even lean on two. But at three, the doubt loop begins:

"MAYBE I'M NOT CUT OUT FOR THIS."

CHECK IN WITH YOURSELF

Too often we skip the triage step. Panic hits, and we lunge for the nearest lever, cancel the vacation, fire off a 2:00 a.m. message to the team, and anything to make the discomfort stop. Often, we solve the wrong problem, because we never stopped to ask, "What's broken?"

THE POP FRAMEWORK

STEP	WHAT TO DO	WHY IT WORKS
P—PAUSE	4-4-6 rhythm for sixty seconds straight	Drops cortisol and gets you out of panic mode[24]
O—OBSERVE	Voice what's happening in one line	Shifts panic to logic-based decisions
P—PICK	Choose a few levers that you can pull now	Agency resets control over the situation

Apply the POP framework before you snap and crackle (sentence brought to you by Rice Krispies...*cue air horn*):[25]

First, pause and breathe. When panic spikes, vision narrows, and cortisol hijacks judgment. A single minute of controlled breathing—inhale for four counts, hold for four, exhale for six—tells the limbic system to stand down. You can do it in a Lyft queue or outside a boardroom. Sixty seconds is short enough to fit anywhere in your day, yet long enough to reopen the mental aperture you just lost.

Next, observe. Distill the crisis into one honest headline ("I overslept" is logistics; "I'm scared she thinks the company matters more than she does" is the truth), yanking the fear from the emotional basement into analytic daylight. Then, with cortisol down, scan every lever—from obvious fixes to far-fetched favors—until five or six paths stare back at you, which proves the situation isn't binary.

Finally, pick and move forward. Decide on a few levers you can yank immediately. Forget the perfect solution, go for the next best move, and then pull them fast: hit send, book the contractor, reschedule the call, whatever the plan demands before clarity fades and rumination creeps back. Decisive action restores agency, punctures anxiety, and builds muscle memory so the next flare-up feels like nothing.

When I slept through six frantic calls and left my wife circling Orange County airport's curb, POP would have rewritten the night. The breathing pause would have cooled the guilt surge; the observe—"I'm scared she feels second to the company"—would have surfaced the real wound. Assessing would have revealed the obvious culprits: five hours of sleep, no lunch, inbox at three hundred. The choice? Text her, order a car, and park any work thoughts until tomorrow. Doing those three acts would have said, "I'm late, but you're first," while setting an alert to never let that happen again.

Picture this: It's a regular Tuesday when your star employee says, "Hey, I got a competing offer. I'm giving my two-weeks' notice." Every entrepreneur will get this at some point. Your gut reaction is to hand over whatever they want, tell them to f*ck off, and/or let the news derail dinner with your family as you spiral through backfill scenarios. With POP, the reaction should be less dramatic. First, breathe (draw out a long "goosfrabaaaaaahhh").[26] Then observe. One person can't crater the company, and they could be leaving for many reasons outside your control. You can't understand why they are leaving until you talk to them, and they aren't leaving for two weeks. So put an invite on both of your calendars for the next morning, preserve your family dinner, and take stock of the situation the next day.

In the beginning, you'll feel like a fish dropped into boiling water—unable to name the stress and clueless how to cool it. Eventually, you'll see every flare-up triggers you to react in at least one of three ways: pointing to your nonnegotiables, grabbing for a release valve, or hitting a system reset. Those are the guardrails we'll bolt down next.

NONNEGOTIABLES

My wake-up call was a blown long weekend in Hawaii.

My wife had planned everything including flights, hotel, and dinner rez with friends, because we both needed a break. Monday, she asked, "You're still good for this weekend, right?" "Absolutely," I said. Wednesday, she asked again; same reflex answer. Then a not-really-urgent "fire drill" hit at work and, without even talking to her, I canceled the trip.

That was one of dozens: "Coachella? I'm in!"—cancelled. "Double-date Friday?"—ghosted. Soon my wife was the designated excuse machine: "Sorry, something popped up at work." The truth was simpler. I could have gone; I just hadn't drawn any lines.

Nonnegotiables are those lines. Without them, every incoming ping feels like a fire drill, dinners get "rain-checked," workouts dissolve, and your calendar turns a dismal, company gray as guilt and resentment pile up at home. With them, the guardrails are visible to everyone—anniversary dinners stay inked, Tuesday runs actually happen, and when a late-night "emergency" arrives, your team already knows the answer is "Catch you tomorrow."

Think of nonnegotiables as policy, not preference. You don't apologize for paying taxes or running payroll; you shouldn't apologize for guarding the three hours that keep your marriage, your lungs, or your sanity intact. Make them public, make them boring, and make them impossible to override except in truly existential moments (hint: most "emergencies" aren't).

When that surprise two-week notice really lands hours before your standing Wednesday family dinner, the boundary you've already drawn makes the decision automatic: The calendar stays blocked, Taco Tuesday is preserved, and the follow-up chat waits until morning. By treating that dinner as nonnegotiable long before any crisis, you eliminate the stressful "Will I? Won't I?" debate.

Founders who stay married to both their startups and their sanity treat these commitments exactly that way—immovable and routine. Following are a few examples.

→ *The Family Anchor* (Satya Nadella, Microsoft). He often credits family—especially raising a son with special needs—with reshaping how he leads, grounding Microsoft's culture in empathy, patience, and perspective beyond quarterly results.

→ *The Email Firewall* (Tim Ferriss, author/investor). He designed strict email boundaries—batching replies and limiting access—so inbound noise doesn't hijack his day. Communication isn't constant. Attention is protected by structure.

→ *The Meditation Constant* (Ray Dalio, Bridgewater). For decades he has practiced Transcendental Meditation twice daily, crediting it with clarity through market swings and leadership stress. Twenty minutes, morning and night—immovable.

→ *The Early Riser* (Tim Cook, Apple). He wakes before dawn—often around 3:45 a.m.—starting the day in quiet before the world floods in. The habit rarely

shifts, anchoring judgment before the inbox and
headlines arrive.

→ *The Sabbath Builder* (Jack Dorsey, Block/Twitter).
While leading two public companies, he organized strict
daily themes—management Monday, product Tuesday—
carving protected blocks for focus so chaos didn't
dictate how time was spent.

I bring up these founder examples not to fill the pages but to
show that people running the most successful companies practice
balance. Each ritual sends a clear signal that preserving personal
priorities makes them sharper leaders, not distracted ones. When
the calendar defends what matters off the clock, the company
benefits on the clock: Decisions arrive clearer, and teams mirror
the boundaries.

RELEASE VALVE

Early in my career, the copy room doubled as a confession booth
for me. A few trusted colleagues and I would grind till lunch, then
slip downstairs to let the steam out. *Can you believe Mark took
credit after not doing any of the work?*

It was a silent pact: Vent hard, say nothing outside the circle,
return to spreadsheets sane.

Founding a company blows that safety hatch clean off. Outside
your co-founder, if you have one, there's no lateral peer to absorb
a rant. When an employee vents upward, you have to referee, not
commiserate, and friends or family can listen but rarely speak the
language of cash burn, churn, and runway scope. The steam still
builds; it just has nowhere to go. That's why every durable founder
designs a release valve as deliberately as a product roadmap.

Your release valve can be whatever you want it to be so long as it settles you; whether that's a ten-minute "rage walk" on the phone with your mom, a hate journal that you scribble on in the bathroom stall, or a Nerf basketball hoop in your office where the rule is you need to score ten times before making a decision. The point is less about the ritual itself and more about carving out time to let yourself "get it out" so you can choose a logical path forward.

Back to the two-week-notice scenario: Once your Taco Tuesday dinner is wrapped and the kids are in bed, you pull out your phone. You drop a raw, two-sentence SOS into the private "brain trust" text thread you keep with three noncompeting founders: *"Bad headspace—our lead designer just gave two-weeks' notice."* Within minutes, the replies roll in: one fires off a sympathetic "been there"; another shares a quick retention tactic; the third reminds you how this is a blessing in disguise. You feel heard. By morning, you're steadier and ready to tackle the conversation logically.

Below are five founders, five stress-release blueprints, each a living reminder that sustained high performance isn't about enduring pressure but about engineering it safely out of the system before it detonates.

> → *The Therapist-in-Chief* (Marc Benioff, Salesforce).
> He has spoken openly about working with therapists and spiritual teachers while building Salesforce, treating mental hygiene as seriously as earnings. Reflection wasn't indulgent—it was fuel.
> → *The Founder Confessor* (Brad Feld, Foundry Group).
> He documents the emotional volatility of venture life and long advocates therapy and founder openness.

Naming the dark days, he argues, reduces stigma and helps leaders carry the load.

→ *The Operator's Journal* (Sheryl Sandberg, Meta). After profound personal loss, she turned to writing and reflection, sharing the practice as a way to process grief while continuing to lead teams, strategy, and operations at global scale.

→ *The Builder's Therapy* (Ben Silbermann, Pinterest). During Pinterest's slow early years, he described leaning on close peers and honest conversations to manage doubt while growth lagged expectations. The pressure was shared, not carried alone.

→ *The Creative Release* (Reed Hastings, Netflix). He has spoken about carving out time for outdoor activity and decompression, stepping away from boardroom pressure to reset perspective before returning to strategic decisions.

Bottle the stress and it will seep into board decks, one-on-ones, and date night. Unfortunately, all it takes is one outburst, and your board will label you as erratic and your team will think of you as volatile. Nobody earns a medal for acting like a sealed vault that finally explodes in year ten. Choose a release valve and lean into it when the first response that comes to mind is emotional, not logical.

SYSTEM RESET

After my deflated childhood basketball dreams floated off, I pivoted to the least-judgy sport I could find: running. You pick a direction, set a pace, no teammates, no referees. It's perfect for a kid haunted by "Am I good enough?" At first, it was just exercise, but somewhere around mile two, the anxiety soundtrack dulled, and the low-grade hum of self-doubt lifted a few octaves. Twenty minutes of pavement could repaint the whole day.

Fast-forward to California and I became *that* guy—hot-yoga pass, sauna nights, cold-plunge mornings, white-noise naps, keto experiments. Different rituals, same medicine: Flush the brain before the doubts mildew. Neuroscience backs the hunch. Moderate cardio spikes BDNF, the protein that rewires stress circuits, while even ten minutes of mindfulness nudges the amygdala off red alert.[27] Translation: Motion and stillness can both reboot the operating system if you schedule them like critical tasks instead of luxuries.

Founders usually spiral the opposite way. Revenue dips → work longer → skip workouts → order DoorDash at midnight → pants allegedly shrink in the dryer. That loop is physically unsustainable and mentally lethal. The antidote is a scheduled reset—a practice that yanks you out of code and back into a body. The best founders protect that reset the same way they protect payroll: nonoptional, nonnegotiable, and visible on the company calendar.

Back to the two-week-notice scenario one more time. Instead of catapulting straight into Zoom at 8:00 a.m., set the alarm for 6:30, slip into a twenty-minute sauna to sweat out the cortisol, sip water, and let your pulse slow. By the time the calendar alert dings, you're walking to the computer clear-eyed, notebook open, already rehearsing the coaching questions your friends suggested the night before. Whether the employee shows up disgruntled, dangling a higher salary, or simply burned out, you enter the call with an oxygenated brain and a game plan. It's proof that one reset can convert into a measured, even optimistic, conversation.

Even the most inspirational, always-positive founders need a reset. The cheerleader on stage is still a human behind the curtain, and their optimism stays credible only because they schedule regular tune-ups. These founders created their own resets:

→ *The Store Walker* (Howard Schultz, Starbucks). During turbulent stretches, he returned to stores, walking floors and talking with baristas to reconnect with the craft. When the noise rose, he went back to coffee—letting the ritual reset his judgment.

→ *The Sleep Evangelist* (Arianna Huffington, Thrive). After collapsing from exhaustion, she rebuilt her life around seven to eight hours of sleep, banning devices from the bedroom and reframing rest as a leadership discipline rather than a luxury.

→ *The Sunrise Athlete* (Richard Branson, Virgin). He rises early and exercises daily—swimming, tennis, cycling—before turning to business. Movement comes first, inbox later. The routine clears his mind before the day accelerates.

→ *The 4 a.m. Reader* (Tim Cook, Apple). He wakes before dawn—often around 3:45 a.m.—and begins the day in quiet, reading customer emails before the world floods in. The calm precedes the call sheet.

→ *The Dancing Founder* (Payal Kadakia, ClassPass). A lifelong dancer, she kept dancing while building ClassPass, calling it the practice that kept her grounded through fundraising and scale. The studio remained her reset button.

Call it a run, a nap, a screen fast, twerking to your favorite big booty mix, or a salsa class, just call it "scheduled." Because a reset missed once is an anomaly, missed twice is a trend, and missed three times is a new habit—one that ends with your body taking your brain hostage.

DON'T BE LIKE ADAM SANDLER

Remember Adam Sandler's magic remote in *Click*? He mashes "fast-forward" on the "boring stuff" only to wake up divorced, estranged from his kids, and horrified that the scenes he skipped were the ones that made life worthwhile. Startup life hands you the same remote: skip the workout, skip the weekend, skip the birthday. Keep pressing that button and—exit or no exit—you can find yourself alone at your own victory screening, stadium lights over an empty house.

Dust, sweat, and a little blood in the arena are nonnegotiable; what is optional are the gate hugs you miss for "one more email," the laugh lost to a Slack ping, the small hand you don't hold on the walk to school. Guarding those moments is not a perk; it's the insurance that keeps victory from feeling like defeat.

The hidden fear says, *If I pause, the company craters.* The cure is a daily loop, lived not listed: Ink your nonnegotiables so fire drills bounce, vent the pressure in a standing outlet before it ruptures, and protect a body-first reset with the same ferocity you protect payroll. When panic still slips through, run POP—pause, observe, pick—so crises shrink. Master that loop and the remote loses its grip. The startup still races, but life keeps its best scenes intact.

SECTION 1 RECAP

EVERY EARLY-STAGE DOUBT is really a prompt for action. The trick is to catch the sentence playing in your head, answer it with practice, and keep moving before the echo grows teeth. The six chapters in this opening section each turn a classic panic line into a repeatable countermove:

- → Choose Your Fuel. When you think, *Why am I doing this?*, nail down one motive: Wealth, Control, Passion, or Ego. Then draw borders and filter every choice with that lens.

- → Question the Insight. When the worry is, *Smarter people skipped this for a reason*, build a Belief Ladder, attack each rung with blunt user feedback and rival clues.

- → Catch the Wave. When dread says, *Am I too late to the party?*, label today's tide: Low, Rising, High, or Receding, and plan accordingly. Timing outperforms hustle.

- → Spot the Swans. When the headline *Founder Flames Out* flashes, draft it, ring-fence the fallout, write the confetti version too, and plant cheap options to ride the upside.

- → Question Yourself. When you hear, *Maybe I'm not the right person for this*, name your superpower and 2:00 p.m. energy, spot the gaps, and recruit partners or do a reset.

- → Brace for Impact. When you panic and say, *If I slow down, we die*, preblock sacred hours, keep a scheduled vent outlet, and lock in a daily body-mind reset to stay levelheaded.

SECTION 2

START OFF ON THE LEFT FOOT

7

THROW SPAGHETTI

DOUBT VOICE: What if the thing I'm about to build is exactly the wrong thing?

NOVEMBER 2023, 4:17 a.m.—I marched up to the coffee shop beside our office and yanked the door.

Nothing. It was closed. Obviously.

I trudged back through the predawn chill, uncaffeinated and crawling toward one of the worst days of my career. In two hours, I'd tell the whole company about the reduction in force, then sit through one-on-one Zoom calls with affected employees, each which was gutting.

Four years earlier, everything we touched had turned green: Our first product vaulted from beta to hockey stick in weeks—wait lists, praise tweets, instant product–market fit. Yet, here I was, doubting every instinct: *The insight was solid…the timing perfect—so how did we face-plant?*

"HOW COULD THIS GO WRONG WHEN WE PLANNED EVERYTHING RIGHT...ON PAPER?"

The logic had seemed airtight. Brands were suffocating under on-site ad inflation and starving for cheaper, organic ways to acquire customers. Amazon's brand-new attribution API looked like a golden bridge to bring new traffic from outside the Amazon walls, and we were uniquely positioned to execute on it. We knew analytics, we knew link tracking (necessary in this case), we knew the brands—of course we would win. Riding high, we assembled a sixty-person launch squad, parked a seven-figure GTM budget, and recorded onboarding videos before the first beta user typed a password. All of it balanced on an Amazon API still labeled "beta," and we assumed it would hold.

It didn't. The spec changed; conversions evaporated; early adopters ghosted. Four months later, we were already in retreat. Less than a year later, LinkedIn slapped me with a headline: a rival—same insight, twelve-person team, shoestring MVP—had raced to $10 million in revenue in six months. Our timing and thesis: right. Scope and DNA: catastrophically wrong.

The self-doubt voice didn't whisper; it roared.

The real phantom behind all that turmoil is simpler: It's the dread that your very first step will be the wrong one. You worry you'll pour months into a dud, or worse, freeze at the microphone while a leaner team wings it and wins. Name that fear now, because once you admit the terror of a bad opener or sudden stage fright, you can design experiments tiny enough to fail fast, cheap enough to repeat, and public enough to keep you moving. That's the cure for paralysis and the antidote to perfect-on-paper plans.

WHY MOST SPAGHETTI DOESN'T STICK

When founders debate "How big is big enough for launch?," the loudest voices cluster at two poles. On one end stand the *Lean Startup* purists: ship a skateboard, watch it wobble, bolt on wheels, iterate forever. On the other end roar the *Blitzscaling* champions: raise a war chest, staff an army, flood the market before anyone can pronounce your name. Both playbooks work and both implode.

What neither one admits is that the right scope is never a moral choice. It's an alignment problem with your DNA, the market timing, and the single riskiest assumption in front of you. These three components, presented in Section 1 of this book, tell you how large or small your first release should be. Together, they tell you where your product (spaghetti) is most likely to stick.

STICKY SPAGHETTI SPECTRUM

STYLE	CUSTOMER SEES	WHEN IT WINS
COMMUNITY	Podcast/newsletter that hand-holds early fans	Authority and insight beat code; no pressure
CONCIERGE	Founders deliver the outcome by hand	High-touch learning validates assumption
TOOL	One painkiller feature in an ugly UI	Market is broad and incumbents are asleep
RENTAL	Leverage 3P integrations to solve pain points	Multiple pain points to solve at once
RAISE THE BAR	Incumbent features plus one painkiller feature	Customers have pain but expect certain things
BLITZ	Brand, GTM cannon, capital to scorch earth	Winner-takes-most and the window is tiny

Start with the assumption. Pick the one rung you can move, such as strangers in cars, one-click checkout, or glamping at Four Season rates, rather than a macro wave you only watch. Think Amazon testing Prime by offering two-day shipping to a slice of ZIP codes, or Netflix green-lighting *House of Cards* to prove viewers would subscribe for originals. If that single bet breaks in your favor while everything else flops, you still emerge with proof investors or customers who care. If it breaks against you, pivot early and cheap.

Next, tag that assumption with a tide reading. Low-Tide calm rewards slow learning through community meetups or concierge pilots. A Rising Tide may call for a quick tool or rental layer that can expand overnight. High-Tide frenzy, where buyers benchmark you against incumbents, often demand a Raise the Bar release: Nail the table stakes customers already expect, and then add one killer twist that gives you the right to win.

Now layer in your founder–market fit. If you and one teammate can describe "great" in this domain with your eyes closed, you can risk a scrappier build. If you're still learning the vocabulary, bias toward smaller, hands-on formats where every interaction doubles as research.

Combine those coordinates and choose along the Sticky Spaghetti Spectrum. Low Tide plus half-baked fluency? Ship a community or concierge test. High Tide, vanishing edge, but deep expertise? A tool or rental play that iterates daily, or do a Raise the Bar launch if customers demand polish out of the gate; it makes more sense. Only in winner-take-most markets where you're fluent, funded, and the window is tiny does the full Blitz feel rational. Let the assumption, tide, and DNA pick the pot.

PUT THE SAUCE BEFORE THE NOODLES

By now you'll notice some subsection titles make sense, and others make you scratch your head saying, "What the f*ck does that mean?" You're seeing one of my superpowers live in action—amazingly awful analogies that hit 60 percent of the time. Sauce before noodles equals the cart before the horse.

Moving on.

A community approach treats your first product as a gathering place, not an item on a shelf. Think of a weekly email bulletin, a breakfast round table you host at the local coworking space, or a short podcast where you surface ideas and invite stories. Success isn't feature velocity; it's audience velocity—opens, replies, and people bring friends. Because the content is cheap to tweak, every discussion becomes fresh intel for whatever you build next.

Choose this path when the only question that matters is, "Will enough people rally around this problem?" If money is tight, the market isn't racing, and you (or someone on the team) can naturally lead a workshop, write an engaging newsletter, or moderate a small forum, you can start by shipping ideas instead of products and watch which topics spark the loudest pull for a real solution.

A community launch maps best to a Passion motive. You're fueled by the topic itself, energized by the dialogue, and willing to trade short-term revenue for the chance to learn out loud with kindred spirits. Ego can add sparkle. Hosting a room puts you on stage, but without genuine Passion the content grind quickly feels like unpaid labor. If the joy of talking shop and sparking a discussion is what gets you out of bed, community first is your spot.

Graduate to building product the moment three signals align: the crowd turns from passive readers to active requesters, their questions converge on one repeat pain point, and back-of-the-envelope math says even a small paid conversion would fund your next few months. At that point, more content yields diminishing insight. A tool or concierge prototype in their hands will teach you faster.

As I reflect on why Assembly's very first product found product–market fit so fast, one truth towers above the rest: We built a campfire before we built code. In 2016, our team suspected that winning on Amazon was a black box, so we lit a public conversation. We had podcast microphones, a Facebook group, and daily "ask-me-anything" threads. Thousands of sellers poured in and almost in unison, they kept asking one question: "Which keywords actually move rank?" That single chorus birthed Black Box, the stripped-down dashboard we shipped that is still our most-used product today.

Assembly's path isn't unique. Other founders have proven that a community campfire can ignite an entire business before a single line of product code is written.

→ Warby Parker paired a mission-driven blog voice with campus pop-ups spotlighting overpriced eyewear. The home try-on kit launched into that early buzz, turning student curiosity into direct orders before traditional retail had time to react.

→ BrewDog's "Equity for Punks" invited drinkers to invest small amounts for equity and perks. Thousands joined, funding expansion while becoming evangelists. The community wasn't just marketing—it fused capital and loyalty before global growth.

→ Monzo built in public, sharing its roadmap and onboarding early users through staged beta waitlists. That transparency turned customers into collaborators.

When access widened, demand surged from a crowd already invested in its direction.

Each story follows the same arc: Spark conversation, listen until one pain point dominates, and then build the tool the crowd is practically begging to pay for.

NOBODY SAYS NO TO HANDMADE PASTA

A concierge launch is entrepreneurship done with rolled-up sleeves. Instead of offering an app, template, or finished widget, you promise an outcome, such as photos edited, bookkeeping balanced, influencer campaign run, and personally walk through every step to deliver it. Because you control the workflow by hand, you spot the hidden frictions no survey or mock-up can reveal. This route shines when processes are messy, data sources unreliable, or trust matters more than scale. The customer's fee funds your learning loop, and the checklist you refine becomes the blueprint for future automation or for hiring a team.

Choose the concierge path when three conditions feel true: Your biggest unknown is how to deliver the outcome, not whether anyone wants it; a handful of high-ticket customers could cover expenses while you learn; and at least one founder can run the service end to end, logging every hiccup for a future playbook. In this stage, manual effort is a feature, each repetition exposes hidden steps, and trust builds faster than any polished brochure.

The concierge play is tailor-made for founders whose dominant motive is Control. You want your hands on every lever, every client conversation, and every tiny process tweak. Because you personally deliver the outcome, you decide what "great" looks like, refine the workflow in real time, and raise prices at your own pace. Passion-driven founders can thrive here too, but it's the control seekers who truly relish running the entire service end to end before handing pieces off to a team or system.

Shift out of concierge when the work feels like déjà vu. If clients beg for a quicker, self-service option, 80 percent of each engagement repeats the same tasks, and a quick margin check shows that systematizing those tasks would lift profit instead of draining cash. It's time to codify. Whether you hire staff, create checklists, or invest in lightweight tools, the goal is the same: bottle what you've learned so far, and free your team to tackle the next issue.

Our product miss brought up earlier in this chapter made this lesson vivid. The rival that lapped us never called itself "software" on Day One. Two founders, a color-coded spreadsheet, and endless Zoom calls ran full-service creator and publisher campaigns for brands that couldn't navigate Amazon's new rules. Every glitch, including a mis-tagged link, late post, or wrong commission went into a living playbook. Six months later, they hired ten developers, turned that playbook into a dashboard, migrated the brands they'd served by hand, and sprinted past eight-figure revenue while we were still doing our postmortem.

Assembly's wake-up call isn't an isolated tale. Plenty of breakout brands started the same way by selling the finished dish, cooking it by hand, and using the glitches as their recipe for scale. The pattern shows up in wildly different industries, from fashion to chores to personal style.

→ Rent the Runway began with its co-founders personally delivering designer dresses to Harvard dorm rooms, gathering fit notes and swap frequency before investing in warehouses or dry-cleaning robots.

→ TaskRabbit launched as a single Craigslist post. Founder Leah Busque ran errands around Boston herself, timing routes and tip sizes; those datapoints became the matching engine once demand outpaced her bicycle.

→ Zappos started when Nick Swinmurn photographed shoes in local stores and posted them online. Whenever an order came in, he bought the pair retail and shipped it himself. The hands-on hustle proved customers would buy footwear sight unseen and mapped every fulfillment step before the first warehouse opened.

Each story follows the same pattern: Promise the outcome, deliver it manually, log every hiccup, and only then build the system that bottles the magic.

NONNA SAYS APPETIZERS ONLY

A tool launch is the digital (or physical) equivalent of a Swiss Army blade with just one razor-sharp edge: a single feature that erases a headache the moment customers touch it. Ugly interface, duct-taped packaging—doesn't matter. What counts is that the user can solve their own problem without emailing you. The goal isn't depth; it's instant self-serve relief that proves demand exists at scale.

Pick the tool route when three clues line up: (1) your riskiest assumption is, "Will people fix this pain themselves if I hand them one button?" (2) the tide is rising—users and rivals are moving fast enough that manual services won't keep pace, and (3) the team already speaks the domain fluently enough to ship fixes daily. This play best fits a Wealth motive: You're hunting a broad market, betting that volume, not bespoke service, will compound returns.

Move on from the tool stage as soon as the pattern gets predictable. If customers keep asking, "Can it handle X as well?" and you notice most users bump into the same limit, it's a sign the single-feature pocketknife has done its job. Add up the numbers: If expanding the tool or layering on a broader solution would raise profit rather than just costs, it's time to upgrade. When the questions repeat, and the value plateaus, add the next thing.

At Assembly, we saw this when we transitioned our community podcast to a self-serve tool. After months of podcast debates and Facebook threads, sellers begged for something—anything —that would rank keywords on Amazon. We answered with Black Box, a self-serve dashboard that looked like a GeoCities tribute to 1997: chunky buttons, clunky tables, zero design awards. But pain outranked polish. The moment people could paste a product ASIN and see winning terms, adoption exploded. Moving from "theory on a mic" to a tool everyone could click was the inflection that put Assembly on the map.

Across food, finance, and fashion, other founders have discovered one unmistakable "aha" moment is enough to launch an empire before polish or breadth ever show up.

> → Typeform launched with one twist on online forms: one question at a time, delivered conversationally instead of a wall of fields. Not an analytics suite—just a better way to ask. Higher completion rates fueled growth before features followed.

> → Discord launched as simple voice chat for gamers frustrated with laggy alternatives. No creator tools, no Nitro tiers—just reliable, low-latency communication

mid-match. Once communities formed, servers, bots, and paid features followed.

→ Venmo began as a simple way to pay friends back without cash or checks. No banking suite, no merchant tools—just split the bill and move on. The social feed spread adoption fast. Cards and business tools came once usage exploded.

Each story follows the same rhythm: Ship one painkiller feature, let users cure themselves, watch the data pile up, and only then decide what to bolt on next. When the headache is brutal enough, even a tool that looks like dial-up internet can become the launchpad for an empire.

MAKE THE SAUCE, BUY THE NOODLES

A rental launch is like hosting a dinner party with ingredients from half the restaurants in town. You don't farm the tomatoes, bake the bread, or distill the olive oil. You plate it all so the guest never wonders who grew what. In business terms, you stitch together other people's capabilities, such as payments, inventory, delivery fleets, and data feeds behind one easy surface. Customers experience a single solution, while your partners carry most of the capital cost.

Choose rental when you spot a pain made of several smaller hassles that nobody wants to juggle. Your key doubt is, *"Will people pay for someone to glue these moving parts together?"* The market is heating up fast enough that building every piece yourself would make you late, and your team already speaks the partner lingo well enough to keep the handoffs invisible. Rental suits founders driven by a mix of Control and Wealth: You choreograph the stage and partners foot the heavy bills.

Shift once the borrowed kitchen cramps the menu. If partners start throttling volume, raise their fees, or fail to keep up with your quality bar, it's time to own a layer or two. Maybe negotiate direct contracts, buy a small supplier, or write your own software to protect experience and profit. When outside links become the weak links, graduate to the Raise-the-Bar playbook. Or if you've gained enough conviction/know-how and the market opportunity is big enough, take a gamble on Blitzing if you've got the risk appetite for it.

Plenty of founders have walked this same "borrow first, own later" path. Here are three that turned smart borrowing into breakout growth:

→ DoorDash began by stringing together restaurant menus, Stripe payments, and freelance drivers who already owned cars. Diners got hot food without leaving the couch, while DoorDash kept overhead low. Only after scale did the company invest in data-driven dispatch, ghost kitchens, and nationwide driver perks.

→ ClassPass's Payal Kadakia didn't build gyms; she aggregated their empty-class slots under one membership that let users hop from yoga to boxing. Studios filled idle inventory, members loved the variety, and ClassPass later layered on premium tiers and corporate perks.

→ TurboTax's Tom Gonser's early online filer pulled government forms, IRS e-file rails, and credit-card payments into one workflow, so taxpayers could finish in an evening. After volume proved the appetite,

Intuit added audit-defense, live CPA chat, and refund-advance loans.

Each story shows: Rent the pieces, arrange them beautifully, charge for the convenience, and upgrade to ownership only when borrowed parts start to limit growth.

OPENING AN ITALIAN RESTAURANT IN...ITALY

A Raise the Bar launch means walking onto a field full of seasoned players and promising everything customers already expect plus one unmistakable edge. You can't show up half-baked. Refunds must flow, receipts must reconcile, security and uptime have to match the incumbents. The point of difference might be price, speed, or a single magical feature, but baseline performance has to be flawless.

Choose this path when three realities collide: (1) your market is crowded, and table stakes are nonnegotiable—think payments, tickets, medical data, or big-ticket consumer goods; (2) your riskiest assumption is *"Can we out-execute on quality while adding a twist?"*; and (3) your team has deep domain chops or regulatory muscle to clear the bar on Day One. Raise-the-Bar appeals to Passion-plus-Control founders—people obsessed with craft and unwilling to launch until the foundation is bulletproof.

Raise-the-Bar is one of the riskiest plays on the spectrum: You're committing to match an incumbent's entire checklist and add your twist, which can soak up capital and patience long before you know whether you're right. Treat it as a rolling audit. Every quarter ask, "Is this still true table stakes, or could we rent that layer—or double down on our killer feature—and get to market faster?" If the answer keeps tilting toward "build it all," be sure the budget and runway can survive a marathon. If not, lighten the load with a rental partnership or refocus on one differentiator that will make customers forgive gaps elsewhere. Continuous testing keeps you from pouring years and millions into a hamster wheel that yields no tangible results.

At Assembly, when we built our first advertising automation product, the stakes were sky-high: We were dealing with clients' advertising spend, and more than fifty tools already crowded the shelf. Brands expected rock-solid budgeting, bid controls, and crystal-clear reporting from the first click. We spent a year grinding out an MVP that met those expectations—hardly an MVP at all by lean standards—because one misallocated dollar would torch trust. Raising the bar on reliability bought us credibility. Only then could we layer on integration to the rest of our product suite that made the product truly different.

Plenty of consumer giants have made the same bet. They met the industry's full checklist before daring to add their secret sauce.

→ Peloton delivered a studio-quality bike with commercial-grade reliability, then layered live classes and leaderboards. No squeaky pedals, no shaky streams. Baseline gym expectations were nailed before "high-five" camaraderie made the bike a phenomenon.

→ Robinhood matched the security, trade accuracy, and FINRA compliance of legacy brokers, then dropped commissions to zero and wrapped it in a two-tap mobile flow. The twist mattered only because the basics felt rock solid.

→ Eventbrite knew arenas wouldn't ditch Ticketmaster unless uptime, scanning speed, and anti-fraud were flawless. The company partnered with small venues

first, perfected those table stakes, and only then
wooed larger stadiums with self-serve dashboards
and data insights.

Different industries, same play: Clear the existing bar so customers don't flinch, then raise it just enough that they'll never look back.

PREPARING FOR A FUTURE
MICHELIN STAR

A Blitz launch is an all-out land grab: Raise more money than feels safe, hire ahead of revenue, flood ads, lock in supply, and aim to become the default before competitors breathe. It works only when the prize is genuinely winner-takes-most—ride-hailing in one city, social video in one feed, meal kits in one suburb—because the first mover that scales often cements habits the rest can't pry loose.

Founders reach for Blitz when three forces converge: (1) speed matters more than elegance—delays let rivals copy, supply dry up, or regulators freeze the lane; (2) capital is abundant and impatient, often nudged by investors who need home-run returns to balance their portfolios; and (3) demand is elastic enough that pouring fuel (discounts, ads, promo codes) really bends the growth curve. The motive here is usually pure Wealth or Ego—build the biggest, fastest, loudest thing and let valuations sort themselves out.

But Blitz is also the most misused playbook. Venture backers love it because portfolio math rewards a handful of outsized wins. Anxious founders love it because moving slowly feels like falling behind. Assembly learned that lesson the hard way. You've already heard our misfire: We tried to Blitz a problem that still needed concierge learning, and we burned cash proving it. The moral: If the market doesn't crown a single king, or if table stakes aren't yet nailed, Blitz becomes an expensive game of chicken.

During every funding round, ask, "Is this still a winner-takes-most race, and have we truly earned the right to scale?" If margins are shrinking under promo spend or growth is buyer-subsidized rather than product-pulled, it may be smarter to downshift to a Raise-the-Bar polish or even rent missing pieces until conviction rebounds.

→ Uber ignored city-by-city frugality and Blitzed with driver subsidies, rider discounts, and lobbyists, betting that dense liquidity would tip each market forever. In most major metros, it worked. Once riders knew a car was five minutes away, later entrants felt invisible.

→ TikTok (ByteDance) poured nine-figure ad budgets into Western markets, including running Super Bowl spots, to seed the "For You" feed with creators and viewers simultaneously. The algorithm's early addictiveness and relentless spend pushed legacy social platforms onto the defensive within a year.

→ CNN+ offers the cautionary flip side: WarnerMedia poured roughly $300 million into splashy promos for a streaming news hub, yet debuted just weeks before the Discovery merger froze budgets and muddied distribution strategy. Daily users never cracked 10,000, subscriber habits never formed, and the service was axed after one month.[28]

Each tale underscores Blitz physics: When the game truly is speed or death, nothing else will do. When it isn't, the cannon recoil can break the ship.

DON'T LET YOUR POT BOIL OVER

Ours boiled over and we felt the scald. We went Blitz on a problem that really needed a slow-burn concierge phase. But worst of all is that we didn't course-correct when we needed, because we didn't think that was an option. Manual hours ballooned, the API kept mutating, and "quick fixes" devoured whole sprints. By the time we faced the mismatch, the burn rate had outrun traction and there was no easy way back.

Plenty of founders change playbooks mid-flight, and it's not "selling out." It's seasoned judgment. The best entrepreneurs read the dashboard, spot the stall, and course-correct before the engine flames out. That ability to pivot on logic, data, and pattern recognition is exactly why second-time founders sit at the top of every VC wish list.

Southwest Airlines began as a single intrastate shuttle (concierge logistics), proved people loved no-frills fares, then Blitzed the country once gates and planes were financed. Blue Apron launched meal-kit deliveries by hand-packing boxes in a rented kitchen (concierge), codified the packing line into a tool, and finally raised capital for national Blitz marketing. Sometimes the answer is a new playbook; other times the Belief Ladder proves shaky and shelving the idea early saves years and dollars.

When those warning lights flash, run this quick gut check before the stew scorches:

STYLE	COMMON RED FLAG	WHAT IT MEANS
COMMUNITY	Nobody joins or the same people engage with you	The problem is not real or the solution already solves it
CONCIERGE	Manual work growths are linear with the number of users	You're proving operations, not product
TOOL	Sign-ups spike but weekly active use flatlines	The problem exists, but the solution falls flat
RENTAL	Bad gross margin or user requests partner features	You picked the wrong thing to build yourself
RAISE THE BAR	Customers find your edge not that interesting	You're picking the wrong fight with incumbents
BLITZ	Platform you're building on is shifting too fast	Your solution will become stale fast

Every style mismatch starts with the same hidden fear: "*If I slow down, I'll lose my shot.*" That self-doubt nudges you to keep ladling water into the wrong pot even as the bubbles hiss. Fight it by returning to the only metric that matters. Are you proving or disproving a single, contrarian rung on your Belief Ladder? If the answer is no, pivot the cookware or, even braver, turn off the stove. Doubt will still mutter, but now it's steam you can safely vent, not a boil that burns the whole kitchen.

MUTE THE ROCK STAR

SOMEONE ONCE TOLD me that Los Angeles sidewalks are covered with those little mint-green, self-serve floss-pick wrappers dentists hand out after cleaning.

The next morning, I spotted three on my walk to work. By lunch, I'd counted nine. By dinner, I was blaming the city's potholes on oral hygiene. When I told friends, they started seeing wrappers everywhere too. I'd get texts: "Dude, this is insane, how have I never noticed this!?"

That's the Baader-Meinhof phenomenon: Notice something once, and you suddenly see it everywhere. The same illusion hit me the first time I read a LinkedIn post that screamed from the mountaintop:

"LOOKING FOR A ROCK STAR CANDIDATE."

Novel, I thought, until my feed turned into a music festival of rock star product managers, growth hackers, and brand gurus. By lunch, I thought the Rolling Stones were going to launch a new company funded by Blink 182.

Then the metaphor cracked.

Who wants a real rock star on Day One? Rock stars trash hotel rooms, show up late, and demand a bowl of green M&Ms, which is opposite of the teammate you need when the shipment goes missing at dawn and a furious customer is already on the phone.

Yet founders still chase the myth of the unicorn hire—someone with unshakable bravado, a résumé studded with big-name logos, and a promise to "10× everything by Friday." Once a company is humming, you can survive a few swing-and-miss hires. On Day One, though, bringing in a diva with an agenda can drain cash, derail culture, and rob you of the runway you need to reach product–market fit.

I learned that lesson the jittery way. Before Assembly, I had never hired a true operating team and was still finding my sea legs. Startup Twitter (now X) screamed, "Find the once-in-a-lifetime unicorn who'll end world hunger!" The doubt loop whispered the opposite fear: *Hire someone too good and they'll expose you, then ask your co-founder why he partnered with a lightweight.* Interviews became ping-pong matches between hero-shopping and defensive panic.

The cure wasn't bravado; it was clarity on what an early-stage company needs.

Early-stage startups run on three workhorse roles, not flashy headliners: Translators, Builders, and Zealots. Translators listen to customers, decode the real pain, and turn it into clear to-do lists. Builders whip up a rough-and-ready version by tomorrow—

even if the paint is still wet—so the next customer sees progress. Zealots keep the energy high when the numbers look scary, reminding everyone why the hard slog is worth it.

If you're one or even two of these, great. If not, your first hiring mandate is to find the missing piece before chasing world-class soloists. Product–market fit (customers pulling the product out of your hands faster than you can ship it) shows up when Translators hear the pain, Builders patch it overnight, and Zealots make sure no one quits before the next release.

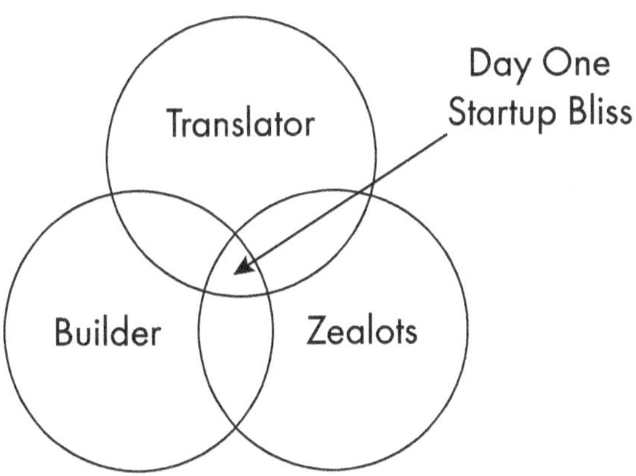

HOW DEEP IS YOUR LOVE?

Before you hunt for designers, engineers, or growth wizards, secure one role first: a Translator who grasps the hidden "why" behind every assumption on your Belief Ladder. Surface-level feedback: "People want consolidation," "This design doesn't feel right" rarely pinpoints what's truly broken. A Translator digs until the root cause, clicks with the ladder's riskiest rung, and then turns it into a clear action.

FLUENCY	WHAT YOU REALLY KNOW	FIRST MOVE
FLUENT	You can diagram industry workflows in your sleep	Skip to Builder; you already have a Translator
WORKING	You speak the lingo but still spot-check on Google	Recruit an advisory circle to support you
TOURIST	Jargon feels foreign and you are uncomfortable	Add a co-founder or early hire to fill the gap

If you're **fluent**, think YETI's founders, lifelong hunters who could list cooler specs blindfolded. You debate jargon for sport and recognize problems customers haven't voiced yet. Comfort comes from intuition; discomfort only appears when the rules change. Treat that edge with humility: Grab an outside skeptic to keep you from solving old pain with yesterday's fix.

A **working** grasp means you speak the dialect but still fact-check after calls. Sweetgreen's college-age founders could preach salad culture, yet farm logistics and food-safety codes made them sweat, so they installed veteran suppliers and a produce adviser early. If that's you, form an informal board of gray hairs who've already tripped on those land mines; their corrections keep your roadmap honest.

Tourists need subtitles; they love the vision but stumble over the basics. Casper's e-commerce founders knew online funnels, not coil counts, so they recruited mattress engineers and retail veterans to steer product R&D. When you're this green, the fastest path is a Translation co-founder, or early hire who has "lived the pain" and can own every customer interview until the language sticks.

When a Translator is missing or speaks only at a shallow level, the product often solves the wrong pain. Juicero, for instance, raised roughly $120 million to build a $400 Wi-Fi–connected juicer, yet its value proposition never aligned with how most people actually made juice at home. When reporting showed the proprietary packs could be squeezed by hand, mockery went viral overnight. The machine solved a problem many customers didn't feel. The moral is simple: If no one on the team can translate day-to-day user grit into a crisp spec, every feature is an educated guess, every sprint a gamble, and even perfect execution can land miles from where customers actually hurt.

As mentioned in Chapter 5, my superpower was to get up to speed on topics incredibly fast. I devoured white papers, prowled forums, met with everyone in the space, convinced I could shorten my lack of previous domain knowledge with sheer force. Before formally launching the company, I gained a working grasp, but by no means was I fluent. We finally admitted no one on the founding team could translate deep Amazon pain points, and we brought on two sharp domain advisers.

You usually won't find a great Translator through a glossy résumé blast. You find them in the places where the real grumbling happens. Lurk in niche sub-Reddits or the comment section of controversial industry topics with one hundred people liking it. The people who speak up with oddly specific complaints, such as "The pH balance on this reminds me more of a low-elevation bean," "FDA lot codes don't fit our label printers are already translating for free." Reach out, buy coffee, and ask them to walk you through a day in their shoes. If their stories keep looping back to the exact rung on your Belief Ladder, you've located your sherpa.

Just remember that depth can be double-edged. Veteran Translators carry scar tissue, and scar tissue can calcify into "That's impossible" reflexes. Your edge as a founder is the fresh perspective that says, "Yes, but what if...?" A Translator's job is to make the pain vivid, not to dictate that the old way is the only way. Let them map the potholes, and then let your Builders test new routes. If the Translator declares every detour is a dead end, you're anchored to yesterday's view. The reason you're here is to chart something nobody's driven before.

Pattern after pattern says the same thing: Companies that secure a true Translator early accelerate; those that bluff, stall. Hire or become the person who can connect customer pain to your riskiest assumption, and the rest of the org stands on rock instead of quicksand.

HOW HEAVY IS YOUR DRUM SET?

Identifying the pain is only half the battle; cutting through that pain with a precise, workable solution is the other, and it's usually harder. Ideas remain hypothetical until a Builder rolls up their sleeves and forges your riskiest Belief-Ladder assumption into something customers can touch, taste, or try.

Crucially, the Builder's skillset must match the lift of the project: A simple fix needs a quick-and-dirty craftsperson who thrives on speed; a hard technical or operational lift calls for someone who's shipped that MVP before, and an abstract R&D leap demands a co-visionary who will explore unknowns for years. Matching the Builder to the lift is what turns insight into proof.

LIFT COMPLEXITY

LIFT	WHAT YOU NEED TO KNOW	FIRST MOVE
SIMPLE	Problem is clear; solution is straightforward	First a scrappy contractor or vibe code yourself

LIFT	WHAT YOU NEED TO KNOW	FIRST MOVE
HARD	Problem is clear, but solution is technically tricky	Bring in a Builder who has shipped this before
ABSTRACT	Even defining the solution takes deep craft	Add a co-founder or heavy equity early hire

A **simple** lift means the path to value is obvious: think Allbirds hand-sewing their first wool sneakers with a contract shoemaker and a borrowed shoe mold. If you can sketch the solution on a napkin, hire a freelancer, or spend a weekend hacking just to watch a real customer use it. Comfort here is speed; discomfort shows up only if you overengineer version one or realize the lift is more than expected.

A **hard** lift crops up when the idea is clear, but the plumbing is gnarly. Peloton needed live-stream video, Bluetooth hardware, and secure payments to feel seamless on Day One. They hired an ex-enterprise video engineer as founding CTO who had shipped stacks before and could own the timeline end to end. If you're at this level, budget for a seasoned Builder who has wrestled similar nightmares and knows which corners can and cannot be cut.

An **abstract** lift appears when even the blueprint is fuzzy. Impossible Foods couldn't just toss soy into a burger. It had to bioengineer plant heme. Founder Pat Brown became the chief Builder, pairing with PhD scientists and raising science-heavy capital because no freelancer could conjure that first patty. When the lift is abstract, your Builder must be a co-visionary who stays until the science, craft, or process is repeatable.

When the Builder is missing or mismatched, the entire plan can implode. Coolest Cooler smashed Kickstarter records, raising $13 million for a "Swiss Army" party cooler, yet no supply-chain veterans could translate the flashy prototype into scalable, cost-controlled production. Component prices spiked, fewer than two-thirds of backers ever got a unit, refunds bled cash, and the startup melted away within five years. A brilliant insight, but the wrong Builder for the lift.

At Assembly, we got lucky. The company we acquired on Day One came with a Builder who'd already shipped advertising tech, email infrastructure, and data products. He knew how to spin up an affordable, high-output engineering hub, had a working grasp of our sellers' day-to-day headaches, and understood his limits. He pulled in outside UX and data-science help when the work fell beyond his strike zone. That awareness kept the solution aligned with our key assumption instead of wandering.

A great Builder should mirror the requirements to solve the riskiest rung on your ladder. Hire a world-class design expert to craft dashboards when the real gamble is a data pipeline, and you'll polish a shell with nothing inside. Hire a backend engineering savant to optimize queries when the leap is consumer trust, and you'll miss the mark in the opposite direction. The Builder's strength should map one-to-one with what must be proven now. They should be confident enough to admit, "I'm not the best at X," so you can supplement before cracks widen. Nail that match, and execution stops being a bottleneck and starts compounding every insight your Translator uncovers.

FINDING YOUR GRATEFUL DEAD FANS

In the early days, founders usually wear every hat: answering support emails at midnight, cold-calling suppliers at dawn, then tinkering in Figma before lunch. That works until momentum arrives. Suddenly, the company's biggest risk isn't product gaps;

it's lost cohesion. Uber felt this in 2010. Travis Kalanick could code surge pricing and pitch VCs, but someone still had to recruit, onboard, and cheerlead every black-car driver in San Francisco. The answer is a Zealot: a teammate who treats the mission like oxygen and welds the seams while everyone else focuses on their lane.

Our glue was Bradley. He started as a power user in our Facebook group and joined "to lead evangelism," which is code for wearing whatever hat was on fire. One week he hosted a twenty-four-hour live stream to gather feature requests; then he overnight shipped swag on his own dime because a fulfillment delay annoyed him. He even flew himself to Dubai, Manila, and Karachi to shake hands with sellers we had only seen as email addresses. That zeal let the rest of us stay heads-down on product.

Uber had the same magic in Austin Geidt. While Kalanick tweaked code, Geidt cold-called chauffeurs, hand-delivered iPhones, triaged payout bugs, and moderated driver forums— sometimes in the same day. Her "one-woman launch kit" became the template for every new city.

Both stories prove the rule: founders can juggle Builder, Translator, and Zealot for a season, but speed compounds the moment a full-time glue grabs that hat.

So how do you find your Bradley or Austin?

ZEALOT CHECKLIST

FILTER	LOOKING FOR	QUICK TEST
ZERO EGO	Shares credit in highs; takes blame in lows	Identify previous projects that went sideways
EDGE SKILL	10× output on one critical task	Find pattern in projects they get asked to do

FILTER	LOOKING FOR	QUICK TEST
MISSION	Recites your why off script easily	Ask what they'd want to fix if they joined
LEARNING	Changes stance when new data is presented	What would they do if they had half the time?
RANGE	Happy heads-down or leading a room	Previous role changed and they were OK with it
TOUGHNESS	Doesn't fold when things aren't working	Company went sideways and they stayed

They have **zero ego**. Great glue players shine the light on others and soak up blame. In Airbnb's early years, cofounder Joe Gebbia often stepped into customer support and host mediation roles, crediting engineers for wins while absorbing frustration when bookings went sideways. Ask a candidate for a flop story; if their instinct is "The team did X well; I fell short on Y," you've spotted the trait.

They've got **edge skills**. In Facebook's early growth phase, product leader Chamath Palihapitiya focused relentlessly on activation mechanics, routing onboarding and engagement experiments through his team until retention improved. When crises hit around growth, people looked to him for one thing: fixing user engagement. Look for that pattern—if teams consistently call someone to solve one critical problem, you've found a 10x output source.

They are **fluent in your mission**. At SpaceX, early engineers weren't just building rockets—they were building toward Elon Musk's stated goal of making life multiplanetary. Employees routinely articulated the long-term vision in interviews and recruiting, reinforcing purpose alongside technical work. Test for the same by asking, "Join tomorrow. What's the first fix and why?" True

Zealots answer in the customer's language and tie it to purpose, not perks.

They have a **capacity to learn**. At Netflix, early product and operations hires had to pivot repeatedly—from DVD logistics to streaming infrastructure—adapting to entirely new technical and licensing challenges as the company shifted models. Drop a new constraint mid-chat—half the budget, double the timeline—and see if the candidate calmly resequences instead of freezing.

They've got **range**. Early Shopify employees often toggled between support, product testing, and merchant onboarding as the company scaled, filling gaps wherever needed. Probe a sudden role swap in your prospect's past. If they leaned in, learned fast, and shipped, you've got the breadth early chaos demands.

Most important of all, they've got **toughness**. During Airbnb's early regulatory battles in New York and San Francisco, small operations teams worked through legal uncertainty and public backlash while continuing to support hosts and guests. Ask for a crisis they endured. The Zealot worth hiring stayed, improvised, and shipped anyway—proof they won't fold when everything breaks.

Finding someone who nails every box on the Zealot checklist is rare; most candidates shine in two or three traits and need time—or teammates—to round out the rest. Decide up front which gaps you can tolerate, then move fast when a near-perfect match appears. Remember, you hire people for their superpowers, not their shortcomings. If a candidate has the range and toughness you need but only "working" mission fluency, you can coach the story. If they live the mission and radiate zero Ego but lack a single edge skill, you can upskill or pair them with a specialist. The danger isn't a few rough edges. It's waiting for flawless and missing the glue that keeps the venture together.

ONBOARDING YOUR ZEALOTS

Welcome a Zealot with the same straight-shooting honesty that attracted them. Begin by laying your true motive on the table. If you're aiming for a three-year flip, say so. If you're chasing a decade-long mission, make that clear instead. Few things drain zeal faster than realizing they enlisted for a crusade and wound up in a quick-flip sprint.

Next, achieve an early significant victory. Hand them one real customer headache or internal snarl they can untangle in the first week. Shipping something visible kills analysis-paralysis, validates their edge-skill in the eyes of the team, and lets them taste momentum right away.

From there, set a thirty-day stress test. Agree on a bold, time-boxed sprint and watch how they set priorities, surface blockers, and bounce back from hits. If the fit feels off now, it will feel worse when the stakes rise.

Finally, remember that a startup's world reshuffles weekly—new data, fresh hires, unexpected fires. Zealots thrive on that churn, but only if you give them room to adjust their own playbook. Decide which one or two checklist traits you must have and be ready to overlook the rest. You hire for strengths, not to patch every weakness. Bring the right glue in early, trust them with real problems, and the self-doubt in your head won't disappear, but it will have to shout over a teammate whose conviction rings louder than doubt.

WHAT IF I'M JUST THE OPENER?

Everyone feels it but few admit it: You scan a résumé that outshines yours, pulse spikes, and the doubt loop hisses, *"Hire this person and everyone will wonder why you're CEO."* Here's the truth: Companies that welcome talent capable of eclipsing the founder don't crumble; they compound.

PayPal is the poster child. Engineer #12, Jeremy Stoppelman, later built Yelp; Steve Chen and Chad Hurley spun out YouTube; Reid Hoffman founded LinkedIn; yet PayPal still sold to eBay for $1.5 billion and minted tech's most famous "mafia." Yahoo hired backend coder Jan Koum; nine years later, he launched WhatsApp and sold it to Facebook for $19 billion, but Yahoo's founders never rued giving him a launchpad. Apple brought in Tony Fadell to run iPod engineering; he went on to create Nest and sold it to Google for $3.2 billion while iPod and iPhone sales soared.

When a hire eventually overshadows you, see it as proof you staffed for scale, not Ego. Their later success validates your talent filter. Future stars notice where today's stars learned their craft. Alumni who build empires become partners, investors, distribution channels, and recruiting magnets. Most of all, they raise the floor: If you remain the sharpest person in every meeting, your company's ceiling is set painfully low.

Yes, it's uncomfortable to bring in people "better" than you, but that discomfort signals you're casting a band that can play arenas you haven't booked yet. Separate authority (you still set the mission and values) from authorship (experts write the pages they know best), then step back and orchestrate. Hire for superpowers, supplement the weaknesses, and remember the hidden fear that launched this chapter: *What if my first hire exposes how little I know?* The only thing that will be exposed is a founder (you) wise enough to surround doubt with teammates who drown it out with results.

9

PICK YOUR POISON

DOUBT VOICE: What if nobody believes
in my vision and slams the door shut?

APRIL 2019, ROOFTOP bar in Los Angeles, spritz in hand.

Two hours earlier, we'd presented to a top-tier family office that owned an NBA team—relaxed jokes, sharp questions, nods at every slide. They swept us to a white tablecloth dinner, uncorked a Brunello (a fancy red wine), and coaxed out the inspirational stories that made us misty. By dessert, we were trading childhood anecdotes. Deal done, or so we thought.

A week later came the polite "not a fit" e-mail.

"WEREN'T A FIT FOR YOU?"

My inbox blurred. We'd iced every other investor conversation to court them, and the "no" felt terminal. The self-doubt voice pounced: *So much for your* résumé and a year of turning over every stone—no one buys your story.

Tunnel vision had blinded us. The family office's pedigree and checkbook gave us beer goggles, and we skipped the important questions: How do you work with founders? What does success look like to you? What's your risk appetite? We never asked ourselves:

"WERE YOU A FIT FOR US?"

The question landed with a thud, right after it was too late to ask. The hidden fear, of course, is that if you push back or probe too hard, the money will vanish, and everyone will decide you're not "fundable." So you over-laugh at the dinner jokes, gloss past vague answers, and interpret every yellow light as amber-tinted enthusiasm. In that approval trance, you miss the signals—slow diligence, small initial checks, allergic reactions to risk—that would've warned you the partnership was wrong.

Postmortem clarity flipped on every red bulb at once. Assembly needed speed and a big first swing; they favored tiny pilot bets. We believed the market was sprinting; they thought the macro was dubious. We wanted to buy a platform company immediately; they preferred a wait-and-see nibble. Their eventual "no" should have been no surprise.

Funny how things work. A moment that felt like the end became the beginning of something special.

Fifty-two days later, we met the investor who already under-wrote our thesis, loved our urgency, and wired a war chest without hand-wringing. Had the first group said yes, we'd have acquired a small asset, watched someone else scoop up Helium 10 (our first big platform acquisition), and spent the next decade recounting the almost-story over pints in an Irish pub. The door that slammed turned out to be the exit from the wrong building.

Investors aren't faceless banks. Each category of money, whether it's your uncle's check, a classic Sand Hill VC, or a revenue-based lender comes with its own antidote (speed, network, patience, operating muscle) and an equal-and-opposite poison (pressure, dilution, hidden vetoes, shifting priorities). Your job is to pick the cash whose cure you absolutely need right now and whose side effects you can survive. The grid below is a quick cheat sheet.

INVESTMENT PATHS

TYPE	ANTIDOTE (GAIN)	POISON (LOSE)
SELF-FUNDED	Full control, no dilution, learn discipline	Every mistake drains personal savings
FRIENDS AND FAMILY	Quick yes from people who trust you, flexible	Guilt and tension if things don't work
EMPLOYER FUNDED	Day-job salary, benefits, resources to launch	IP ownership murky; capped ownership
ANGEL INVESTORS	Fast money, founder empathy, warm intros	Small checks run out; advice quality varies
MICRO OR SEED	Hands-on help to PMF; bridge to your Series A	Limited follow-on; bandwidth spread thin
CLASSIC VENTURE	Big brand, board leverage, hiring magnet	High-growth bar, unicorn-or-bust mindset
GROWTH OR PRIVATE EQUITY	Large lump sums, late-stage playbook	Rigorous dashboards, push for efficiency
FAMILY OFFICE	Patient capital, long-term mindset, flexible	Slow decisions, priorities can flip quickly
STRATEGIC INVESTOR	Distribution channels and industry credibility	Roadmap can skew toward parent's agenda
DEBT LENDER	Nondilutive cash ties to performance in biz	Go from swan to shark when things go south

Seem overwhelming? Start by grabbing a pen and looking at the table above. Circle the antidotes that jump off the page to you—speed, distribution, all hands on deck—and X out any poison your company simply can't absorb yet: dilution, board pressure, talking to your family. Then, layer in what you already know from earlier chapters: your dominant motive, the riskiest Belief Ladder rung still unproven, the tide you're surfing, and the lift that lies ahead. The right investor path is who will ultimately: (a) give you money, and (b) be aligned to the foundation of your strategy/choices.

Let's walk through each:

Self-funded capital works when Control is your motive. The key risk on your Belief Ladder sits squarely inside your skillset, the market tide is still low, and the "lift" (the amount of work to get a first offer in front of customers) is simple. The gain is complete freedom: You can launch, tweak, or ditch an idea overnight without asking permission. The loss is that every wrong turn withdraws straight from your savings and your confidence, so pace experiments to cash burn and force yourself to kill weak ideas quickly. GoPro began exactly this way. Nick Woodman bankrolled homemade surf-camera prototypes with bracelet money, proved surfers would pay, and still owned the whole cap table when big retailers came calling.

Friends-and-family capital best fits Control, who can tell their family to buzz off, and Passion founders whose biggest unknown is, "Will anyone care enough to show up?" These are classic, early-stage community or high-touch test projects. The gain is a fast, trusting yes plus flexible terms; the loss is emotional debt, because every late delivery or pivot resurfaces at the next wedding or holiday dinner. Ring walked this line: Jamie Siminoff raised doorbell seed cash from relatives, iterated without board pressure, yet felt personal heat to ship on time and get to the next level.

Employer incubation works when you want steady income while you prove a simple idea and the corporate tools, data, or factory floor can speed you up. The gain is salary, resources, and a safety net; the loss is murky ownership rights and the risk the parent company shuts the project down or claims it once it succeeds. Gmail began as Paul Buchheit's 20 percent side project at Google. He tapped internal servers and talent until user demand made the product too valuable to ignore.

Angel capital shines when the tide is clearly rising, the concept is a lightweight tool or service you can sell without hand-holding, and the motive tilts toward Wealth through fast experimentation. Quick checks, personal introductions, and empathetic coaching are the gain. The loss is a short runway and advice that can conflict week to week depending on who you are talking to. Calm used well-connected angels to crack media partnerships while the founders tested meditation formats until downloads exploded.

Micro- and seed-fund money bridges a proven concept to clear product–market fit when the tide is picking up speed and the lift is harder. Maybe it's a technical hurdle or a regulated process, but still well defined. Intensive partner time, design help, and a path to bigger rounds are the gain. Limited follow-on cash and a ticking clock are the loss. Notion rebuilt its note-taking engine under First Round's "roll-up-your-sleeves" support, hitting usability milestones fast enough to land a larger round before money ran dry.

Classic venture capital fuels a full Blitz play in winner-takes-most, high-tide markets where motives blend Ego (we want to dominate) and Wealth, and the bet is that moving first locks in network effects. The gain is brand halo, giant checks, and a Talent Magnet; the loss is unicorn-or-bust pacing that can bend culture and strategy. Robinhood took NEA's rocket fuel, spent ahead of revenue, and took zero-commission trading mainstream before incumbent brokerage giants could react.

Growth-equity and private-equity funding suits profitable companies entering Raise-the-Bar territory. The tide is still rising, the lift is repeatable but capital hungry, and the motive is Wealth via disciplined scale-up. Deep pockets and IPO-tested playbooks are the gain. Data-heavy dashboards, quarterly efficiency targets, and less forgiveness for stumbles are the loss. SimpliSafe bootstrapped to strong revenue then partnered with Sequoia Growth, swapping freewheeling sprints for structured national expansion.

Family-office capital matches decade-long Passion missions in steady waters, where growth can be patient and craftsmanship matters. Ultra-flexible, low-pressure money is the gain. Slow decision cycles and heirs who may change priorities overnight are the loss. Tracksmith tapped the Walton family funds to open stores and refine heritage-grade supply chains, comfortable that success would be judged in years, not quarters.

Strategic investment is ideal when distribution, not invention, is the big gamble. It's often a scaled rental play, and the motive tends to be Wealth, as you prioritize buying the fast-pass ticket instead of waiting in line. Instant access to shelves, factories, or customer lists is the gain. The loss is that your product roadmap can drift toward the parent's agenda, and you have a single point failure (a recipe for a black swan event). Beyond Meat sold Tyson Foods a minority stake, gaining factory bandwidth and freezer space while fiercely guarding its plant-based mission.

Revenue-based lending or venture debt appeals to owners who crave Control, already have predictable margins from a working product or service and need extra fuel without giving up equity. Nondilutive cash tied to revenue growth is the gain. Repayment spikes if sales waver are the loss, so you must be confident the tide won't suddenly turn. Ilia Beauty used Clearco advances to load holiday inventory, repaid from receipts, and kept every share. They traded strict cash-flow discipline for full ownership.

With all that laid out, remember these lanes blur in real life. Family-office capital can swing for the fences on a moon-shot brand. An employer-incubation route may give you far more day-to-day Control than a late-stage growth-equity board ever will. Even some angel rounds come with corporate-grade dashboards, while a "hair-on-fire" classic-venture firm might let you run wild as long as the numbers climb. Treat the labels as guardrails, not guard dogs. Map the antidote you need, weigh the poison you can stomach, and pick the partner whose reality, not reputation, matches the business you're building.

The most important thing is getting to know who they are IRL (in real life). Shake hands, lock eyes, and confirm they believe in every rung of your Belief Ladder. They should buy into both the sweeping macro tide and the contrarian micro leap that underpins your plan. If they wobble on either, keep searching. Once alignment is clear, ask which investment cratered and insist on talking to that CEO. An investor's behavior when everything implodes reveals more than any victory lap. If these things check out, you'll know they see you as a partner and human, not a line item.

CHANNEL YOUR INNER ADAM NEUMANN

If you're twenty pitches deep and investors keep vanishing into "circle-back" limbo, the odds are the idea isn't the real problem. Yes, some notions are truly bonkers; someone raised millions to deliver pizza by drone in 2014, yet the checks cleared because the story was airtight. Most founders, by contrast, shuffle into the room at 1,000 feet, pour every detail of their six-month vision board onto the table, and hope volume substitutes for vision. That isn't a pitch; it's a brain dump, and no spreadsheet pedigree can rescue a narrative that drowns the listener in minutiae.

Most pitch decks die because they stay in the cerebral cortex. You fire facts, such as addressable market, growth, and retention curves, while the listener's gut stays flatlined. Story beats data every time, so flip the order: Hook the feeling first, then lace it with facts. Think of the deck as a five-scene movie trailer. If an investor can sense tension, stakes, and inevitability in two minutes, the diligence that follows becomes confirmation, not persuasion.

There are many things I've screwed up over the years, but with the thousands of founder pitches I've heard, professional pitch coaches I've worked with, and trial and error, I'm very confident in the following information.

THE MOVIE TRAILER

STORY BEAT	YOUR JOB	EMOTION TRIGGERED
WORLD SHIFT	Name an irreversible change reshaping space	"Oh-oh, status quo is toast."
WORLD DIVIDED	Show there will be a divide of winners/losers	"I want to be on the winning side."
PROMISED LAND	Paint life for the end user at the end state	"I want to live there. How do we get across?"
THE BRIDGE THERE	Sprinkle the milestones that make it palatable	"Alright, this is getting more realistic."
MAP IN HAND	Give evidence that you are the best navigator	"These are the people who can take me there."

World shift hits when a habit you thought was permanent flips overnight. Picture that oat-milk lattes outsold whole-milk cappuccinos at Blue Bottle. That quiet menu stat signaled a mainstream craving for plant-based everything, and every café owner who'd scoffed at alt-dairy suddenly felt late to the party. You're looking for an instinctive nod that the change is real and irreversible. If the room pauses to debate whether it's "just a fad," stop. Belief Ladders don't climb themselves.

World divided makes the line visible: Cafés that leaned into plant-based options now post "sold out" signs by noon, while old-school diners tip unsold jugs down the drain. The split should feel so sharp that investors picture themselves on the winning side before you finish the sentence. If they defend the laggards (people will come back to regular milk), you've uncovered a mismatch.

Promised land lets them taste tomorrow. Imagine baristas frothing zero-carbon oat milk, commuters snapping photos of "cow-free" lattes, and farmers earning more per acre growing oats than feed corn. When you land this picture, the table leans in, eager to know how fast it arrives. If eyes drift to laptops, the vision didn't stick.

Bridge turns the dream into realistic next steps: locking a regional oat supplier at fixed prices, piloting ten high-traffic cafés, and rolling out keg dispensers that cut cost and waste. Each milestone makes the idea feel more real and easier for investors to wrap their heads around. The moment investors jot numbers instead of objections, you know momentum is showing its face.

Map proves you're the guide worth backing. You already doubled sales at a test café, have the former procurement lead from Stumptown on payroll, and hold a letter of intent with the West Coast's biggest distributor. When investors hear that, still call your toughest reference, and then return more excited, you've converted curiosity into conviction.

This was Assembly's storytelling arc in one breath:

Marketplace retail has hit a breaking point: New selling channels appear every quarter, while spinning up an e-commerce brand is cheaper than ever. That change has split the field. Incumbents are still chained to one storefront, and a contrarian camp (ours) is already moving wherever the shopper scrolls. In the promised land, a three-person team runs ads, inventory, and profit analytics for ten marketplaces from a single Assembly screen. The bridge starts with our keystone move: acquiring an Amazon toolset, planting a flag on the world's largest marketplace, and unlocking real-time data, seller trust, and API firepower that compound with every new channel we wire in. We have the map. We've fully charted and have an inside angle within the ecosystem, and we have our next five moves in motion.

As you build your own story, season confidence with a pinch of self-doubt. Naming the blind spot that still unsettles you, and showing the plan to kill it, signals self-awareness, invites partnership, and earns trust much faster than glossy bravado. But close the loop: You've logged the reps, pressure-tested the numbers, and believe in the outcome. If you don't back yourself, whether it's body language, words, or energy, it will show.

DON'T ANSWER THE QUESTION
THEY'RE ASKING

If your movie-trailer story lands, the meeting usually drifts into what sounds like softball questions: "How big is the market?" and its polite cousins. Do not be fooled. Those lobs are X-rays: Investors watch how you parse the subtext to see whether the discipline behind the story is as sharp as the poetry. Nail the answers, and the momentum keeps flowing; flub them, and the earlier magic dissolves.

THE SOFTBALLS THAT ARE ACTUALLY CURVEBALLS

QUESTION	QUESTION BEHIND THE QUESTION
HOW BIG IS THE MARKET?	Have you pressure-tested your addressable market with realistic segmentation?
WHO ARE YOUR COMPETITORS?	Do you understand the battlefield and your offensive/defensive edge?
WHAT'S THE BUSINESS MODEL?	Which monetization paths have you weighed, and why did you choose one?
HOW WILL YOU ACQUIRE USERS?	Is there a single repeatable channel—with early signal—or are you dreaming?
WHY DO YOU WANT TO DO THIS?	What's your motive: Control, Wealth, Passion, Ego? Are you honest about it?

How big is the market? Tell them you've run the numbers, not dreamed them up. Start with the customers you can realistically reach in the next few years. Glossier, for example, launched by counting the loyal readers of its beauty blog and pricing how many would buy a $16 Boy Brow, not by waving at a $500 billion cosmetics pie. Once you've nailed that "reachable slice," widen the lens to show how new products multiply it. A grounded base plus a believable path to upside says, "I know where the first dollars come from, and I know how to stack the next ones."

Who are your competitors? Investors really mean, "Can you describe the playing field and why you still score?" Acknowledge the toughest rival. Think of Yeti tipping its hat to Igloo for dominating cheap coolers. Then point out the built-in edge they can't copy overnight (in Yeti's case, indestructible design and premium branding that let it charge five times more). Respect for your elders plus a clear moat trumps loud bravado.

What's the business model? Investors know your revenue engine will evolve. What they need to see is that you understand the full palette of options, have picked one for now, and can explain when you'd switch gears. Walk them through the menu: one-time sales, subscriptions, usage-based, ad-supported, and why today's choice best matches how customers receive value and it keeps margins healthy.

When Mailchimp moved from pay-as-you-go credits to tiered subscriptions, it did so because small businesses wanted unlimited sends without surprise bills. That shift smoothed cash flow and lifted margins, but the team could still point to scenarios (enterprise volume spikes, international SMS) where usage pricing might return. Showing you've mapped the roads you might take later is far more reassuring than pretending the first route is carved in stone.

How will you acquire users? Here, they're hunting for one repeatable and affordable way people will find you. Dropbox won early by giving every new user extra storage for bringing in a friend—a loop that drove millions of sign-ups with almost zero marketing spend. It kept cost to acquire (CAC) far below lifetime value (the total revenue one customer brings in over the entire time they use your product). If you already have data, share that single channel and explain why it scales. If you're in prelaunch, lay out the experiment you'll run next week, the success metric that says, "Double down," and the kill switch that sends you back to the drawing board. Depth on one proven path beats wishful breadth on ten.

Why do you want to do this? That answer is your motive, and investors need it served straight so everyone rows in the same direction. Say you're chasing control, fortune, or a problem that keeps you up at night; just be explicit. When Hamdi Ulukaya bought a shuttered Kraft plant to launch Chobani, he told early backers he simply missed the thick, tangy yogurt of his childhood and believed American shoppers deserved better. Profit mattered, but great yogurt and good manufacturing jobs in a rural town mattered more. Because his motive was crystal clear, every board conversation filtered through that lens. Give investors the same clarity: Own the fire that drives you, acknowledge the risk it drags along, and pair it with the confidence of someone who's already betting their time and money. Alignment beats platitudes, and transparent motive lets partners coach you through the valleys without ever questioning why you're on the trail in the first place.

You'll field a million questions, each dressed up in a different outfit: charts, small talk, even "just curious" hypotheticals. Don't get hypnotized by the costume. Almost every prompt hides a deeper probe: Do you understand the numbers? Can you spot the land mines? Will you remain standing when the wind shifts? Investors rarely say that outright; they like to think their riddles are subtle. So listen for the beat beneath the melody, answer that, and you'll keep the momentum you earned with your story trailer.

JUST BECAUSE THEY SAID NO DOESN'T MEAN THEY'RE AN IDIOT

The first dozen refusals sting like a slap: *"What am I doing wrong?"* After the fiftieth, you grow pitch callouses and the inner monologue flips: *"These people do not know what they're missing."* Pause before you harden into that Marlboro-red growl. Investors spend their days speed-dating founders, and many have already backed companies that look eerily like yours. Or they buried the post-mortems. Their pass might be lazy groupthink, but it might also be a pattern recognition you haven't earned yet.

So when the "no" lands, don't rage-tweet. Autopsy it. Consider if they doubted the Belief Ladder, the timing, or the MVP scope (possibly you're still proving the wrong assumption). Their baby-ugly comment might be brutal, but ignoring it guarantees the next "no" will sound the same.

AM I ALONE?

Fundraising turns even the steadiest operator into a head-noise jukebox. Someone across the table can approve or reject your next eighteen months with a single "yes" or "no," and that power imbalance unsettles founders more than any other milestone. You're not alone. In the 2025 Slush Startup Struggle survey, 58 percent of founders named raising capital as their number one worry—above growth, hiring, or product.[29] So remember that a spike of doubt is normal. Focus your attention on finding partners who fit your mission instead of chasing the fastest check. The critic in your head quiets when the right "yes" lands.

10

FEEL THE BURN

DOUBT VOICE: What if I lose everyone's trust in the first one hundred days and get fired?

THIRTEEN DAYS AFTER our Series A cleared, I woke up convinced this was my Rocky-on-the-steps moment—adrenaline high, destiny queued, world cheering. By 10:00 a.m., that bravado had melted into a spreadsheet comparing seven dental plans, an Illustrator file with twenty-four shades of blue, and a Google Doc full of motivational quotes for a press release no journalist had even agreed to read.

I was paralyzed by perfectionist quicksand.

"HOW YOU DO ANYTHING IS HOW YOU DO EVERYTHING."

My dad drilled that into me at a young age. Fueled by his mantra, I treated pixel-perfect logos and pristine benefit decks as proof of professional rigor, because if I couldn't nail the small stuff, who would trust me with the big stuff?

While I debated which emoji was most appropriate, a knot grew in my gut. Something besides cash was draining. Cash burn I understood, and our runway math was tattooed on my skull. Yet a heavier cost was quietly accruing, one I could feel but not track on a dashboard.

That's when the hidden fear pounced. What if every minute I spent polishing PowerPoint alignment was a signal to my team that I had no idea how to ship the product? If the launch slipped, the press yawned, or a board slide looked thin. The people who just bet their careers on me could decide I wasn't the adult in the room after all. *Lose their trust once*, the self-doubt voice whispered.

Over time, I could name those hidden burns. It was attention burn: The best hours of my brain poured into threads about nonmaterial things. And behind it lurked credibility burn: Every minute lost to dental-plan micromanagement pushed out the product roadmap and the revenue model I'd promised the team and our investors.

THE THREE-BURN DASHBOARD

BURN	HOW YOU DETECT IT	WHAT'S HAPPENING?
CASH	You see it in your financial statements	On track, but spending money on the wrong things
CREDIBILITY	You hear it in the questions you get	Overpromise to make everyone happy
ATTENTION	You feel it in your body when working	Your schedule is busy, but nothing progresses

For years I read "burn" in black and white: dollars draining, runway shrinking. Thirteen breakneck days rewired that naivete.

A startup smolders on three fuses: cash you can count, attention you can feel, and credibility you notice only when it's gone. The last two are smokeless killers—igniting first, scorching deepest, and leaving the money fuse looking tame by comparison.

THE BURN WE KNOW, OR DO WE?

Most founders—self-funded or venture backed—still use a Stone Age dashboard: "How many months of runway do we have?" The board aligns, the team aligns, and you feel either "on track" or "off track" and go about your day.

Wrong.

Cash burn is not a calendar countdown; it is a dynamic betting machine. Dollars aimed straight at proving your core assumption are fuel. Dollars that wander elsewhere are lighter fluid on the runway. So, the real metric isn't how fast the money disappears but where every dollar lands.

To keep yourself honest, bucket each of your current or expected expenses into one of three categories.

SAME DOLLAR, DIFFERENT CURRENCIES

CATEGORY	WHAT IT IS	YOUR NEXT MOVE
VALIDATION	Anything that helps prove core assumption	Triple down
SCALING	Helps you grow after product–market fit	Be selective
VANITY	Perks, office, filler roles, premature marketing	Trim or cut bait

A healthy early-stage budget looks a lot like a barbell: 70 percent of every dollar should sprint straight at Validation spend,

about 25 percent fuels Scaling spend, and the crumb that's left—
5 percent at most—pays the unavoidable Vanity tax. Shift the mix
only when facts prove you've graduated. When the core thesis is
tattoo-level true, Validation can taper to 25 percent, and Scaling
rises to half the pie. Vanity never earns a promotion; it floats in
single digits forever.

Validation spending—your prove-it pot—covers whatever it
takes to show that the core assumption on your Belief Ladder can
hold weight. If you're crafting a physical gadget, that might pay
for the first aluminum mold or 3D printing ten rough units to
break in a garage drop test. If you're building software, maybe it's
a handful of contractor hours to stitch together a click-through
demo, or a part-time engineer to wire a proof-of-concept backend.
A service startup might fund a single-city pilot with real customers
who hand over real money. The rule: Every dollar must turn a
"we believe" into a "we know."

Scaling spending is the momentum engine, money you'll deploy
when early proof says, "This works—now grow it." Maybe that's
lining up a second supplier so shelves never go bare, training
a manager to replicate your service standard, upgrading your
website so it won't crash on a busy holiday, or mapping the marketing channel that keeps customer-acquisition costs predictable.
You don't swipe the card on Day One, but you sketch the plan
early, so the foundation is ready when demand spikes. It's the
same mindset you used for a possible white-swan (10x) upside:
optimistic enough to prepare, realistic enough not to rebuild
everything later at premium rates.

Vanity spending is the stealth arsonist—think reclaimed-
wood desks, espresso taps, monogrammed hoodies, or that ping-
pong table nobody uses after Week Two. The mid-2010s are
littered with gorgeous offices from companies that no longer

exist. Customers don't care how Instagram-friendly your lobby is; investors see right through catered-lunch bravado; and a neon "Hustle" sign never shipped a product. Do the minimum that keeps the lights on and the team motivated. Then funnel the rest back to Validation or Scaling where it can actually earn its keep. Reality check: Until revenue proves otherwise, culture is forged by results and shared purpose, not kombucha on tap.

Once the buckets are set, your next mission is to make every Validation dollar sweat. Hire a contractor before you lock in a full-timer, rent a shared mold before you commission your own, and white-list the third-party API that gets you a demo next week instead of coding one from scratch. Micromanage tasks, not people. Insist every sprint card states which Belief Ladder rung it's trying to snap from "maybe" to "proven," and then kill or rescope anything that drifts. Lean teams move faster and break cheaper, and every penny you save buys you an extra experiment.

Picture 2011's photo-sharing race: Instagram and Color both chased the same "post a picture, see friends' pictures" itch. Instagram's small team funneled its early funding into one validation question: "Will people stick around if we make posting and filtering dead-simple on iPhone?" They stripped features, launched quickly, and iterated off real usage. Color, meanwhile, raised about $41 million before launch and built a proximity-based social network backed by heavy PR—but struggled to demonstrate sustained engagement. Twelve months later Instagram sold to Facebook for $1 billion, while Color pivoted and ultimately dissolved. Same market, opposite burn dynamics.

And remember, the budget you pitched on Day One isn't scripture. As experiments turn guesses into facts, redirect cash without apology. Shift payroll from contract designers to supply-chain ops, pause the marketing test that flopped, or jack Scaling spend when demand outruns inventory. Investors don't reward rigid fidelity to an outdated spreadsheet. They reward momentum toward a fully validated Belief Ladder. Your only constant KPI is proof, so move the money wherever proof is hiding next.

THE PINOCCHIO EFFECT

Startup lore says you must radiate irrational exuberance 24/7: "We'll triple revenue this quarter!" "Our product is pretty much all AI-powered." The crowd cheers—until the calendar flips and nothing ships. Every overhyped promise lights an invisible match; eyebrows rise, team jokes start behind your back, and suddenly each new claim costs twice as much belief. Cash burn drains the bank, and credibility burn drains the room.

To keep the story honest, run future-tense statements through a three-lane filter.

THE FIBBING MATRIX

CATEGORY	WHAT IT SOUNDS LIKE	YOUR NEXT MOVE
EARNED	"We've closed five pilots, two more contracts in legal."	Shout it
STRETCH	"We expect to hit one thousand users based on the trend."	Flag the assumptions
FANTASY	"We'll own 10 percent of the market once we go viral."	Delete or downgrade

Earned reality can be shouted from rooftops, but in measured doses. These are the milestones you have already delivered:

contracts signed, features live, NPS tracked. Feel free to tell investors, customers, and your grandma, yet pace the hits. If you trumpet ten wins in a week and then go radio-silent for six months, shareholders will wonder what blew up. Drip-feeding proof keeps excitement steady and stocks a reserve of goodwill for the inevitable bad days.

Credible stretch belongs on whiteboards and monthly investor updates—never on the front page of TechCrunch. A stretch goal missed looks heroic to an employee (We swung big!) but smells like Fantasy land to a seed fund and counts as an outright strike with a debt lender. Show the math: Conversion rate times traffic trajectory equals target. Expose the kill switch if inputs wobble. Investors want aggression wrapped in logic; the tighter the capital provider—growth equity, private equity, venture debt— the narrower your acceptable miss.

Fantasy land dazzles at off-sites and Series-A pitch decks but poisons day-to-day execution. Fantasies carry brute-force optimism that eclipses smaller, still-remarkable wins; hitting five thousand users feels flat after promising "viral by summer." Use moon-shot slogans sparingly—annual kickoffs, culture posters— then retire them when heads go down to build. During execution, your team can smell the gap between ambition and delusion and will call BS before your board does.

At Assembly, we carved out a weird middle lane I've nicknamed **Credible downgrade**. We were in a white-hot market, yet we budgeted like we were crossing Antarctica—ultraconservative forecasts that left room for every blizzard. With growth-equity investors, the safest music to play is "beat and raise," and for a while, we hit the high notes. We outperformed for fifteen straight quarters and quietly nudged guidance up. The hitch? After three cycles, the board figured out our game and inflated our next-quarter numbers for us, erasing the cushion we'd built. The sandbagger label felt noble, even dad-approved (*Reputation is rarer than money*), but in hindsight, we should have swapped the padded parka for straight talk: realistic stretch goals up front and fewer post-hoc surprises.

Consider the IPO-era contrast between WeWork and Airbnb. WeWork's filings leaned heavily on mission language—"elevating the world's consciousness"—while obscuring unit economics and governance complexity. Investors balked, the IPO collapsed, and the credibility burn was immediate. Airbnb, by contrast, went public amid a pandemic downturn, openly acknowledging collapsing bookings while clearly outlining contribution margins and path to recovery. One narrative strained belief; the other rationed it. Same public markets, opposite approaches to trust—and the market kept score.

Credibility is a startup's rarest asset—slow to earn, lost in a headline, and fiendishly hard to win back. Yet keep your word, even if the venture flames out, and investors will still pick up the phone. A 2024 Data-Driven VC review of 30,000 funding rounds found that repeat founders whose prior companies failed raised their next round only two months slower, on average, than founders coming off successful exits.[30] Founders can replenish money; trust, once scorched, almost never is—so guard it.

THE MAGPIE SYNDROME

The first time I felt the fuse fizzing wasn't in the P&L; it was in Google Calendar. I spent six hours refereeing Slack threads, two hours polishing an internal deck, and exactly zero minutes interviewing the three critical hires we still hadn't made. My lizard brain whispered that tidy slides proved I was "on it." Reality said I was taxiing in circles, torching jet fuel while the runway lights blinked in the distance. Panic sent me to the productivity aisle: Covey, Newport, Allen, Pomodoro's, 5:00 a.m. clubs. Most hacks crumbled under startup chaos, but five frameworks stuck.

GUIDE TO GETTING SH*T DONE

TRICK	WHY IT HELPS
LOWER ACTIVATION ENERGY	Puts high-value work within arm's reach and hides temptations
MEMO FORMAT OVER SLIDE DECKS	Slashes formatting time; forces clear thinking in plain text
THIRTY-MINUTE SPARK, THREE-HOUR TRENCH	Creates a momentum jolt, then protects a deep-work block
MANUFACTURE ACCOUNTABILITY	Adds weekly outside pressure so you can't negotiate with yourself
BUILD SCHEDULE AROUND BODY CLOCK	Schedules cognitively heavy work when your brain is in fifth gear

Lower activation energy came straight from *The Happiness Advantage*: make good choices stupid-easy, bad ones annoying. Like, move your treadmill beside the bed—step off the mattress, and you're basically jogging. The same principle applies at work: customer-chat tab on the bookmark bar, TikTok buried three folders deep. Every click you remove from mission-critical tasks—and add to dopamine traps—tilts the day toward shipping instead of scrolling.

Memo, not slide deck is a Bezos special. Presentations seduce you into picking fonts and animating bullet points; memos force narrative clarity fast. Amazon's internal study found teams cut prep time by 30 percent after ditching PowerPoint for six-page documents.[31] One page of prose uncovers fuzzy logic before your audience does, and nobody burns an afternoon debating hex codes.

Thirty-minute spark versus three-hour trench shrinks the intimidation gap. Fire off a tiny win: Answer an email from the outsourced engineering firm that's bugged you for the last two months. Finish a series of eSignatures, and then dive into a barricaded three-hour block on the one thing that matters. The quick hit floods dopamine, hijacks procrastination, and greases entry into flow.

Manufactured accountability works only when the referee isn't your investor—or a direct report who's grading you, not vice versa. Pair with a peer founder, coach, or even a Slack bot that pings every Friday: *Did you finish the deep-work block you swore on Monday?* Shared skin in the game creates healthy pressure; alone, the binge on the latest season of *Love Island* always wins the negotiation.

Body-clock matching saved me from noon-hour brain meltdowns. I can draft strategy at midnight and design prototypes at dawn, but ask me to fill out a spreadsheet at 12:00 p.m., and you'll question my IQ. Audit a week, then slot the hardest work into the high tide. Your 5:00 a.m. might equal my 11:00 p.m.; the trick is aligning, not conforming.

While I stand by those core rules and credit them for hauling me out of the mud, I'm no guru with a magic bullet. So here, in plain English and one breath, are thirty other productivity hacks you can try:

1. Turn phone grayscale; color feeds dopamine loops.
2. Use noise-canceling headphones with no music.
3. Set Slack "away" and check at 11:00 a.m. and 4:00 p.m.

4. Swap your chair for a standing desk during deep work.

5. Stack meetings on Tuesdays; keep other days sacred.

6. Disable desktop email alerts—fetch, don't receive.

7. Keep a water bottle on your desk; thirst mimics fatigue.

8. Two-minute rule: If less than 120 seconds, do it now.

9. 52/17 rhythm: fifty-two minutes of work, then a seventeen-minute break.

10. Block addictive internet sites with Cold Turkey Blocker (actual site).

11. Write tomorrow's top three tasks before shutting off your laptop.

12. Chew mint gum—mild cognitive arousal bump.

13. Micro stretch for sixty seconds every thirty minutes to reset your focus.

14. Keep room temp around 68°F; cooler air perks alertness.

15. Lock your phone in a timed box when drafting a strategy.

16. Do box breathing (4-4-4-4) before big tasks.

17. Use a white-noise app at 70 dB for creative work.

18. Set a countdown timer on a second monitor— visible urgency.

19. Eat a protein-heavy breakfast; avoid 10:00 a.m. carb crash.

20. Five-minute sun break at noon—kills circadian dip.

21. "Later list" for random ideas; clears mental RAM.

22. Blue-light glasses after 8:00 p.m.—sleep fuels focus.

23. Watch vibrate hourly: posture plus breath cue.

24. Caffeine microdoses (½ cup) every ninety minutes.

25. Do a "walk and talk" when meeting people live.

26. Desk plant—proven microrest for eyes, steady calm.

27. Call your parents and tell them you love them.

28. Use scent cues—dab peppermint oil before writing.

29. Take eight- to twelve-minute micronaps to jump alertness.

30. Write with wrong hand before brainstorming.

At the end of the day, every productivity trick is just a hypothesis, so treat it like any other experiment. Whether you're plunging into an ice barrel at dawn, swearing by keto and apple-cider-vinegar shots, or revving your morning with a Megan Thee Stallion rap session, the only metric that matters is whether your attention stays locked on the work that validates your next Belief Ladder rung and moves the company forward. Run the test, keep what works, scrap what doesn't, and remember, trial and error is the only to-do list that always ships.

WHY BUILDING THIS MUSCLE MATTERS

Most founders miss the target on the first swing—the ten-year failure rate is north of 70 percent, and "ran out of cash or runway" still tops the list of postmortem causes.[32] That odds board isn't meant to scare you; it clarifies the real prize of this chapter. Mastering cash, credibility, and attention burn is less about saving this company and more about wiring a skillset that survives whichever one succeeds.

The hidden fear we opened with, *What if I lose everyone's trust in the first one hundred days and get fired?*, is really a fear of becoming unbackable. Curb it by running the Three-Burn Dashboard as religion: Point every dollar at proof, label every projection earned/stretch/fantasy before an investor has to, and guard the calendar. When the slide slips, or the forecast misses (and it will), you'll draw on a reservoir of goodwill instead of sparking a board revolt.

Remember, discipline doesn't guarantee a win; it guarantees a finish. Even if this idea tanks, you'll walk away with a track record of blocking and tackling a hypothesis—exactly the currency investors wire to serial founders. Treat each experiment like money, each promise like an IOU, and each hour like scarce oxygen. Do that, and whether the company lands or flames out, you stay fundable.

So ship the memo instead of the deck, kill the vanity spend, mute the dopamine pings, and drip-feed only the truths you've earned. The fuse keeps burning, but at least now you control the flame.

11

BE MONOGAMOUS

 What if I launch my
product and nobody blinks?

IF I HAD a time machine, I wouldn't bother with the Roman
Empire;[33] I'd punch 2012 into the dashboard, step out in a hoodie,
and watch customers fall into my lap.

In 2012, you could spin up a landing page, dump rent money
into Facebook's primordial advertising pool, and clock out before
happy hour. App-store charts updated in real time, costs were
pocket change, and a half-competent drip campaign made your
grandma say:

"MY GRANDSON IS HANDSOME...AND A GENIUS!"

Those kind words of affirmation and marketing napalm are
ancient history, and that's where the hidden fear creeps in today.
You can ship a brilliant product and still hear nothing but can-
yon echo. Product-led growth (simply building a product on the

expectation users will flood in) once rode two game-changing tailwinds: untapped channels and investors who mistook cash burn for strategy.

Both winds have died.

Facing that silence, founders overcompensate like late-night infomercial hosts—"But wait, there's more!"—rattling off SEO optimization, TikTok content, podcast tours, community flywheels, and blockchain airdrops before lunch.

The result is predictable: cash on fire, credibility smoking, and a random grab bag of customers who ghost you before the next board meeting.

The cure for the invisible launch fear isn't frantic polymarketing; it's ruthless monogamy. Pick one channel, master its physics, and let every cycle compound inside that funnel until the market can't ignore you. Monogamy turns the spotlight from "Will anyone notice?" to "How bright can we make this beam?" and that flips the fear into fuel.

GO THROUGH THEIR TRASH CAN

Before you decide how you will acquire customers, slip into detective mode. Shadow your customers the way an anthropologist trails a tribe. Observe not just how they use your product but how they power through their mornings, where their attention drifts when they're tired, and which chores always get postponed. The goal is to stalk their real life, not their dashboards, until you can predict what time the coffee brews, what scares them at night, and what tiny victory makes the day feel worth it.

On paper, your customer reads like a tidy robot: "Steady foot traffic, tight-knit staff, always seeking efficiency." In real life, she's Maria, the third-generation donut-shop owner who starts rolling dough at 2:00 a.m., keeps the radio low so the night crew can hear drive-through orders, and jots tomorrow's batch sizes on a grease-spotted clipboard. She checks her phone only during glaze cooldowns, reconciles receipts after the last maple bar sells out, and collapses for a nap while most offices are just pouring coffee. If your acquisition plan pictures her sipping lattes at a nine-to-five desk, scrolling LinkedIn at lunch, or opening an 11:00 a.m. email blast, you're working off a fantasy schedule. Knowing the real rhythm of her day is the difference between talking to data points and talking to a person.

We stumbled upon this at Assembly. Conventional playbooks told us to woo prospects with ROI calculators, testimonial decks, and polished case studies—classic enterprise courtship. Spending real time with customers surfaced the opposite: Our "companies" were moonlighting strivers hunting for inspiration between shifts. These first-time e-commerce sellers toggled from YouTube how-tos to Instagram success reels, then into bleary 1:00 a.m. Tony Robbins "Get off you're a$$" clips, gulping down any tip they could before crashing for a few hours—only to wake to a day job they dread, a third kid on the way, and no clue how they'll cover summer camp. They needed help fast, delivered with grace, from a voice they could trust not to torch their savings on a pipe dream.

Knowing what keeps Maria rolling dough at 2:00 a.m. is fear of empty racks at dawn, pride in a third-generation recipe, the calm that comes only after the last maple bar—and immediately narrows the universe of ways to reach her. The moment you name that hidden motive of your customer, just like your motive, things become clearer. That clarity never arrives by copying the hottest playbook. It comes from deliberate soul-searching. Spend time in the customers' shoes, buy them coffee, map the spikes of hope and panic, and write what they whisper.

PLENTY OF FISH IN THE SEA

Choosing a channel is a bit like speed dating: Every suitor flashes promise, but most reveal a deal-breaker the moment you ask for a second drink. Use the table on the next page as your cheat sheet of the art of the possible.

FIRST-DATE OPTIONS

CHANNEL	THE LURES	THE TURNOFFS
FREE TOOLS	Wide top of funnel, gives users a taste	Ongoing overhead, may never pay
WORD OF MOUTH	High trust, close to product-led growth	Hard to engineer, can reverse just as easy
SEO CONTENT	Evergreen traffic, compounding flywheel	Slow ramp, SEO algorithm whiplash
PLATFORM LISTING	Built-in demand, ride off the coattails	Compete for visibility with other companies
MAJOR INFLUENCER	Lightning-bolt reach, borrowed authority	Huge fee, one-off spike, no control
MICRO INFLUENCERS	Niche credibility, diversify audiences	Ops nightmare, plus ghosting is common
AMBASSADOR PROGRAM	Cost tied to revenue, advocacy flywheel	Needs airtight attribution, rogue reps
PAID ADVERTISING	Instant traffic, precise targeting, testable	Auction costs rise, creative fatigue, costs
SOCIAL MEDIA	Social following, large reach, creates brand	A lot of trial and error, may not convert
FOUNDER SALES	Deep product insight, signals hustle and care	Founder bandwidth evaporates at scale

CHANNEL	THE LURES	THE TURNOFFS
SALES TEAM	Repeatable pipeline, relationship depth	Ramp time, needs high ACV to work
INDUSTRY PARTNERSHIPS	Borrows someone's audience if aligned	Slow deals, road-map compromises
LIVE EVENTS	Face-to-face trust, demo on the spot	Costly booths, dead weeks between shows
BILLBOARD ADVERTISING	Massive local aware-ness, social proof	Hard to measure, need to pay cash up front
PUBLIC RELATIONS	Free reach, third-party valuation, SEO benefit	Unpredictable timing, message control limit

Free tools work like pocket-size screwdrivers: You hand out a mini-app or calculator that fixes one nagging issue for nothing, just as HubSpot's early "Website Grader" diagnosed site flaws and quietly funneled hundreds of thousands toward its paid product. The lure is a vast crowd sampling your value up front; the limitation is the ongoing cost to maintain something many users won't graduate from.

Word of mouth spreads when delighted customers turn into unpaid town criers. That's exactly how Stanley tumblers leaped from rugged camp gear to TikTok must-have after nurses, teachers, and moms raved about ice that stayed frozen through double shifts. Trust is unrivaled and the budget is near zero, but the spark is hard to manufacture, and a single bad story can race back just as fast.

SEO content wins by publishing answers people keep Googling, then letting search results drip buyers into your lap; Beardbrand's beard-care tutorials still reel in traffic years after posting. Compounding evergreen clicks are the reward, while monthslong ramp times and sudden algorithm shakes are the headache.

Platform listings plug you into marketplaces customers already trust. Klaviyo rocketed its early user base by ranking high in Shopify's App Store, where one-click installs and instant reviews built credibility overnight. Built-in demand and endorsement come free, yet you jostle for visibility beside dozens of copycats.

Major influencer campaigns unleash a single celebrity shoutout that detonates reach. Liquid Death's limited skateboard painted with Tony Hawk's real blood sent sales soaring. Borrowed authority lands instantly, but fees are huge, the spike fades, and you surrender control of the narrative to one voice.

Microinfluencer swarms tap hundreds of niche creators, as Daniel Wellington did by mailing free watches to sub-50K-follower Instagram accounts. You gain targeted credibility and diversified risk, but herd management—payments and ghosting—can feel like juggling cats.

Ambassador programs turn superfans into commission-earning reps. Pura Vida's campus reps logged every bracelet sale with a personal code, fueling an advocacy flywheel whose costs scaled only with revenue. Success demands bulletproof attribution and constant brand policing.

Paid advertising buys eyeballs on demand. Purple Mattress blitzed quirky Facebook videos and climbed from its first $10,000 day to seven-figure weeks. Instant traffic and granular testing shine, while auction prices, creative fatigue, and runaway burn rates lurk.

Social media organic growth comes from posting your entertaining or helpful content. Duolingo's wisecracking owl turned TikTok jokes into millions of free impressions. Building personality is powerful, but algorithms change overnight, and likes don't equal dollars.

Founder-led sales put the maker in every demo. Wade Foster personally cold-emailed and onboarded Zapier's first hundred users, mixing product insight with hustle. Prospects love direct access, yet the founder's calendar becomes the growth ceiling long before demand does.

Sales teams bring repeatable pipelines once deals justify the cost. Gong staffed experienced enterprise reps early, turning $30,000 to $60,000 contracts into a predictable revenue drumbeat. Relationship depth and forecasting improve, but salaries, ramp times, and quota relief require high-average deal sizes to work.

Industry partnerships hitch your wagon to a complementary brand's audience, like Headspace inserting guided breathing tracks into Nike Run Club workouts. Credibility transfers quickly, though negotiations crawl, and roadmap compromises often follow.

Live events deliver face-to-face trust. GoPro's Nick Woodman demoed cameras at surf contests, selling straight from his van. In-person demos convert, but booth fees, travel costs, and long gaps between shows drain resources.

Billboard or out-of-home ads plaster your message everywhere commuters look. Brex blanketed San Francisco with "Get a corporate card in five minutes," signaling legitimacy to every rideshare passenger. Local ubiquity and social proof pop, yet it is hard to trace, and the cash is up front.

Public relations secures earned coverage from journalists or podcasters. Sara Blakely faxed a handwritten pitch to *Oprah*, landed on "Favorite Things," and Spanx inventory evaporated overnight. Third-party validation is gold, but timing is unpredictable, and you surrender control of the angle once the story leaves your hands.

The crazy part? Those fifteen options barely graze the menu. Channels rise and fade with algorithms and attention spans, but their popularity is irrelevant if your customer never shows up there. Remember Maria, our donut-shop owner rolling dough at 2:00 a.m.? She listens to a crackly local radio station to stay awake, not TikTok, LinkedIn, or a random "Can I get a minute?" call from your sales rep. If you chase the "hottest" channel instead of the one that intersects her midnight soundtrack, you're wasting money.

IS THIS MY ONE TRUE LOVE?

Your temptation right now is to eye that buffet of fifteen channels, lick your fingers, and attack it Golden Corral–style: "A few paid ads, one scoop of TikTok, ooh look, partnerships!" Don't. (Also, please don't do that at Golden Corral). Big-budget marketers preach "test and learn," because they have the runway to burn ten plates of shrimp before deciding what's edible. You don't. With limited cash and calendar, picking two or three channels means you'll never go deep enough on any of them to know if they ever had a fighting chance. So before you pile your tray, run each option through the framework below. Whichever channel scores highest, pick that single plate and keep going back for refills until you've mastered the recipe.

THE ONE TRUE LOVE TEST

CRITERIA	SANITY CHECK
DAY IN THE LIFE	Does the product appear exactly where the user's pain flares up?
TRUST TRANSFER	Is the message delivered by a source the user already trusts?
SIGNAL SPEED	Can you see clear value within hours or days (not months)?

CRITERIA	SANITY CHECK
RESOURCE FIT	Can you adopt without stretching your current team or budget?
DEFENSIBILITY	Is the channel protected by data, access, or anything else?
PROFITABILITY	Based on your business model, does this channel make you money?
SCALABILITY	Can this customer type grow to—or beyond—your target volume?

For Assembly, we went all-in on an ambassador program—offering existing customers 25 percent of every dollar their referrals spent, as long as they launched a YouTube channel showing exactly how our tool made them money. That single decision now drives more than half our new users. Let's walk through why it worked for us.

Day-in-the-life fit means the channel must appear exactly when and where the pain spikes; our e-commerce strivers were doomscrolling YouTube at midnight searching "How to make my first $1,000 online," so ambassador tutorials slid into the very minute their anxiety peaked. If your audience's pinch point is the morning commute, maybe podcast prerolls win; if it's a donut shop, maybe it's the channel that worked fifty years ago: a radio placement.

Trust transfer happens when a familiar, respected voice carries your message—think Oprah's "Favorite Things" list transforming Spanx into an overnight sellout. Our ambassadors delivered that same credibility: Viewers saw creators who looked and talked like them, screen-sharing real sales dashboards, and skepticism melted before any polished ad could load asking them for money.

Signal speed gauges how quickly value shows up. Our program went from idea to live videos in under thirty days, and Stripe pings hit the very next night. SEO might take quarters to rank, and enterprise partnerships can crawl through legal. If your runway is six months, you need channels that light up results in weeks, not quarters.

Resource fit asks whether your existing team can keep the engine humming. Ambassadors became our content factory, freeing a lean staff from producing endless how-tos. Paid ads need daily creative tweaks—deadly if you have one part-time marketer. Marry only a channel your current crew can actually feed.

Defensibility measures how hard the playbook is to steal. Lifetime commissions turned our ambassadors into caretakers who nurtured their audiences and kept churn low because every renewal paid them too. A rival can mimic payouts, but not the personal bonds or libraries of success stories already forged.

Profitability insists the math helps you. We paid bounties only after a referral activated our ninety-nine-dollar-per-month plan, so customer-acquisition cost was self-governing and ROI was outrageous. A free tool might drown you in hosting bills long before conversion. Run the numbers and skip motions that can't pay their own rent.

Scalability checks the ceiling. Every niche—Spanish-speaking resellers, sneaker flippers, stay-at-home parents—needed its own trusted voice, so we added more ambassadors. Founder-led sales would have capped us at my calendar; a single influencer would have limited us to one demo. Choose a ladder tall enough for your ambition.

Walk every candidate channel through these seven lenses. When one scores high across the board—like ambassadors did for us—marry it, master it, and keep refilling that plate until you know the recipe cold. Only then think about adding a new channel.

WHEN A SECOND DATE MAKES SENSE

Sooner or later, investors—and your survival instinct—will ask for a second channel. Channels age. Google rewrites its ranking playbook, Meta throttles targeting, and trade shows hit saturation. A second or third lever lets you sleep when the algorithm gods have a bad quarter. The right moment is when the leading channel shows predictable month-over-month performance, and you can afford the ramp time of the second channel without starving the core.

It's important to flag slow-burn tactics—public relations outreach, long-form SEO, marketplace listings—because they can take months (or years) to pay off. If you launch them only after sales stall, you'll face an ugly revenue gap. Instead, spin one up while your primary channel is already footing the bill; think of it as planting next season's crop while eating tonight's harvest. In the early days, borrow capacity with a specialty agency or freelancer rather than hiring a full-time employee. When the channel finally catches, and you can see a clear path to it covering that salary—and then some—that's the moment to bring someone in-house.

But remember, every new channel is another dashboard, another attribution argument, and another hire lobbying for budget. Slack threads about "Who sourced this customer?" grow exponentially. So, run the candidate through the scorecard again, this time including the overhead of people and politics. If it still clears the bar, start wooing. If not, keep dancing with the partner who brought you and revisit the roster when that relationship is bankrolling.

WHEN YOU'RE LEFT WITH YOUR HIGH SCHOOL SWEETHEART

Paid marketing.

At some point, you need it; at some point, it needs you.

Paid advertising is the first crush most founders run back to when newer romances sputter. It's familiar, always answers your texts, and if you're willing to swipe a card, never says no to dinner. If you're going to lean on paid advertising, do it with intention.

The first intention is **product R&D**. Instead of waiting for strangers to wander in and test your product, you can hunt them down and probe specific rungs on your Belief Ladder. Spin up micro ads—each headline testing a single assumption—and watch who bites, what it costs, and whether your solution actually satisfies them. Suppose you believe "People want an all-in-one platform." Launch an ad that promises exactly that. If lots of users click through but rely on just one of your tools, you've learned that the all-in-one pitch attracts attention, yet the bundle itself doesn't deliver perceived value. You can iterate the product (or the story) long before engineering spends months stitching features together—all because paid traffic handed you a real-time focus group.

The second intention is **pure growth**. Yes, the average return on ad spend has slipped as with every platform, but paid advertising still works, especially when the market is racing toward "winner takes all." If you're fighting for mindshare in a crowded category—think food-delivery apps (DoorDash) or buy-now-pay-later services (Affirm)—you may need a Blitz of paid reach just to stay visible while the land grab is happening. Treat those dollars like an accelerant, not a forever fuel: Lock down your unit economics, set hard targets, and know exactly how many months of cash burn you can stomach before losing credibility. Paid can vault you onto the podium, but in a lot of cases, you're just buying fireworks on a credit card.

WHEN TO GO YOUR SEPARATE WAYS

Halfway through any marketing push, the self-doubt voice whispers, *This is a dumpster fire. Shut it down before people notice.* The only way to know whether it's panic or wisdom is to look at numbers you chose before emotions showed up. Pick one leading sign (click-through, demo requests) and one trailing sign (paid conversions, churn drop). Mid-flight you ask, "Are the early signs climbing toward the goal or sitting flat?" If they're flat and you've already tweaked the obvious stuff, cut the budget and recycle the lesson. If they're climbing—even slowly—keep breathing; some crops take a season.

Our own test of patience came with Sell & Scale, the first customer summit we ever ran. We blew the doors off: rented a Las Vegas corridor, booked panels, and because we secretly loved him, we hired Nelly for the after-party. In the weeks before the show, the self-doubt voice was ruthless: *This is rent money on pyrotechnics. What if nobody comes?* Day-after numbers seemed to prove the fear. We'd spent seven figures and saw only a small bump in trials. The spreadsheet said, "Never again."

Then Week Two hit. Organic sign-ups doubled, partner emails quoted the event, and our sales pipeline was the largest it had ever been. Three months later, we traced a massive lift in our organic traffic to the halo effect of people tagging us on LinkedIn and sharing with their network. The data was right; it just took its time to speak.

So trust the dashboard, but give it the right clock. Set a first checkpoint for quick signals—did people click, share, or show up? Set a second one long enough for revenue to echo. Kill fast when both fail, but don't pull the plug just because applause hasn't reached the bank account by Monday when you launched on Friday.

12

OPEN YOUR EYES

SWEAT AND BLOOD bounce off the cymbal. Dramatic.

Whiplash, the 2014 Oscar darling, opens on first-year drummer Andrew Neiman hammering paradiddles in a dim hallway while maestro-terror Terence Fletcher circles like a hawk. "Not my tempo!" And the count resets. Chairs fly, knuckles split, a car flips through an intersection, yet the drummer drags himself onstage—bloodied, broken—because one credo burns in his head: Greatness is chosen, not bestowed. Push hard enough, the film illustrates, and the universe will finally applaud.

I bought that creed wholesale.

"I DON'T KNOW IF I CAN STOMACH BEING WRONG, SO I'LL JUST WORK HARDER AND TRY TO BE RIGHT."

In late 2019, we acquired Ordermetrics—a lightweight data analytics application we imagined as the footbridge between our Amazon and Shopify customers. The bet felt harmless: House both data sets in one pane and we'd see the customer's whole business, unlocking cross-sell after cross-sell. Cheap chip. If it flopped, no blood; if it landed, one more arrow in the quiver in our path toward domination.

What followed was three years of disproving every assumption in slow motion. Ordermetrics never cracked 1 percent of our revenue, yet it hijacked far more than that in mindshare. The founders who "lived the pain" left, our Amazon customers shrugged, and the code base we rebuilt from scratch still didn't move the needle. We kept rotating A-players onto the project, kept telling ourselves, "It's tiny—no harm if it fizzles," even as board decks and executive meetings ballooned with Ordermetrics slides.

By 2022, the verdict was obvious: sunset it. Founder–market fit? Gone. "Analytics as beachhead?" Not really. The bridge between marketplaces? Still a gap. The decision was easy. Why did it take three years to pull the plug?

Because we never opened our eyes.

We clung to our launch-day narrative instead of asking the first-principles questions: Do our customers actually need unified analytics? Does this solve their biggest pain? Is this our DNA or a distraction? The opportunity cost was compounding in our core platform while we nursed a vanity experiment. Ordermetrics wasn't a disaster, just off-mission, and the slow burn hurt more than a fast no.

The hidden fear crouching behind every pivot is simple: Every pivot is public proof you called the play wrong. You imagine your archenemies muttering, "I told you so." Admitting error feels like handing ammunition to everyone watching, so you keep drumming—louder, harder—hoping sweat can drown out the misfire.

I still love *Whiplash*, but its moral has an asterisk.

Pushing past pain only matters if you're pounding on the right drum. When you're heads-down or staring at the wrong metric, you can miss the signal to pivot and react years too late. Other times, the first wobble triggers premature panic, and you bail on a good thing.

Before you decide whether to grind harder, sidestep, or call it a day, determine if your business has *true* product–market fit, stripping away any biases that you have. It's not enough for the product to "make sense." The market side—your core assumption about who will love it and why—must click at the same moment. A product everyone praises but no one buys, or an audience that loves the idea but isn't the one you built for, both are problematic.

ARE YOU THERE YET?

STAGE	ASK YOURSELF	ACTION IF NO
MARKET (INSIGHT)	"Do I still believe in my assumptions?"	Stop spend, rethink idea, conserve runway
PRODUCT	"Does my product address the assumption?"	Adjust your minimally viable product
FIT (CHANNEL)	"Am I reaching the right customers?"	Adjust your segment or channel strategy

As you saw in Chapter 2, everything starts with the market insight—the core truth on your Belief Ladder that says, "Here are the assumptions that make my idea real." Chapter 7 then showed how the product is the lightest, fastest embodiment of that insight, designed to prove or disprove the assumptions you make. Finally, Chapter 11 drilled home that channel is the repeatable lane where the product and the prospect collide at a price that keeps the lights on. When those three clicks line up, momentum feels effortless. When even one slips, things feel off.

While product–market fit is the phrase everyone parrots, the sequence runs the other way: from market to product to fit. First, you confirm the market's pain, then you build the lightest product that relieves it, and only after those two align do you engineer the "fit" that lets them scale together. Do that in any other order, and you will most certainly drive yourself crazy.

Although that order is real, the journey is anything but linear. Picture a Rubik's Cube—the moment you line up the green face, a twist scrambles the red, yellow, and blue sides you'd just polished. Progress comes from short, deliberate sequences that realign several colors at once, repeated until the whole block locks into harmony. I'll hand you those sequences in this chapter.

SO PEOPLE ARE OKAY WITH STRANGERS WATCHING THEIR KIDS?

Before you can tweak product or channel, you need a clean read on whether the market agrees with the story you're telling. Five quick, clinical checks expose a sick insight long before the runway bleeds out.

MARKET DIAGNOSTICS

DIAGNOSTIC	WHAT TO CHECK	FIRST MOVE
FUNNEL SILENCE	"Does initial interest turn into converted buyers?"	Sharpen the pain, rewrite the hook
QUICK DESERTION	"Do new customers return after a first look?"	Surface the "aha" sooner, cut cruft

DIAGNOSTIC	WHAT TO CHECK	FIRST MOVE
LECTURE SALE	"Can I close this without a TED Talk?"	Simplify the promise or pivot the problem
RELATIVE GAP	"Is anyone else winning in the market?"	Copy their play— or drop the rung
PRICE FLINCH	"Will buyers pay for the product?"	Reframe value or pick a new segment

Funnel silence is your first siren. When Burbn launched with check-ins, badges, and photos, ad clicks evaporated at the sign-up screen. Kevin Systrom's team assumed the pain was "share every moment." The crowd disagreed. They ripped away every feature but photo sharing and rewrote the hook—Instagram's conversions shot from trickle to torrent. Treat silence as a *serious* blockage: If strangers won't even smell the dish, change the recipe before you turn on another burner.

Quick desertion means curiosity exists, but commitment doesn't. Tote, the forerunner to Pinterest, watched shoppers try the app once and never return. Ben Silbermann noticed users kept saving images but not buying products, so he rebuilt around visual pinboards. Desertion starts as a surface-level bruise—often one missing "aha" screen—but festers fast if ignored. Pull the magic moment forward, delete the rest, then reread retention.

Lecture sale shows up when every deal needs a walk-through worthy of a late-night infomercial. Early Vitamix blenders sold only when demonstrators spent ten minutes blitzing soup on state-fair stages. Sales rocketed once the company swapped jargon for the blunt tagline "Whole-food meals in sixty seconds" and plastered stores with a single demo video. If a lecture is still required after you strip the pitch, the wound is serious—pivot the promise, not the discount.

Relative gap is your external mirror. Chick-fil-A's chicken-sandwich dominance left Popeyes languishing—until Popeyes copied the core idea, added brioche, Cajun seasoning, and a cheeky social-media brawl. The "stalled" brand vaulted to record sales and forced rivals to play catch-up. When a peer explodes on your thesis, the ladder is sound—your execution isn't. Borrow their distribution trick, bolt on one unmistakable edge, relaunch; unaddressed, the gap grows terminal.

Price flinch is what happens when momentum looks real—until numbers hit the table. Prospects engage, nod through demos, and talk rollout, then stall, negotiate early, or vanish once pricing appears. That tension isn't always about cost. More often, the value hasn't crystallized: the pain feels optional, the buyer lacks budget authority, or the outcome sounds theoretical. In strong markets, price causes a pause, not paralysis. When flinch repeats, it's a signal you're selling to the wrong segment—or solving a pain they don't urgently own.

Sometimes the landscape proves you wrong even with pattern recognition or sound logic. Assembly assumed sellers craved one console for both Amazon and Shopify. Why wouldn't they? But data begged otherwise: Amazon merchants spent hours in rank-tracking dashboards. Shopify merchants lived in pixel-perfect brand builders. Bundling the two felt like forcing a square peg into a round hole. After three years, the usage split screamed oranges, not apples, and we exited the business unit to double down on marketplaces.

Misreading an assumption doesn't always shrink the world; sometimes it blows the doors off. Play-Doh began life as a wallpaper-cleaning putty until teachers discovered kids loved sculpting with the stuff. One packaging change later, a cleaning supply became a toy-aisle staple. Wrigley entered business peddling soap and baking powder, but customers raved more about the complimentary sticks of peppermint gum that came in each box; the freebie turned into a global gum empire. Even Kickstarter was born as a ticketing service for New Orleans jazz shows; when strangers asked to fund totally different creative projects, the founders scrapped events and unlocked a platform that has raised billions. The rung may snap, but if you study where the splinters land, you might find a ladder twice as tall.

Assumptions are hypotheses wearing nice clothes. The moment they hit daylight, the crowd starts voting. The signal that you misread a rung is rarely subtle. Prospects ghost the demo. Trial users never cross the paywall. Marketing tweets get polite silence, while a rival's thread goes viral on the same day. Customers are a blunt instrument: When they don't feel the pain you diagnosed, they walk away.

GO BACK INTO STEALTH MODE; YOUR PRODUCT IS WHACK

Jeff Bezos is quoted saying, "When the anecdotes and the data disagree, the anecdotes are usually right." The only sure signal of product–market fit is listening to flesh-and-blood customers. Do they find you, finish setup, and then rave to a colleague without being asked? No dashboard can answer that as loud as a buyer saying, "Don't shut this off. I need it tomorrow."

However, once you've heard that music, you still need a scoreboard everyone can see. One "holy grail" metric—clear, movable, and pain-linked—keeps the team aligned and the anecdotes honest.

STAGE	ASK YOURSELF	WHAT "NO" MEANS
TRACKS CORE PAIN	"If this goes up, did a user's life get better?"	If no, then it's a vanity or misleading metric
MOVABLE WEEKLY	"Can we actively move this in a sprint?"	If no, it's hard to derive the insights you need
STANDS ON ITS OWN	"Does it tell the whole story or part of it?"	If it needs footnotes, it's a cog, not a beacon

Tracking the core pain keeps you from celebrating ghosts. Early Facebook first monitored total sign-ups, but growth stalled when new users failed to connect with anyone meaningful. The team discovered that users who added at least seven friends within ten days were far more likely to stay. Instead of chasing registrations, they optimized onboarding to help members find friends fast. When that activation number rose, it meant real social value had formed. If sign-ups climbed while connections lagged, the product wasn't delivering its promise.

Movable weekly turns the metric into a game every squad can play. Slack discovered that teams exchanging roughly 2,000 messages were far more likely to stick. Instead of celebrating sign-ups, the company focused on helping new workspaces reach that threshold quickly—inviting teammates, integrating tools, and prompting early conversations. When early message volume accelerated, engineers knew friction had dropped. If growth stalled, the team tightened onboarding until the curve bent again.

Standing on its own prevents dashboard sudoku. Airbnb emphasized "Nights Booked" because it captured both sides of the marketplace—guests completing stays and hosts supplying inventory. Tracking registrations alone ignored whether transactions actually happened. When trust concerns surfaced in the company's early years, bookings dipped, signaling the core experience needed attention. Strengthening host verification and reviews restored trust and bookings recovered.

Find the metric that clears all three bars, paint it on the wall, and filter every roadmap item through a single question: Will this move the grail? If it won't, park it.

Locking onto a North Star metric feels like crossing a finish line, but it's really a starting gun. When that number stalls, the market is whispering—sometimes politely, sometimes with a bullhorn—that something upstream is off. Three quick "Why isn't it moving?" diagnostics keep you from blaming the metric when the fault lies elsewhere.

PRODUCT DIAGNOSTICS

DIAGNOSTIC	WHAT TO CHECK	FIRST MOVE
INPUT STARVATION	Are you getting enough data points?	Remove access bottlenecks
ACTIVATION DIP	Are customers getting a win fast enough?	Shorten the path to payoff quickly
COUNTER DRAG	Are gains getting offset somewhere else?	Hunt down the drag and relieve it

Input starvation is like watering cans left in the shed: no flow, no growth. In its early years, OpenTable struggled in cities where restaurant inventory lagged diner demand. Instead of tweaking marketing copy or discounts, the company focused on signing more restaurants and installing reservation systems directly into venues. As supply expanded, bookings followed. When starvation stalls your metric, the fix is surface-level—widen distribution, remove bottlenecks, or increase inventory—and the dial should respond quickly.

Activation dip happens when people sample but never feel the magic. Early Twitter users who followed only a handful of accounts often churned quickly because their feeds felt empty. The company learned that helping new users follow more accounts during onboarding dramatically improved engagement. Instead of celebrating sign-ups, the team focused on making sure every newcomer immediately saw a lively, personalized feed. If the payoff lands too late—or feels empty—pull it forward and retest.

Counterforce drag appears when one hand fills the bucket while the other pokes a hole. Uber saw ride volume surge in new cities, yet driver churn and regulatory battles offset growth. Expanding aggressively without aligned local operations created friction that slowed momentum. By investing in driver incentives and city-level teams, Uber worked to stabilize both sides of its marketplace. Counterforces signal structural tension—serious but solvable with cross-functional work across pricing, operations, or policy.

Sometimes the metric edges upward, but it's still not fast enough to topple an incumbent. Here, Peter Thiel's ten-times rule bites: customers rarely abandon a tolerable solution unless the alternative feels dramatically better. Ticketmaster endures frustration because—fees aside—it reliably processes massive on-sale traffic without collapsing. SeatGeek leaned into clearer pricing, interactive seat maps with real views, and consumer-friendly guarantees to differentiate the experience. The shift wasn't about being marginally cheaper; it was about making the buying process feel more transparent and intuitive. If your North Star creeps instead of leaps, assume inertia is winning and pile on speed, savings, or clarity until switching feels obvious.

WHY WON'T GRANDMA USE MY SOCIAL MEDIA APP?

Most founders hear "product–market fit" and zero in on product. The other half of the phrase—the market—gets waved through security without a passport. Build for the wrong crowd (the fit), and their feedback mutates your roadmap into Frankenstein: lots of parts, no heartbeat.

Think of your early users as a mirror, not a mandate. If Grandma wanders in and declares your video-chat startup "confusing," that's data—about Grandma. Your first step in determining customer fit is making sure the trash can that you dove into in Chapter 11 was the right trash can.

IDEAL CUSTOMER PERSONA (ICP) SCORECARD

ICP TEST	WEAK FIT	STRONG FIT
AGREES	Agrees with some of your Belief Ladder	Agrees with all of your Belief Ladder
PAIN LEVEL	Like it, but if it goes away, not a big deal	Love it, and it's going to save their day
SATURATION	Many competitors targeting them already	Nobody is addressing this audience's needs
EXPANSION	Interested in MVP, but nothing else	Love the roadmap as much as the MVP

Most founders chase "anyone who bites" then wonder why contradictory feedback drags the roadmap in four directions. The ICP scorecard forces you to grade early users before you let their opinions hardwire your product.

When a prospect **agrees** with every rung on your Belief Ladder, you've struck ideological gold. Early Tesla buyers weren't just car shopping; they already believed batteries could outgun combustion engines, so they forgave rattly panel gaps and limited charging stations. Their alignment let Tesla double down on range and acceleration instead of watering the vision to placate skeptics.

The **pain-level test** asks whether your solution is an aspirin or a vitamin. Calendly soared because sales reps loathed the back-and-forth of email scheduling; one link replaced ten messages, and users reached for credit cards unprompted. Contrast that with the parade of habit-tracker apps that people call "cool" yet delete after a week—the inconvenience they solve just isn't acute.

Market saturation looks beyond enthusiasm to see who else is courting the same wallet. Fenty Beauty exploded by aiming at an untapped segment: makeup users with skin tones long ignored by legacy cosmetic lines. Because no incumbent made foundations in forty-plus shades, Rihanna's brand met immediate, unopposed demand and converted shoppers into evangelists overnight. If rivals already blanket your ICP, carve a neglected subsegment—or sharpen your headline until the incumbents' copy feels tone-deaf— before adding more features.

Finally, **expansion potential** gauges whether today's fans can grow with you. Shopify aced this: Merchants who started with a storefront soon adopted payments, fulfillment, and lending, stacking lifetime value far beyond the twenty-nine dollar basic plan. If your ICP loves the starter pack but yawns at the roadmap, you're courting a one-night stand. Either redesign future releases around their bigger ambitions or pursue a neighboring persona hungry for what's next.

Once your ICP passes the scorecard, lay it side by side with the audience who is walking through the front door. Go back to the acquisition lane you chose in Chapter 11—was it TikTok "how-to" clips, a Kim Kardashian promotion, founder-led demos, or a bright yellow billboard? If the people converting through that channel don't match the age, budget, or worldview you just defined, you have a channel-to-ICP mismatch, not a product flaw. Fix the targeting (creative, keywords, partnership criteria) or switch lanes entirely before you pour more money into promotion. Otherwise, you'll keep buying Grandma's clicks and blaming grandma for the bounce rate.

WHEN TO CHOOSE A DIFFERENT OUTLET VERSUS PULLING THE PLUG

Every variable in this book—insight, assumptions, market timing, channel, product—can be bent, swapped, or rewritten. The one constant is you (and the team standing next to you). A company can survive ten pivots, but only if the people turning the wheel still want the destination and still have the skills and stamina to get there. When those human inputs erode, no refresh will save the mission.

First, check your motive the way you check runway. Do you still jump out of bed? Founders who once evangelized daily sometimes wake up dreading their own Slack channel. Phil Libin felt that moment at Evernote. He was obsessed with building the magical note-taking tool, but as the company's next chapter demanded global distribution deals and enterprise sales, his personal "why" evaporated. Libin ceded the helm to a growth-stage CEO, keeping equity and goodwill intact instead of grinding through a mission that no longer matched his motive. When the "why" turns into "why me?" with a legitimate reason, handing off the baton—or winding down—can be the smartest capital-allocation move you'll ever make.

Jawbone's founders were masters of sleek consumer hardware, but as the company expanded from Bluetooth speakers into wearable fitness devices, the challenges multiplied: supply-chain strain, product reliability issues, and fierce competition from Fitbit and Apple. The shift demanded operational depth and capital intensity beyond the company's earlier sweet spot. Lawsuits, recalls, and margin pressure mounted, and the company eventually liquidated. When the battleground shifts beyond your native strengths, hire the missing ace fast—or admit the mismatch before the burn multiplies.

In the same breath, consider team capacity and investor interest. Fab.com rocketed on flash-sale momentum then pivoted to a global design marketplace that required sophisticated supply-chain muscle the staff had never built. Engineering costs soared, operations buckled, and cash fled faster than new talent could arrive. Shutting the laptop a year earlier would have preserved capital and reputations for the next venture. If the pivot you're eyeing demands a wholesale retraining of the crew while the bank account counts down, closing with grace today beats a panicked fire sale tomorrow.

Pulling the plug is never about conceding defeat; it's about reallocating scarce human and financial capital to a hill you and your team can—and want to—take.

WHEN YOU NEED TO
TELL PEOPLE

Nothing knots a founder's stomach faster than typing "We're pivoting" into an update deck. The words looks like *failure* in a seventy-two-point font. Relax: Most stakeholders don't need a play-by-play every time you trade one feature for another, or if you're changing your target customer. However, they do need a heads-up when a change rewrites the ladder they first bought into or shortens the runway they funded.

The rule of thumb is simple. If the underlying assumptions remain intact and burn stays flat, keep iterating and spare the inboxes. But if a rung on the Belief Ladder snaps—or the new direction will devour cash—surface it quickly. A brief memo that links the old rung, the new evidence, and the revised plan earns you more trust than a glossy postmortem months later. Overcommunicate and you'll whiplash people who lack your day-to-day context; undercommunicate and you'll ambush them when the bank balance tells its story. Treat updates like medication: The right dose heals; too much makes the patient woozy.

SAYING IT OUT LOUD

A year after we shuttered Ordermetrics, I stood in front of the company for our quarterly "values" all-hands. The card said, "Humility," so I admitted the problem: "I was the one who decided on Ordermetrics, and it used up your time, and I apologize." Saying it felt like phoning my mom from the principal's office in first grade after dropping an f-bomb—raw, throat-tightening, public shame.

What followed was anything but shameful. Slack lit up with a dozen thank-you notes: "I've been sitting on a busted experiment of my own." More interestingly, people started surfacing riskier ideas knowing that risk was an accepted and practiced standard, and not a trigger for termination. By admitting a very real miss—and showing that pivoting isn't a scarlet letter—we widened the runway for smart bets and faster course corrections.

The lesson is simple: Failure and pivots are the price of ambition, not evidence of incompetence. When leaders speak their misfires aloud, they normalize experimentation, unclog the feedback loop, and free the team to swing hard at the next pitch. So say it out loud. The company you build will be braver because you did.

SECTION 2 RECAP

MOST MID-STAGE DOUBT is really a call to move. You've got a strong foundation underneath you, yet the maze of possible turns can freeze your next steps. Section 2 turns this paralysis into a structured discipline and early momentum:

→ **Throw Spaghetti.** When you fear, *What if I build the wrong thing?*, make sure the scope matches what's needed on the spaghetti spectrum and see what sticks.

→ **Mute the Rock Star.** When you fret, *My next hire might expose me*, favor reliability over pedigree: a Translator to decode pain, a Builder to ship, and a Zealot to fuel morale.

→ **Pick Your Poison.** When you spurt, *Nobody will back me*, prepare your movie trailer and answers behind the hidden questions, and be mindful of investor side effects.

→ **Feel the Burn.** When the gut says, *Something is on fire!*, guard your three fuses: cash you see, credibility you hear, and attention you feel. Let any fuse blow and the others ignite.

→ **Be Monogamous.** When worry mentions, *Nobody is going to show*, go deep on one customer acquisition channel that targets your customer, read the results, then iterate.

→ **Open Your Eyes.** When dread murmurs, *Time to quit*, run diagnostics on your market, product, and channel; keep pivoting until your motive changes or your team isn't a fit.

SCALING WITH SELF-SABOTAGE

13

BUILD A BEAR

I WALKED INTO my first day at Assembly with zero management reps, so I defaulted to the only play I knew: be the office golden retriever, which manifested as an approachable demeanor, always-on optimism, heavy usage of emojis, an everyday black T-shirt, and a hat I wore with a smiley face that said: "Have a nice day." ☺

Twelve months later—with a hundred heads in—I unwrapped a gag gift from one of our engineering management team members. It was an ironic T-shirt that said:

"LIFE SUCKS AND THEN YOU DIE."

I laughed on the outside, but my internal self-doubt jumped in: *Nice isn't having the hard conversations, boss.*

I deeply read too much into the gag gift, but there's a shard of truth in every joke. I took that truth as gospel—the entire company had gone Canadian-polite: No one pushed back, consensus felt easier than conviction, and accountability kept getting smothered under, "It's okay."

It didn't happen right away, but being nice started to impose a tax we didn't want to pay anymore, so we course-corrected in the other direction.

Out went the cap, and in came a starched, button-down, new persona: Stoic Adam™, dispenser of hard truths and zero emojis.[34] We even hired accordingly—battle-scarred execs whose resting face said, "F*ck around and find out." The vibe shift felt like oil dumped in a koi pond.

Twelve months of that act and everyone—including me—looked exhausted. I'm not a drill sergeant, and a culture built on collisions alone scorches earth faster than it grows crops. The pendulum had swung from family to everyone-is-replaceable—and both extremes sucked.

The hidden fear isn't about whether you show up as a golden retriever or drill sergeant. It's that most founders have three full-time jobs already: (1) keeping revenue alive, (2) steering an ever-shifting product strategy, and (3) managing investors and fundraising cycles. How in the world can you also foster a world-class culture? With no been-there-done-that blueprint, culture feels like a luxury project you'll "get to once the fire hose slows down." You worry that while you're heads-down, the team is silently writing a culture for you—one that might calcify into mediocrity or toxicity long before you notice. The dread is that by the time you craft the values slide deck, the real values have already been set, and you'll spend the next five years jack-hammering your own foundation.

The cure to this spiraling is building a bear.

A bear can rocket after salmon yet lumber for miles. Deliver one decisive swat and then move on. Gorge in the fat seasons and hibernate through the lean, all while looking oddly huggable from a distance and still flashing claws when the den is threatened. That blend of warmth and muscle—speed when it matters, patience when it doesn't—became the blueprint for how to build a successful team.

THE BEAR PACK

PERSONA	DAY-ONE SUPERPOWER	HIDDEN TAX
FRIENDLY CHAMELEON	Learns any domain and becomes the glue	Conflict avoidance; "Let's circle back"
GENERAL ATHLETE	Can play multiple roles at any point	May bail if they move around too much
QUICK STARTER	Gets things done as fast as possible	Hates maintenance; can do messy jobs
SYSTEM THINKER	Turns duct tape into highways	Requires real budget and patience
CONFLICT CATALYST	Says the thing everyone is tiptoeing around	Can torch morale if action doesn't happen
FINANCIAL STEWARD	Translates strategy into numbers, and vice versa	Reflex "no" on spend can choke ideas
RADAR OPERATOR	Spots issues before they happen	Might look like boy who cried wolf
CULTURE CONDUCTOR	Turns values into rituals, brings good vibes	Ignores performance for how people feel
TALENT MAGNET	Attracts A-players who anchor the team	Star-power bias can led to mismatches
WEATHERED VETERAN	Twenty years of scar tissue, has a good gut take	"In my last company" on repeat all day

In Chapter 7 we stripped the founding crew down to three essential hats: the **Builder**, who can turn an idea into something a customer can touch; the **Translator**, who converts customer grumbles into clear specs; and the **Zealot**, whose energy glues the first two together when coffee runs out. Those roles get you from zero to "People want this." When the basic engine is humming, however, you need ten complementary personas that keep the momentum from stalling, culture from curdling, and growth from collapsing under its own weight. What follows shows how each persona joins the dance, one after another, as the company moves from first sale to full stride.

Momentum usually sneaks in on the back of a **Friendly Chameleon**—the adaptable teammate who is ready for anything and can tape a shipping box at nine, smooth-talk a tense customer refund at ten, and still charm finance over lunch, all with a smile. Tasks that once felt like speed bumps suddenly roll, but harmony is this person's oxygen. They'd rather promise "Let's circle back" than plant a firm "no" and their attitude doesn't necessarily equate to skillset.

Those skill gaps expose holes you can't staff with full departments yet, which is when a **General Athlete** proves priceless. On Monday, she's pitching a small retailer; by Wednesday, she's designing the shelf tag; on Friday, she's untangling a freight snafu. Her range of skills turns emergencies into blocking and tackling, but that shuffling can last only so long before she requests a more stable role.

Speed matters even more than range when the first purchase order is on the line, so a **Quick Starter** barrels in, grabs the half-baked idea, and has a sellable sample online by the weekend. Early traction beats flawless theory—until the work they whipped through requires someone to come in and fix everything they built from the ground up.

That someone is the **System Thinker**, who looks at the rattles and drafts a simple map: order form here, supplier check there, follow-up two days later. If that system is implemented correctly, the business hums, but only if leadership gives him the checkbook and the room to run. If they don't, momentum freezes, and the company ends up in an awkward middle ground that doesn't help anyone.

With a business ready to scale, the conversation shifts from "Where did the money go?" to "Where should it go next?" A **Financial Steward** turns performance into a score everyone understands. Strategy translates into numbers, and decisions get sharper —unless her reflex answer to new spending is no, which strangles the small experiments that could fund next year's scoreboard.

Sharper numbers surface real tension, and a **Conflict Catalyst** names it out loud, "Our oldest customers pay more than first-timers. "Why?" That hard question pops the bubble of complacency, provided the leaders act. But ignore two of her flare-ups, and she'll learn that honesty hurts more than silence, and candor will leave the room quickly.

Good decisions still need an early warning, supplied by a **Radar Operator** who tracks a wobbling courier partner, a rumored regulation, and a social-media grumble before any of them hit payroll. One heads-up can save a fortune until so many pings land that the team calls him the "boy who cried wolf," and misses the one that mattered.

Growth then demands new hands, and a **Talent Magnet** turns the company's mission into an irresistible sales pitch. A day later, an unattainable hire you thought was impossible to get signs on—sometimes with half her network. But star power can blind; hire the brilliant misfit, and you inherit morale puzzles far costlier than an empty seat.

As newcomers arrive, a **Culture Conductor** stitches purpose into everyday life—Friday "win" toasts, a slack emoji for thrifty fixes, onboarding stories people repeat at dinner. Those rituals make identity stick, yet if belonging outranks results, you'll wake up with a friendly country club instead of a contender who can execute your strategy.

Just when the roster feels complete, a **Weathered Veteran** adds ballast. He's steered teams through recalls, recessions, and ugly PR storms. His scar-tissue intuition can spare you months of pain—so long as he remembers that what rescued a different firm in '09 might not fit today's market. Even the bear with gray fur has to learn new tricks.

Why ten personas?

Since fewer profiles leave blind spots, you won't notice until the roof caves in, and many more turn the org chart into a petting zoo. Think of them as vitamins: Overdose on one and you get hives; skip another and the entire body limps. The magic isn't variety for variety's sake. It's the balance that lets the company sprint in June, hibernate in January, and maul a competitor in March.

Balance is delicate: lean on too many veterans, and ideas ossify; rely solely on Quick Starters and you'll spend nights patching their loose ends. Under $10 million in revenue, prioritize Friendly Chameleons to keep information flowing, General Athletes for whatever's on fire, and Quick Starters to turn sketches into sales. Between $10 million and $50 million, add a cash-savvy Financial Steward, a Culture Conductor to hardwire values, and a couple Veterans for seasoned judgment. Cross the $50 million mark and you'll need heavyweight System Thinkers to scale routines, a few Conflict Catalysts to puncture groupthink, and a Talent Magnet to reel in specialists.

Think back to Netflix's leap from DVDs to streaming. A

nimble product lieutenant hacked the first "Watch Now" button in days, a friendly cross-functional partner kept Hollywood lawyers and engineers talking, process minds quietly replaced duct tape with playbooks, number wonks translated wild content bets into guardrails the whole company could understand, and a culture maven turned "freedom plus responsibility" from a slogan into a daily habit. Because speed, glue, structure, prudence, and spirit all showed up at once, the shift survived bandwidth bugs, studio sticker shock, and a recession. Today, Netflix is iconically known for its distinct and recognizable culture.

Ignoring balance is what doomed Theranos. Holmes walled the company off with intimidation specialists and unquestioning cheerleaders but skipped the bridge builders who translate lab data into doctor's language, the money minders who ask whether promises match the budget, and the forward-lookers who spot regulatory squalls before they break. With no glue, no guardrails, and no early-warning radar, every claw pointed inward, and the organization tore itself apart long before the ultimate end.

Why use archetypes over specific roles?

Archetypes keep the company nimble. One person can wear two personas—maybe you're a founder plus a Financial Steward while your growth marketer moonlights as a Quick Starter and Culture Conductor—so payroll stays lean, and decisions move fast. Seeing themselves as shifting personas rather than fixed titles lets teammates swap hats without Ego, spot gaps early, and grow alongside the business. Think LEGO bricks, not cinder blocks: easy to restack, tough to topple, and leaving you feeling proud when you're finished.

When you stand back, the Bear Pack isn't a recruiting checklist —it's the living circulation system. Each persona pumps a different nutrient: adaptability, range, velocity, structure, discipline, candor, foresight, magnetism, spirit, and seasoned judgment. That rhythm is what turns a loose crew into a culture that can outlearn, outlast, and outmuscle whatever the wild throws next.

BUT WHO'S GOING TO GIVE THE INSPIRATIONAL SPEECH?

Recognizing which personas you have on the team is only step one; step two is deciding when each person should stop cranking out individual work and start directing others. Get that transition wrong and you either smother output, because nobody is pointing which direction you should be going, or you promote too soon and watch projects unravel because the hands-on experts are stuck in meetings instead of finishing the job.

MANAGEMENT STAGES

STAGE	MINDSET	HIRE/PROMOTE
DOERS (0–5 FTE)	"Give me the ball—I'll score or die trying."	Do nothing. Embrace the chaos of stage.
DRIVERS (6–20 FTE)	"The outcome is my entire identity."	Promote best Doer; test with project
MANAGER (21–80 FTE)	"My wins are the squad's dashboard."	Making progress, but not the right progress
LEADER (80–250 FTE)	"I design systems, not schedules."	Functions need their own playbooks
GURU (250+ FTE)	"I see around corners and coach the coach."	Team lacks foresight on what's coming

When you're fewer than five people, everyone is a **Doer**. The mindset is simple: Hand me the ball and I'll find the net. A founder packs boxes at dawn, codes at lunch, and answers support emails at midnight. That all-hands chaos is healthy this early—every task teaches something you'll automate later. Just resist the urge to add managers; titles eat speed, and speed is your only edge before real revenue.

Cross the ten-person line and pure hustle stops scaling. You need a **Driver**—usually your strongest Doer—who owns an outcome instead of a personal to-do list. Drivers thrive when the goal is crystal clear (ship the beta by July) and the team is still small enough to huddle around one whiteboard. Promote cautiously, though: If the new Driver keeps grabbing the work instead of delegating, you've traded output for bottlenecks. A short, one-project test run lets everyone learn whether leadership suits them.

At roughly twenty-five people, work begins to sprawl across functions and time zones. Enter the first true **Manager**. Their scoreboard is the squad's progress, not personal heroics. They spend weekdays unblocking designers, nudging timelines, and making sure customer feedback lands in the roadmap. Hire or promote when you notice work is getting done, but the *right* work isn't surfacing until the eleventh hour. Also watch for the opposite risk: Managers who create process for its own sake will slow a sprinting culture to a crawl within months if unmonitored.

Around eighty teammates, the business turns into an ecosystem of teams, and you need a **Leader** who designs systems rather than schedules. This person thinks in playbooks, metrics, and feedback loops; they can build a hiring funnel, not just fill a role, and spin up whole regions or product lines without you in the room. Bring one in the moment you catch yourself making the same decision twice for two different teams—an unmistakable sign that structure, not heroics, will unlock the next milestone.

Above 250 employees, only a handful of calls shape the entire year, and that's the turf of the **Guru**. Gurus see around corners:

They spot a regulatory shift eighteen months out, notice culture fraying before Glassdoor does, and mentor the leaders who manage the line managers. They're expensive, so draft them when your leaders start losing sleep over problems they've never faced. The danger is overreliance; a guru who hovers too close keeps emerging leaders from learning their own instincts.

At Assembly, we rocketed from zero to seven hundred people in under four years, hiring many, and onboarding the rest from companies we acquired along the way. Trends in remote work, comp, and org-design flipped every quarter, but the bedrock principles of running a healthy company, regardless of the stage you were at, never budged. Here are the field notes I wish someone had handed me on Day One.

LEARN FROM MY MISTAKES

STRATEGY	WHAT IT IS	WHY IT WORKS
RESIST BLOAT	Every role is guilty until proven essential	Prevents "muffin top" that slows org down
AUDIT THE TOOLS	Scrutinize the budget every new hire asks for	Keeps hidden costs from eclipsing payroll
PROMOTE ON PULL	Promote the person the team looks to for answers	Rewards real influence, not tenure
LIMIT TOURISTS	Keep outside hires to < 10% of management	Protection against cultural whiplash
ROOKIES PLUS VETERANS	One pro mentors a handful of first-timers	Best training ground for future leaders
REAL OWNERSHIP	Leaders need to own P&L or hiring funnel	Links authority to measurable results

Practice **resisting bloat** first. When Shopify paused after its 2021 pandemic hiring binge, it still wound up cutting roughly one thousand people—about 10 percent of staff—only a year later;[35] proof that saying, "Let's wait thirty days before green-lighting wish-list roles" costs far less than reversing.

Once salary taps are under control, move straight to a quarterly **tool-stack audit.** Zylo estimates that roughly one-third of the average SaaS bill goes to licenses nobody logs into;[36] listing every subscription, its owner, and its price usually reveals three apps doing one job.

Leaner systems surface real leaders, and the best leaders come internally. **Promote-on-pull:** If half the Slack channel already pings Jamie for help, give her the badge. LinkedIn's Global Talent Trends shows companies that fill roles internally keep those employees 41 percent longer, turning organic authority into retention.[37]

Along the same lines, **cap your tourist ratio**—outside managers should fill no more than one in ten leadership seats. During Uber's hypergrowth years, internal controls and culture lagged rapid expansion, culminating in the widely reported 2017 crisis and leadership shake-up. When scale outruns stewardship, the original DNA thins.

As teams crystallize, **pair vets with rookies** and let knowledge run both directions. General Electric popularized reverse mentoring in the late 1990s, requiring senior executives to be coached by junior employees on internet and digital trends. Structured two-way learning keeps veterans sharp and newcomers absorbing scar tissue.

And finally, **enforce real ownership.** Amazon's "single-threaded leader" model gives every owner a slice of P&L or a hiring funnel; if they control neither, they're spectators in meetings, not decision-makers. Teams know exactly who signs the checks or approves the head count, and those leaders feel the cost of every delay in real time. The clarity shrinks meeting invites and slashes handoffs.

PUTTING A KIBOSH ON THE CLICHES AROUND CULTURE

At some point every founder gets the cupcake question: "So… what's the culture like here?" Early on, I'd mumble something vaguely—Integrity! Humility! Customer-First!—because that's what the slide decks say. The honest answer? When you're still sprinting for product–market fit, there **is no culture**; there's only oxygen. Ship or suffocation.

Fast-forward and you will eventually block a day in your calendar to "define values." It feels like picking crystals in Joshua Tree: Close your eyes, grab four buzzwords from the fishbowl, and declare them eternal truth. Then the market sneezes, and you pivot and throw them in the trash.

Below is what you'll hear and what to do instead.

QUOTES WITH NO LEGS

GO-TO PHRASE	REALITY CHECK	WHAT TO DO INSTEAD
"WE'RE ONE BIG FAMILY"	Don't we all wish you could fire your family?	Stick to the mission and the scope of role
"HIRE A-PLAYERS ONLY"	An A at five people can be a billion at fifty	Grade against what you need in business today
"STRATEGIC AND HANDS-ON"	Ninety-nine percent of candidates tilt one way or another	Decide on one: strategic or hands-on

GO-TO PHRASE	REALITY CHECK	WHAT TO DO INSTEAD
"LOOKING FOR A CULTURE CARRIER"	So you are saying there is no culture?	List the tangible values the team works with
"PASSIONATE ABOUT PROBLEMS"	Passion without skill is expensive fan fiction	Hire for competence; Passion comes in time
"LOOKING FOR AN INDUSTRY EXPERT"	I thought you were trying to disrupt	Hire them, but keep in mind exactly where

"We're one big family" sounds warm until the first layoffs. WeWork's all-hands once closed with "Thank you for being part of the family," but when cuts hit in 2019, the goodbye emails arrived just the same—as did the security escorts. A company is a team chasing a goal, not a reunion that lasts forever. Keep the rhetoric grounded: Promise fair play, clear expectations, and respect on the way out, then back it up with transparent severance and references.

"Hire only A-players" shows up on countless job posts, yet the grading curve changes with company size. Stripe's first dozen engineers really were Olympic-level generalists; by two thousand employees, the same firm happily staffed whole pods with solid B+ specialists who loved doing one thing brilliantly. Instead of chasing Ivy League résumés, rank candidates against the next eighteen months of work you actually need done. Someone who is an A for today's problems will always beat the future prodigy.

"Strategic and hands-on" is the purple-squirrel request that sent us to a top recruiter. Thirty minutes later, we had a Marvel-grade spec: "Strategic yet tactical, culture carrier, drops into the weeds but speaks in narrative arcs, equally adored by engineers and CFOs." Translation: impossible hire. Decide which half you need more—big-picture architect or sleeves-rolled executor—

then interview for that. If you truly require both, hire one of each.

"Looking for a culture carrier" is often a confession that no culture exists. After Uber's 2017 meltdown, they brought in Bozoma Saint John to "fix" the vibe, but one magnetic exec couldn't offset thousands of employees waiting for permission to behave. Culture lives in repeated actions, not one person's charisma. Instead, start with one observable behavior you want to see (ruthless accountability) and bring it up in every meeting.

"Passionate about the problem." Fyre Festival's Billy McFarland sold a Bahamas mega-fest with influencer sizzle, but filled his team with party-promoter hype, not veteran logistics pros; guests arrived to FEMA tents, cheese sandwiches, and a founder later jailed for $26 million in fraud.[38] Hire for competence first: Can the candidate move tomorrow's KPI with the tools they already have? Genuine Passion usually follows impact, and if it doesn't, you've still got someone who can hit the next milestone.

"Seeking an industry expert" feels safe, but experts bring baggage. Warby Parker's early team resisted pressure to poach execs from Luxottica precisely because those veterans kept insisting customers would "never buy glasses without an optician." Instead, Warby hired a handful of insiders as advisors, and coupled them with digital natives who questioned every retail assumption. Bring expertise in as seasoning, not the whole recipe, and make sure the mandate is "Show us the rules so we can break the right ones."

Buzzwords survive because they sugarcoat hard trade-offs. Family erases performance management; rock star pretends you can skip onboarding; strategic-yet-tactical ducks the choice between vision and velocity. They're slogan hypocrites—sweet on an all-hands slide, sour in practice.

SO WHICH ONE ARE YOU?

I spent my first three years at Assembly trying on the wrong costumes. When hypergrowth exposed every soft spot, I tried Conflict Catalyst barking, then told "Weathered Veteran" war stories I hadn't earned. None of it fit. The day I finally wrote **Friendly Chameleon** next to my name—quick study, room-temperature Ego, connector-in-chief—the tension evaporated. I stopped apologizing for not throwing elbows and started hiring people who loved doing exactly that. My job returned to shape-shifting between teams, translating vision into bite-sized next steps—the thing only I could do extremely well.

Before you pin a label on yourself, run a gut check with people who have shared a deadline or a war room with you. Old bosses, co-founders, that grinder from your first startup—they'll be brutally honest about which hat you really wear. You might swear you're "chill and adaptable," but the folks who watched you at 2:00 a.m. know whether you calmed the room or fanned the flames.

Know your lane, then plug the gaps. A Friendly Chameleon unsticks cross-team chatter; a General Athlete jumps on whatever's on fire; a Quick Starter ships the test version tomorrow. When the scraps pile up, a System Thinker stitches a process; a Conflict Catalyst forces the hard call; a Financial Steward prices every idea. A Radar Operator flags storms early, a Culture Conductor lifts morale, a Talent Magnet reels in specialists, and a Weathered Veteran steers clear of rookie cliffs. Org charts are scaffolds—great for today's climb, rebuilt for tomorrow's weather.

That brings us back to the hidden fear that started this chapter: *How can I juggle revenue, product, investors...and still build a culture?* The answer is painfully ordinary—one persona, one promotion, one ritual at a time. Ship the next feature, hire the missing archetype, tighten the value you already named. Momentum feels like a stampede, but progress is just the bear taking steady, deliberate steps through the forest—claw, paw, claw—until the path behind you quietly turns into a trail teams will follow.

BETA BLOCKER

DOUBT VOICE: How do I inspire confidence when I'm sweating self-doubt?

THE NIGHT BEFORE our first board meeting was supposed to be a casual rapport builder: tapas, a splash of red wine, a few "So how'd you meet?" stories to thaw the room. Instead, I disintegrated. I slouched like a teenager at Thanksgiving, words came out in 1.5-times playback, and every punch line landed with the thud of a dropped mic—no laughs, just sympathetic fork clinks. My body acted out the monologue in my head:

"DON'T F*CK IT UP, DON'T F*CK IT UP, DON'T F*CK IT UP."

I f*cked it up.

The next morning, the slide deck looked gorgeous; the presenter did not. I recited the strategy, but my voice wobbled, throat glued to the inside of my shirt. Q&A felt like dodgeball in slow motion—numbers I'd rehearsed two hundred times scattered the moment a director raised an eyebrow.

Two days later, I met our independent board member for a "no-pressure" breakfast and knocked over the orange juice before bungling the first question. Friendly nods, polite exits, radio silence.

I'd choked again.

I went back to the office to meet my co-founder after that. I was as pale as a ghost and in a dark place.

The irony of self-doubt is that you can build a billion-dollar product while privately shredding yourself, yet the only metric the outside world sees is confidence. Under the waterline, I'd mapped every KPI, modeled six downside scenarios, even memorized the engineering locations of all our competitors in case it came up. Above the water, all they saw was a shivering tip of doubt.

That dinner-to-boardroom implosion taught me the one variable I control: the switch from self-audit to outward certainty. Leading a company isn't just plotting the Promised Land; it's convincing investors, employees, and your limbic system you belong at the helm—then installing a beta blocker ritual that keeps the switch from short-circuiting when the seas get rough.

This chapter is about wiring that circuit—your mental beta blocker. The confidence you project to your board, the calm you lend your team, and the habits that keep the hull steady when the self-doubt voice pounds below deck are all part of the dosage. No prescription required.

TELLING YOUR PARENTS ABOUT YOUR BAD GRADE

Your board exists for one reason: accountability. They're the parents inspecting your report card, not the cheer squad pinning ribbons. A well-run board applies productive pressure—challenging forecasts, surfacing blind spots, and insisting on crisp, measurable next moves. They're legally bound by a fiduciary duty to act in the company's best interest, which means making you a little uncomfortable, so the business performs a lot better; if the room feels cozy while metrics burn, you don't have a board.

Start by reverse-engineering the future. Picture the company you must unveil in thirty-six months, list the scariest gaps between that vision and today's reality, and then recruit a board built to seal each one. Whether you're venture-backed or bootstrapped, treat every seat as a strategic patch. Fill metrics accountability with financial investors, the market-savvy blind spot with industry insiders, and operational bottlenecks with battle-tested company operators.

BOARD MEMBER BUCKETS

MEMBER TYPE	WHAT THEY WANT	HOW TO PREP
FINANCIAL INVESTORS	Data, lots of it. And comparisons of data	Ask them for other board decks they like
INDUSTRY INSIDERS	Proof you're pushing the vision forward	Do quarterly vision and competitor resets
COMPANY OPERATORS	Proof of an efficiently run organization	Go one layer into levers you are pulling

Financial investors are the spreadsheet extremists: venture capitalists, growth-equity funds, or endowment managers in fleece vests. What they crave is data: cohort curves, burn multiples, margin trends, and a tidy comparison against last quarter's promises. Show up light on numbers and they'll assume you don't have a handle on things. Prep by reverse-engineering their taste—ask for sample decks they prize, study the format, and preanswer every benchmark question inside your own narrative. Nail that rhythm, and the pot of gold at the end of the rainbow is that they'll open doors to more money—whether it's from their pockets or the deeper ones they influence.

Industry insiders are domain veterans—former competitors, strategic partners, or sector pundits—who joined precisely because they've seen the movie you're trying to film. They measure progress by storyline, not just box-office receipts. Are you extending the product into the white space they predicted, outflanking incumbents, and staying true to the original thesis? Satisfy them with quarterly "vision and battleground" updates: refreshed market maps, competitor postmortems, and a clear explanation of how each new feature marches the plot forward. Keep the narrative sharp, and they'll open doors to partners in your ecosystem who can step function the company.

Company operators are your pragmatic mechanics—C-suite alumni who have scaled messy orgs before and can smell process rot from the hallway. Their scoreboard is execution efficiency: hiring velocity, cash-conversion cycle, on-time ship rates, and the little levers you're yanking to make each metric budge. Preparation means getting one level deeper than vanity KPIs you showed your financial investors. Walk them through the exact workflow you just rebuilt, the funnel step you shaved to seconds, and the incentive tweak that moved sales productivity. When operators see a cockpit of levers—each labeled, measured, and actively pulled—they'll usually begin pulling out their Rolodex and plugging team gaps on your org chart.

Because we raised exclusively from financial investors in the beginning, our board ended up mirroring the cap table—four money people and the single independent operator we brought in. In hindsight, we should have treated the board itself as a portfolio: rotate in fresh specialties as the company evolves, seed early seats with operators and industry scouts, and keep rebalancing. Instead, predictably, every meeting tilted toward spreadsheets and projections, while whole conversations on talent and go-to-market nuance were used as the board's excuse for a bathroom break, a call they "had to take," or an early flight out they couldn't move.

You are allowed—expected, even—to remix the cast as the company and strategy evolve.

By charter, you'll convene the whole board four times a year: the only dates everyone blocks flights for, and the minutes become part of the company's permanent record. Between those pillars, you can (and should) spin up ad-hoc calls or coffee walks whenever a metric wobble or a deal gets real. The cadence is whatever keeps directors current enough that they understand how your business works.

In your formal quarterly board meetings, while each one will take on a journey of its own, they are all functionally the same pressure chamber that asks three ruthless questions: Do we still believe the macro tide? Does product cure the pain? Are channels surfacing the right users? If any rung in that ladder cracks, you surface it before someone else points it out. The cardinal sin is a director finding bad news for the first time in the room.

Two days before go-time, run a preread circuit (or as my co-founder coined it, the "meeting before the meeting"): ten-minute one-on-ones with every director. No surprises, no big-reveal theatrics. By the time the Zoom lights turn green, everyone knows the plot twists and can spend live minutes sharpening, not decoding, the strategy.

After the circuit, send the board deck, and assume every slide is forwardable. Treat the board deck like a press release you forgot to embargo. Once it leaves your laptop, imagine it ricocheting through inboxes until it lands on a rival's desk. That mindset forces you to scrub sensitive customer names, frame competitive strategy at altitude, and annotate any potentially alarming metric with context right on the slide. If you'd be anxious seeing the page on TechCrunch tomorrow, rewrite it today.

If you want to be extra neurotic like we were, control the takeaway in writing. In the email you send out, craft a one-page narrative that states, in plain English, what happened, why it matters, and what you need next. Lead with the conclusion you want them to walk away with (that'll make it explicit what lens they'll use, "This is a bad quarter" versus "This looks bad, but it's actually fine"), and spell out the topics of conversation so it's clear what everyone needs to come prepared to talk about. When someone forms their own opinions that aren't correct, you can steer them back to your written document that framed it.

When the board meeting starts, begin with prepared remarks that anchor the conversation. Structure your talking points with your fibbing matrix from Chapter 10 in mind: facts are free reign but should be dribbled; forward-looking assertions should be backed with data; and the seductive but dangerous "promised-land" chatter in a red box you purposefully avoid. Open with the indisputable numbers, segue to the assumptions that still need proof, and flag exactly where you're seeking the board's help instead of painting castles in the clouds. That mix—firm footing plus selective vulnerability—signals confidence without delusion: Here's what we know, here's what we're testing, here's where I'm unsure and need you in the trenches.

As a final note, let's talk about the elephant in the room: the parent–child dynamic you have in your head about your relationship with the board. While effectively reporting to someone (your board) is a trigger for self-doubt, as it was for me, it's in your head.

When the boardroom doors close, you're still the king (or queen) of the castle—the one who signs the checks, ships the code, and lives with every consequence. Their job is to poke holes; your job is to show up with a plan so sturdy it welcomes the pressure. Do that with conviction—clear numbers, clear asks, clear next steps. Confidence isn't swagger; it's the calm, evidence-backed certainty that says, "I've got this." That's the signal your board is scanning for, and it's up to you to show them.

MANAGING A PRESCHOOL AS AN ADULT WITHOUT KIDS

Running a hypergrowth startup is that split second in the hallway when a preschool teacher inhales—sweater still lint-free, lesson plan crisp—then pushes the door open to twenty screaming kids flinging finger paint like confetti. One breath earlier, you're composed; one step later, you're triaging chaos with wet wipes and crowd-control instincts you didn't know you had. That's first-time management.

My rookie-manager phase looked like a hostage-negotiation drill. I'd burn six hours combing through a leader's dashboards before our one-on-one, then open with a Gatling-gun of questions meant to prove I'd done the homework—really, I was just masking how young, green, and uncertain I felt. It backfired: Reports clammed up, the call clocked out tense, and nobody left clearer on who owned what.

Over the years, I've realized what everyone does: These are just people. The antidote was **actionable empathy**: less Hallmark, more operating manual. Empathy isn't "being nice"; it's taking their perspective long enough to diagnose what moves them, then acting on that intel. That perspective on what moves them is baked in a long-term macro desire and short-term micro needs.

A **macro desire** is the long horizon "why" that powers someone's day-to-day hustle. A macro desire sits deep in the career cortex and keeps pulsing until it's satisfied—or until the person leaves to chase it elsewhere. Spotting which one lights up for each teammate lets you tailor projects, feedback, and rewards so motivation becomes renewable energy instead of a quarterly bribe.

LONG-TERM MACRO DESIRES

MACRO	TELLTALE ASK	MANAGER MOVE
PROMOTION	"Where did you find your leadership team?"	Guidance on when and how it hits next level
COMP AND PERKS	"When do we find out our bonus amount?"	Be transparent about comp and best paths
CULTURE AND MISSION	"Can I ask, why does this matter?"	Bring them into the fold on decisions
IMPACT SCOPE	"Who's running that new project?"	Give them scope before a title bump

When an employee's primary fuel is **promotion**, every conversation circles back to altitude: they study the org chart like a subway map, quiz you on where today's VPs came from, and angle for stretch projects that showcase leadership chops. Balance that ambition by laying out a transparent rubric—skills, outcomes, and scope required for each rung—and use check-ins to grade progress against it. Tie the next title to milestones (owning a P&L slice, mentoring hires) so the path feels earned, not political.

For those motivated by **compensation and perks**, the loudest heartbeat is financial security—bonuses, equity refreshers, remote stipends. You'll hear questions about bonus calendars or see keen interest in option-pricing models. Meet the need with radical clarity. Share the logic behind pay bands, explain which levers (performance, market shifts) move them, and calendar regular comp reviews so money angst never festers. Offer concrete "level-up" projects that unlock the next bracket and help the company.

Employees powered by **culture and mission** crave a sense that their work bends the world in a direction they admire. Their tell is a gentle "Why does this matter?" when a feature feels off-brand, or pushback when decisions dilute the origin story. Fold them into the narrative early. Invite them to customer interviews, share the investor pitch's "Why now?" slide, and assign them as values guardians on cross-team projects. When they help draft the story, alignment becomes intrinsic rather than enforced.

Those driven by **impact scope** want a bigger canvas, not just a loftier title. They volunteer for messy greenfield projects and ask, "Who's running that new initiative?" Reward the hunger by handing them sandbox authority before formal promotions—let them spearhead an experiment, own a critical metric, or lead a tiger team. Pair the expanded remit with tight checkpoints so ambition translates into shipped outcomes, not sprawling chaos.

While satisfying macro desires retains employees long term, getting them through the day are micro desires.

A **micro desire** is the short-fuse "what" that sparks motivation in the moment. Unlike macro desires, which live deep in a person's long-term career wiring, micro desires surface daily and can be met—or missed—in minutes: a public shout-out after a big deploy, or fifteen extra minutes of face time. Spotting these small but potent cues lets you deliver rapid-fire rewards that keep energy high between the bigger milestones, and turning routine workdays into a string of tiny, confidence-building wins.

SHORT-TERM MICRO NEEDS

MICRO	QUICK READ	TINY FIX THAT LANDS
AFFIRMATION	Lights up at public praise	Impromptu shout-out on public channel
QUALITY TIME	Asks about coming to visit HQ	Make an impromptu trip to visit them
ACTS OF SERVICE	Notices when blockers vanish	Proactive attempt to clear things out of the way
GIFTS AND SWAG	Wears the onboarding swag to daily stand-up	Ask them to take part in the next swag decision
AUTONOMY	Scoffs when you begin to micromanage	Give them room to run, but watch

When someone's battery runs on **affirmation**, watch their eyes light up the moment praise goes public—a Slack shout-out, a company-wide "Great job!" slide, or a quick mention in the weekly stand-up. Feed that circuit with spontaneous recognition. Tag them in the team channel the hour a milestone ships, cc the exec room on an email high-five, or kick off the all-hands with a one-minute mini case study of their win. Public applause costs nothing and recharges them for weeks.

Teammates driven by **quality time** crave proximity to the mothership. They ask about visiting HQ, linger on Zoom after the agenda ends, or propose off-sites just to "sync in person." Meet that need by flipping the travel script: Book a quick trip to their city, grab coffee, and shadow their day. Even a half-day side-by-side signals, "You matter enough for me to get on a plane." The face-time deposit pays compounding trust interest.

If **acts of service** is the motivator, they notice when blockers vanish before they ask. You'll hear a surprised, "Thanks for escalating that ticket" or see productivity spike after you quietly reroute a dependency. Maintain a habit of unblocking—catch process snarls in daily stand-ups, slip them a solution link, or nudge another team to expedite a review. Every unseen favor writes a silent IOU of loyalty.

Those who light up over **gifts and swag** wear the onboarding hoodie to every stand-up and photograph new stickers on their laptop. Keep the dopamine flowing by letting them help design the next drop. Ask their opinion on colorways, invite them to vote on mock-ups, or ship a surprise limited-edition pin when a sprint lands. The token isn't about price; it's the proof they're on the inside.

For colleagues fueled by **autonomy**, nothing deflates them faster than a hovering manager. You'll catch the telltale eye roll when you prescribe how to do the task they already own. Step back; define the "what" and "why," then hand them the "how." Schedule milestone reviews instead of daily check-ins, and be ready with guardrails (budget, timeline, dependencies) so freedom doesn't drift into chaos. Trust first, verify at the agreed checkpoints, and they'll sprint without looking over their shoulder.

This all sounds academic, but it's very applicable. Once you build a muscle for it, it's a superpower that is unfortunately not a common practice among managers.

Bradley, our Glue Zealot from Chapter 7, was my proving point. Year one we tugged the macro lever—bigger paycheck—meh. Year two we minted a new title—still flat. The breakthrough? Loop him into every product review so his fingerprints shape launches (**Impact**) and ship him overseas to evangelize Assembly (**Autonomy**). He lit up like Times Square. Two tiny tweaks outperformed two years of raises and ribbons.

HOW DO YOU SPELL MANAGEMENT IN YOUR SELF-HELP BOOK?

Amazon's search bar drowns you in sixty-plus thousand management titles: GROW models, servant leadership, radical candor, situational coaching, blue-ocean cultures, teal organizations, you name it. I spent two years impulse buying half of them, hoping the next acronym would crack whatever people-puzzle was smoldering that month. Eventually, the pattern clicked: Every glossy framework just relabels one of a handful of root failures. Spot which root you're facing and the fix is very easy.

ROOT CAUSE ANALYSIS

CAUSE	SYMPTOM IN WILD	PRIMARY FIX
EXECUTION	Deadlines slip or the output is wrong	Tooling, staffing, unblocking
DECISION	Endless meetings, whiplash pivots	Verifying if we have product–market fit
IDEA	Good build velocity but zero traction	Clarify they believe in the assumptions
MANAGEMENT	Metrics look good but team is not	Wrong hires or bad performance management

A handful of culprits sit beneath almost every "people problem." Spot the right root and the cure is obvious.

When **execution** is the culprit, projects miss deadlines, quality slips, or the finished product just isn't what you asked for. You'll hear, "We're almost there" month after month, while the shipment date keeps moving. The cure is almost always practical, not motivational. Give the team the right tools, hire or contract-in the skills that are missing, and bulldoze any process roadblocks so people can focus on the work instead of fighting the workflow.

A **decision** problem shows up as meeting overload and constant course corrections—Tuesday's plan is obsolete by Friday. That chaos usually means you haven't locked in a clear market target or a simple way to decide who owns what. First, confirm you really have product–market fit; then install a lightweight decision rubric (single owner, deadline, success metric) so choices stick.

With an **idea** failure, the team is shipping plenty, but customers aren't biting. Revenue flatlines, user growth stalls, and no one outside the building seems excited. Time to rewind. List the core assumptions about who wants your solution, why, and at what price. Then run quick experiments—calls, landing pages, pilot offers—to prove or kill each one before you pour more money into building.

A **management** issue is sneaky: Headline metrics look okay, yet morale tanks, side-chat sarcasm spikes, and your best people quietly update their résumés. Dig deeper and you'll find mis-hired roles left to drift or solid performers starved of coaching. Reset expectations, run honest performance reviews, and be willing to move or exit people who can't meet the bar. The right talent in the right seats recharges culture faster than any off-site ever could.

When performance wobbles, ask: (1) who they hired, (2) the options they surfaced and recommendation they chose, and (3) what they executed. Two greens and a red point to the real culprit—no tarot cards, no four-hundred-page manifesto.

Great teams aren't pep-talked into greatness; they're diagnosed, paid in the currency that matters to them, and freed to solve problems their way. Read the room, match the lever, and most "people issues" melt before they harden into churn. Get lazy with the diagnosis and no amount of Monday-morning GIFs will save you.

DEALING WITH A FIRE DRILL

No matter how tight the rituals, someday a Slack ping labeled "URGENT" will shatter your calm: servers down, a client poached, Twitter roasting a feature. In that moment, founders swing between doomscrolling hysteria and chest-thumping heroics. Neither helps. Remember the seesaw: Nothing is as catastrophic—or as glorious—as it feels. Most growth echoes plans from a year ago; most crises are sparks, not forests on fire. The trick is staying neutral long enough to see which it is, and then act.

STOP, DROP, AND CHILL

BEAT	WHAT YOU DO	WHY IT MATTERS
FREEZE THE PANIC	Orient what is fact vs. gossip or hoopla	Stops rumor mill and preserves credibility
SIZE THE BLAZE	Gauge the impact it will have on business	Triage focus and determine if it's a big deal
ASSIGN AN OWNER	Name one owner and let them run point	Trains your team and drives accountability
GIVE AN UPDATE	Publish an update to relevant team(s)	Transparency wins credibility points
CHECK BACK IN	Document root cause and do any follow-up	Turns panic into playbook for next time

If Chapter 6's POP framework showed you how to handle personal crises, think of Stop, Drop, and Chill as the corporate remix. Different acronym, same discipline—steady hands turn fire drills into routine maintenance.

Start by **freezing the panic.** Take a literal pause, list only what you know to be true, and separate facts from Twitter rumors or hallway chatter. That snap audit anchors everyone in reality and preserves your credibility before the rumor mill can spin and take on a story of its own.

Next, **size the blaze** by putting numbers to it—how many customers, how much revenue, how much reputational risk per hour? Clear impact math focuses resources where they matter most and keeps the team from overengineering a fix for a paper cut that doesn't need urgency.

Then **assign an owner** so one name, not a committee, holds the hose. A single commander gathers resources, makes the calls, and trains up the next wave of leaders who'll run point when it's their turn in the hot seat. If you create a committee, nothing will get done fast.

With a plan in motion, **give an update** to every stakeholder who needs to know: what happened, what's being done, and when the next check-in drops. Honest, timely broadcasts prevent customers, investors, and teammates from inventing scarier stories in the silence.

Finally, **check back in** after the smoke clears: Document the root cause, timeline, fix, and prevention steps. Turning chaos into a written playbook converts tonight's crisis into tomorrow's muscle memory, which means the next fire drill ends even faster.

Here's how this worked at Assembly. One night, traffic from one APAC country exploded overnight. Real customers lived there, but the volume screamed botnet. We froze the panic by pulling fresh logs and confirming there was no breach. We sized the blaze—the spike threatened uptime yet touched less than 1 percent of paying users. A mid-level engineering lead was the assigned owner; the risk didn't warrant yanking C-suite resources. Within two hours, we gave an update to the broader management team, outlining options. The call: geo-block the country for a week, patch a filter, and personally email the affected customers. Seven days later, we flipped the switch back on, retained every account, and filed a crisp postmortem—now part of our "traffic surge" playbook.

Employees watch the how more than the what. Knee-jerk overreactions teach them that chaos is normal; glacial indecision tells them you don't have the wheel. Neutral triage followed by visible action keeps the trust account full. Even small rituals— mandatory sleep after 2:00 a.m. incidents, Uber Eats credits so on-call engineers don't code hangry—signal that urgency and sustainability can coexist.

Fire drills test the wiring you've built throughout this chapter— confidence up top, empathy in the middle, rituals in the bones. Run the protocol, learn the lesson, and get back to shipping before the smoke even clears.

BEING GENUINE IS A BAND-AID FOR SHAKY CONFIDENCE

If I'm honest, when I bombed my first board meeting—and the "meet-the-director" breakfast that followed—it took five or six full cycles to shake the collateral damage. I got to a point where I thought, "Maybe I should just be the wizard behind the curtain."

But then one day it just clicked.

The frameworks and rituals always seem straightforward on paper, but they rarely land on your very first outing, and that's okay. One rocky session won't spark a board coup, and your team won't abandon ship because you weren't a leadership guru on Day One.

What rescues the moment is sincerity: Admit what you don't know, show the work you're doing to get better, and keep the Ego dial at zero. People instinctively root for someone who owns their gaps and improves in public; they recoil from bravado that tries to wallpaper those gaps. So care hard, learn fast, and be straight—the confidence will compound, and so will your team's trust.

15

DON'T TRUST DATA

ESCAPE VELOCITY FELT like freedom…until the day we tried to instrument it.

We were four hundred people deep, so we did what every grown-up startup does: hired the sharpest program manager we knew, licensed the most robust software, and spent three glorious months threading one pristine OKR (objective and key results) tree—from our North Star revenue target down to the intern who A/B-tested the footer color—so we could translate every corner of the business into data, spot problems before they surfaced, and react at sprint speed instead of at a postmortem pace.

In concept, this made logical sense: Understand your data better. In practice, it's what some call a "clusterf*ck."

Friday 10:00 a.m. became metric-upload o'clock. Engineers stopped refactoring to hunt down event tracking; marketers copy-pasted from six Tableau tabs; sales filed JIRA tickets because "someone overwrote my Salesforce." Strategy reviews devolved into courtroom cross-examinations:

"WHERE DID YOU PULL THAT NUMBER?"

Within six weeks goals shifted, tracking drifted, and the dashboard that was supposed to illuminate the "aha" moment turned into "oh sh*t" moments. The team wasn't building product faster; they were doubling as data-entry clerks. We'd engineered a sophisticated reporting system so overdesigned that nobody could use it.

That fiasco birthed our rule of thumb.

"START MEASURING MOUNTAINS, OR YOU'LL DIE ON A HILL."

Okay, I didn't actually say that. But it'd be cooler if I had. Ayyyyyyyy. Alright, alright, alright.

Rewinding.

That fiasco was the first of many myth busters in my operator playbook—and it flipped my perspective on which data matters, how to value it, and when it deserves to be leaned on for making decisions.

Hidden beneath the dashboards lurk a deeper dread: For most of my career, data had been my bulletproof vest. Whenever the self-doubt voice whispered, I could point to a chart, a cohort curve, a conversion rate, and say, "See? The numbers have my back." But once the metrics turned to mush, that safety blanket disintegrated. If I couldn't trust the spreadsheet—or my own gut, which I'd been trained to second-guess in favor of "what the data says"—then which compass was left? The fear wasn't just that we might miss a target; it was that I might be steering blind, exposed and undecided, unsure what the appropriate next step was.

In the pages ahead, you'll learn how to catch bad numbers before they harden into gospel, a simple framework for qualifying any metric, and a playbook for turning data literacy into a company-wide muscle—so every teammate can flex it instinctively.

MYTH BUSTERS: DATA EDITION

DATA MYTH	WHAT HAPPENS	FRESH LENS
"MORE DATA IS BETTER DATA"	Teams chase curiosities, not decisions	Less data that's relevant cleanses the soul
"DASHBOARDS EQUAL INSIGHT"	Static charts become wallpaper in months	Require input of "so what" to validate it
"KPIS ARE UNIVERSAL"	Industry North Stars vary extremely widely	Reset what normal is based on in the industry
"GUT AND DATA ARE ENEMIES"	Data that clashes with intuition is ignored	Treat instinct as a hypothesis generator
"DATA IS OBJECTIVE"	Collection bias: garbage in, garbage out	Audit lineage and assumptions carefully
"PAST PREDICTS THE FUTURE"	Today is based on calls made six months ago	Build leading, not lagging, indicators
"IF YOU CAN'T MEASURE IT, IGNORE IT"	Intangibles (brand, morale) are important	Use surveys and qualitative loops as well
"ONE METRIC TO TULE THEM ALL"	Ignores blind spots and usually changes	Balance a metric stack if metrics check out

"More Data Is Better Data" tells you to capture everything because more numbers must mean better decisions. Before Money-ball, baseball teams tracked piles of traditional stats—batting average, RBIs, pitcher wins—yet still misjudged player value because they measured what was familiar, not what predicted wins. More data didn't mean better insight. Fewer, sharper metrics that connect directly to outcomes beat sprawling stat sheets every time.

"Dashboards Equal Insight" assumes that posting numbers automatically creates understanding. The Challenger space shuttle launched despite charts showing O-ring concerns; the data existed, but it was buried in slides and never forced a clear go/no-go decision. A display without consequence is decoration. Insight only emerges when a metric compels action. If no one knows what must happen when a number shifts, the dashboard is theater, not management.

"KPIs Are Universal" claims that a benchmark from one field applies everywhere. When we showed our investors that 30 percent of new customers left our small-business platform in the first month, they saw a product failure. But in reality, those customers were testing side hustles that often close quickly. The real question was how much revenue we earned from the businesses that stayed. Key metrics must fit local realities—borrowing them blindly from another company or industry leads to bad calls that miss the nuance.

"Gut and Data Are Enemies" says you must pick sides, but the two work best together. Ben & Jerry's built its brand on chunky textures partly because co-founder Ben Cohen, who has a reduced sense of smell, prioritized mouthfeel. A founder's instinct shaped the product; sales data validated it. Treat instinct as a hypothesis generator, then wrap measurement around it. Hunch plus tracking beats either alone.

"Data Is Objective" says numbers never lie, yet in the mid-2000s, lenders approved waves of low-documentation mortgages that models labeled safe because inputs assumed rising home prices and borrower honesty. When those assumptions cracked, so did the ratings. Metrics inherit the bias of how they're gathered and coded. Before saluting a spreadsheet, trace the lineage—who collected it, what was excluded, and what assumption sits quietly underneath.

"Past Predicts the Future" comforts leaders with tidy trend lines, but Blockbuster's rental revenue looked steady even as Netflix's DVD-by-mail service quietly reshaped consumer habits. Historical sales described yesterday's behavior, not tomorrow's shift. Lagging indicators tell you what happened; leading signals hint at what's coming. Pair backward numbers with forward clues—search spikes, waitlists, or sales velocity—before the curve bends without you.

"If You Can't Measure It, Ignore It" tempts teams to skip anything fuzzy. After Apple launched its retail stores in 2001, early analysts questioned the revenue per square foot, yet the stores built brand loyalty and ecosystem control that compound metrics later proved enormous. Not every advantage shows up instantly on a dashboard. For intangibles like morale or reputation, use surveys, interviews, and field stories alongside hard numbers.

And finally, while you should lean on a handful of reliable metrics, betting everything on a single number will blindside you. **"One Metric to Rule Them All"** promises that one headline figure can steer the whole company, but Assembly's guiding measure changed constantly: first weekly active users, then accounts using all three tools, then gross merchandise value (the total dollars sellers moved) across multiple marketplaces. Each switch felt awkward yet simply showed we were still learning how growth really worked. Keep a short set of complementary measures—say growth, profit, and customer satisfaction—so they cross-check one another and alert you when something drifts.

Every one of these myths will get its own fifteen minutes of fame—they won't ambush you all at once. What matters is that you notice when each one steps into the spotlight, call it by name, and remember not to accept any number, chart, or hunch at face value.

WHEN UP IS DOWN AND DOWN IS UP

Anyone can grab the very same metric and see a completely different movie. Hand last month's churn to the Weathered Veteran and he'll shrug, "Five percent? I've seen worse." Pass it to the Conflict Catalyst and she'll pound the table like it's DEFCON 1. Even the Friendly Chameleon can nod along with both sides in the span of a single stand-up. The point is simple: Numbers don't speak for themselves—we ventriloquize them.

After a while, the bright-yellow "Have a Nice Day" smiley on my ball cap curled into a weary frown that muttered, "It's Been a Day." If I couldn't lean on data—my secondary superpower from years of investing—as a first-time operator, what was left to keep the team accountable, or worse, to tell me whether we were winning or not?

Over time—and after watching metric debates implode at more companies than I care to count—I realized the real skill isn't piling up numbers but qualifying them. Back in Chapter 12 we hunted for the holy grail metric: one number that tracks the customer's core pain, moves week-to-week, and stands on its own without footnotes. That single beacon is priceless while you're fighting for product–market fit because it tells you—fast— whether the product is solving the right problem.

But once the business expands beyond that first beachhead,

one beacon won't light every corner. You need a small constellation that shows how product, marketing, sales, operations, and engineering are really performing. To get there, you need to separate noise from insight, which can be cured by the SIGNAL framework.

SIGNAL FRAMEWORK

TEST	LITMUS QUESTION	FAIL EXAMPLE
S—STRATEGIC	Does this tie directly to a core bet?	TikTok follower count for Enterprise
I—INTUITIVE	Can anyone explain it in ten seconds?	Rolling three-week average DAU/MAU
G—GRANULAR	Can we slice it to reveal why, not what?	Total monthly cash-based revenue
N—NEAR-TIME	How tight is the feedback loop?	Annual eNPS scores from your team
A—ACTIONABLE	Do we have a pre-loaded playbook?	Brand sentiment index with no next step
L—LONGEVITY ADJUSTED	Does it protect tomorrow's moat?	Daily ROAS spike from an ad Blitz

Strategic metrics line up directly with your biggest goal. Tracking how many Instagram followers a neighborhood accounting firm gains may look impressive, but it doesn't say whether clients sign on for tax season. FedEx, on the other hand, lives and dies by "overnight packages delivered on time," because every on-time drop proves its core promise. So, measure the mountains, not the hills.

Intuitive metrics are easy to grasp in ten seconds. A "thirteen-week rolling customer-engagement ratio" makes most people squint. A grocery store's "average items per basket" is crystal clear; if the number rises, shoppers are discovering more products each trip, and if it dips, you can work to figure out what's causing that and adjust accordingly.

Granular metrics let you slice the story to uncover causes, not just totals. "Monthly sales" lumps everything together; you can't tell if growth came from new buyers or one huge order. A regional clothing chain fixes this by splitting sales into "first-time shoppers" and "returning shoppers." If the repeat slice dips, the team knows to revisit quality and fit of their clothing lines.

Near-time metrics talk back quickly enough to steer the next move. Waiting a year for an employee-satisfaction score leaves small problems to fester. A coffee shop that pulses staff every Friday on "How was your week, 1 to 5?" can spot morale trouble before it shows up as turnover.

Actionable metrics come with a ready next step. A generic "brand buzz score" might rise or fall without anyone knowing what to do. A hotel group that tracks "minutes to clean a room" has a playbook: If the time creeps up, call in a housekeeper or adjust the checklist so there aren't delays.

Longevity-adjusted metrics protect tomorrow's moat, not just today's spike. A one-day sales jump from a deep discount feels great but can train customers to wait for deals. A magazine publisher prefers "subscribers still active after twelve months," because healthy renewal rates signal durable loyalty and steady cash flow.

Together, when your metrics clear each step of the SIGNAL framework, you're left with data you can trust. Whether that filter leaves you with one crystal-clear number or a dozen well-chosen indicators doesn't make you any more or less connected to your business; it means every data point you keep is built to guide real decisions instead of cluttering the dashboard.

So what actually clears the SIGNAL gauntlet? Let's look at a few companies you know well and choose their metrics:

Airbnb zeroing in on **nights booked per active listing**. It's Strategic—directly tied to the bet that homeowners will trust strangers; Intuitive—any host understands "more nights, more income"; Granular—sliceable by city, season, or host tenure to see why some markets lag; Near-time—updates nightly; Action-triggered—underperformers get automated pricing tips; and Longevity-adjusted—boosting bookings today also strengthens tomorrow's supply.

Duolingo achoring on **learners with a seven-day streak**. The metric is Strategic—committed learners power its freemium model; Intuitive—even beginners know a streak means progress; Granular—viewable by language, skill, or region; Near-time—updates the moment a streak breaks or extends; Action-triggered—a break fires an instant nudge; and Longevity-adjusted—longer streaks predict subscriptions and referrals.

Starbucks focusing on **monthly purchases per active rewards member**. It's Strategic—loyalty visits drive long-term value; Intuitive—baristas and execs alike grasp it at a glance; Granular—breakable by store, day part, or beverage; Near-time—refreshed each morning for managers; Action-triggered—a dip prompts an app offer to lure members back; and Longevity-adjusted—steady visits signal durable sales without constant discounts.

Different industries, same through line: Each company ferociously pruned its dashboard until the surviving metric passed every SIGNAL gate. Once the noise was gone, debates shrank, action sped up, and impact spiked. Pick your own North Star that clears those six hurdles.

AWESOME. NOW WHERE DO I FIND THAT METRIC?

Finding your North Star metric takes time, team alignment, and a willingness to iterate in public. Every company I've met slots into one of two camps: **Data Desert** teams ship features and then pray, collapsing every debate into "I feel…," while **Data Deluge** outfits drown in thirty tabs of pivot-table purgatory. Neither survives long. The target is a temperate middle—just enough instrumentation to prove or kill a bet, not a head-count-heavy dashboard farm nobody reads or decisions based on horoscopes.

The first order of business is accepting it's your fiduciary duty to know the numbers that matter. Boards will probe, customers will vote with their wallets, and nothing erodes credibility faster than a leader who needs their slide deck explained back to them.

Next, take an honest look at where you stand and how your industry works. A consumer-payments app might need second-by-second feedback to keep users from jumping ship, whereas a medical-device firm can still win with quarterly analytics because incumbents steer by the rearview mirror. Knowing your maturity level and your market's rhythm tells you how hard to lean on data and how fast it needs to flow.

Finally, get something into the wild and iterate. If you're a Desert crew, ship a single live dashboard before writing another line of code; If you're a Deluge squad, Marie-Kondo your metrics until only the ones that clearly drive revenue, satisfaction, or efficiency remain. Float three candidate KPIs, plaster them everywhere, and run a two-week test. Archive any metric that doesn't change behavior or live on everyone's lips and keep cycling until the chosen number feels like the company's heartbeat.

When you finally hit pay dirt—your Uber "two rides and

you're hooked," your Facebook "seven friends in ten days"—the room feels different. Conversations shorten, side quests die, and the goal becomes muscle memory. That's the moment you're golden: The metric is no longer a number on a screen; it's the heartbeat of the company, audible in every meeting, Slack thread, and product decision that follows.

WHAT ABOUT THE OTHER STUFF?

Yes—LTV/CAC, retention curves, burn ratio, ARR growth, NPS—all the greatest hits your board deck can't live without. You still have to track them; any investor, acquirer, or half-awake CFO will drill you on each one:

They'll ask for Net Dollar Retention (> 120% good, < 100% bad), CAC Payback (< 12 months sharp, > 24 sluggish), Rule of 40 (≥ 40% healthy, < 20% worrisome), Gross Margin (> 70% software-sleek, < 40% tractor vibes), Gross Revenue Retention (> 90% tight, < 80% leaky), LTV ÷ CAC (> 3 champagne, < 1 bonfire), Logo Churn (< 5% saintly, > 10% bucket with holes), Quick Ratio (new vs. lost revenue 4:1 cruise, 1:1 cement shoes), Burn Multiple (< 1.5 disciplined, > 3 flamethrower), ARR per FTE (> $200K lean, < $100K bloated), Pipeline Coverage (3× target comfy, 1× dice-roll), DAU/MAU Stickiness (> 30% habit, < 15% tourist), Activation Rate (> 25% click, < 10% bounce), Average Contract Value (rising smile, sinking frown), Cash Runway (> 18 months pillow, < 9 tightrope), ARR Growth YoY (triple-triple-double rocket, single digits snooze), Churned Revenue (< 3% monthly tidy, > 6% hemorrhage), Sales Cycle (< 60 days sprinter, > 120 days glacier), Time-to-First-Value (< 5 minute magic, > 30 minute migraine), Expansion Revenue Rate (> 20% seconds please, < 5% "check please"), Engineering Deploys per

Week (daily rocket, monthly rowboat), Support CSAT (> 90% hugs, < 75% rants), Tickets per 1,000 users (< 20 zen, > 50 circus), Gross Profit Margin (> 30% solid, < 15% razor-thin), Net Profit Margin (> 10% comfy, losses blood-red), EBITDA Margin (> 15% sturdy, < 5% brittle), Operating Cash-Flow Coverage (> 1.5× safe, < 1.0× choke-point), Inventory Turnover (> 8 nimble, < 4 dusty), Days Sales Outstanding (< 45 days smooth, > 75 days stuck), Return on Assets (> 8% efficient, < 3% hog), Return on Equity (> 15% investors cheer, < 5% yawn), Debt-to-Equity (< 1 conservative, > 2 heavy), Employee Turnover (< 10% healthy, > 20% revolving door), On-Time Delivery (> 95% promise kept, < 85% fire drill), and First-Pass Yield (> 98% factory gold, < 90% scrap heap).[39]

Thanks for coming to my data TED Talk.

Here's the curtain call: The numbers that guide the company and the numbers that prove the company aren't the same species —confusing them turns dashboards into fog. You'll still face moments when the spreadsheets crumble and you feel exposed, but now you have a playbook. Spot the wobble, run your sniff tests, push the survivors through the SIGNAL filters, and let a trimmed-down set of metrics steer the ship. That's the antidote to the naked feeling: You don't need perfect data, only disciplined data—numbers sturdy enough to earn your trust yet light enough to let your judgment breathe.

16

LISTEN TO THE NOISE

NOISE SHOWS UP uninvited the moment you file your LLC. Mine began in the car one Friday when my mom—hands at ten and two, minivan cruising from picking me up at the airport to visit for the weekend—asked, "Don't you think Assembly is kind of confusing? There are already a bunch of companies called that." I did the mature thing: launched into a five-minute mansplain on brand architecture, derivatives, and why *our* Assembly was totally different.

On the flight home, I caught up on emails ahead of the next week, which included a final report from a pricey pricing consultant: "Our exhaustive regression says bump every tier thirty bucks," they announced, promising a 20 percent revenue pop. On paper it sang, but we'd pledged to customers we'd never raise prices without adding commensurate value. Keeping that promise meant scrapping the recommendation and metaphorically lighting money on fire.

"SPOILER: MOM 1, CONSULTANT 0."

As we scaled, that throwaway car-ride comment kept winning. Prospects who googled us found machine-parts suppliers; enterprise buyers asked whether Helium 10 and Pacvue, the actual products that our customers downloaded, were "plug-ins." Internally we chanted, "We're the Intuit of e-commerce," yet the analogy never landed. The name that felt clever in a branding brainstorm was now tying our shoelaces together mid-race.

Years after my mom's comment, what did we do? We changed our corporate name from Assembly to Pacvue, the name of our enterprise software product. I should have known—when I was growing up, my grandma always used to tell me in her thick East Coast accent:

"YOUR MOTHER (PRONOUNCED *MUTHA* IN CONNECTICUT) IS ALWAYS RIGHT."

Yet my knee-jerk rebuttal to Mom's question wasn't really about branding at all—it was about self-preservation. I was already juggling product fires, payroll math, investor pings, and my own voice; the thought of one more critic felt like an ambush. When an outsider questions you, the reflex is: *You don't live this every day—who are you to judge?* That flash of defensiveness masks a deeper worry that their comment might uncover something you've missed.

That flash taught me what classrooms never did: Off-key remarks we dismiss—competitor launches, employee grumbles, even a parent's musings—often contain razor-sharp truth. Chapter

15 showed why blindly trusting every data point is a trap; the cure is to qualify only the data that matters. Chapter 16 flips the script: We're wired to disqualify outside opinions by default, yet the smarter move is to qualify more of them—probe for context, test the insight, and keep the remarks that sharpen your picture.

And that starts with one question: What do you gain from this information? Let's walk through the **GAIN** framework.

WHAT DO YOU GAIN

SLIDER	KEY QUESTION	WHY IT MATTERS
G—GOAL FIT	Is this input directly tied to our mission?	Keep shiny objects from hijacking time
A—AMPLITUDE	Is the input coming from multiple places?	Separates pattern from daily anecdote
I—INCENTIVE	What does the messenger stand to gain?	Surfaces any hidden biases that exist
N—NEXT STEP	Can we run cheap experiment to test?	Converts chatter into actionable learning

Goal fit asks whether a piece of feedback links directly to the mission you've already declared. When a neighborhood bakery built on "fresh, local, organic" hears a suggestion to sell frozen cookie dough nationwide, that idea fails the test—it veers off-mission and would soak up time and capital better spent on core customers. A pitch to add gluten-free muffins, however, aligns with serving health-minded locals and sails through. Checking if something aligns to your goals keeps shiny objects away.

Amplitude measures how wide and loud the signal is. A lone Yelp gripe about lukewarm coffee might be a crank; five complaints in the same week plus baristas hearing it at the counter form a chorus you can't ignore. Treating amplitude this way separates one-off anecdotes from patterns, so you fix systematic problems instead of chasing noise.

Incentive digs into what the messenger stands to gain. A web-design agency insisting you "must" redo your site—while waving a proposal—has a clear financial motive, so their advice needs extra salt. Contrast that with a long-time customer who volunteers the same critique with no stake beyond faster checkout; their view deserves weight. Surfacing incentives protects you from decisions warped by hidden agendas from the person telling you.

Next step asks whether you can run a quick, low-cost experiment to prove or disprove the idea. Rebranding that requires six months of work before any data comes back is a nonstarter. Swapping in a clearer home-page headline for one week and watching click-throughs is cheap, fast, and informative. A solid next step turns chatter into actionable learning and keeps momentum.

When an insight clears all four GAIN sliders, park the Ego that whispers, "Why didn't I think of this first?" and take it seriously. Your job isn't to originate every good idea—it's hard enough to run a business. Sometimes a free, good idea here and there is just the break you need.

WHEN THE NOISE LIVES
NEXT DOOR

A rival's product is the loudest slider on most soundboards. Ours blared when a startup rolled out a tool that sniffed out supply-chain overcharges and clawed back refunds for customers. Our knee-jerk reaction was "Lumpy revenue, totally noncore," we shrugged—and kept shrugging. It took two full years, customer pings, and a surge of case-study screenshots before we finally built our own version. By then, we were playing catch-up, stitching together an MVP that could have been live eighteen months earlier.

Let's be honest: Whenever a new competitor crops up, a rival launches a shiny feature, or their name merely surfaces in conversation, our first instinct is to scoff. Out loud or under our breath, we list all the reasons their move is naive, off-brand, or destined to flop. That reflex isn't analysis—it's Ego and fear teaming up to tell a comforting story: If their idea is dumb, mine must still be brilliant. But that story can cost you big time. Before dismissing the next "dumbest idea in the world," run it through GAIN.

Remember Garmin?

In 2009 Google released free turn-by-turn navigation on Android phones. The dedicated-GPS giants brushed it aside: "Phones drain batteries and lose signal; drivers will still buy our units." Again, GAIN was flashing green. *Goal fit?* Real-time directions were literally their business. *Amplitude?* Every Android review highlighted the feature, and forums filled with drivers ditching windshield mounts. *Incentive?* Google's motive—sink hooks deeper into mobile search—didn't diminish the benefit to users. Next step? Garmin or TomTom could have tested a freemium app within weeks but instead poured resources into ever-cheaper hardware. Navigation revenue cratered as smartphones ate the category, and the late-to-market apps never caught up. Treating a high-GAIN competitor move as background chatter turned into an existential crisis.

So catch yourself the next time someone—especially a paying customer—mentions a competitor by name. Pause the eye roll, run their comment through GAIN, and decide with clear eyes whether it's throwaway chatter or the spark of your next big idea...or worse, an early warning of the hit that could level you if you ignore it.

NOISE TWO DESKS AWAY

The chorus inside the building can be sharper than anything outside. Engineers, customer service, even recruiters kept joking that "Assembly" felt like a parent company, not the product they worked on. It echoed my mom's critique almost word for word, yet we brushed it off as cafeteria humor—until candidates started asking which "class" they'd be hired into. Nothing kills culture faster than an accidental caste system baked into your org chart.

Most firms wave off in-house rumblings as harmless gossip: *They don't have the full context…We can't fix every complaint… That junior analyst isn't qualified to critique strategy.* It's a comforting rationalization, and exactly how noise turns into missed opportunity. When you hear grumbles in Slack or jokes at the coffee machine, the impulse is to tag them "background chatter" and move on. But those off-key notes often carry frontline truth your management dashboards will never show.

Take Wells Fargo's cross-selling fiasco.

Years before the headlines, branch employees warned that impossible sales quotas were driving fake-account tactics. Headquarters brushed it off as griping from underperformers who "didn't get the culture." *Goal fit?* The critique was dead center on the company's mission of trusted banking. *Amplitude?* Complaints spanned states and escalation hotlines. *Incentive?* Employees risked their jobs to speak up—hardly a biased lobby. *Next step?* A pilot to rebalance quotas or audit account openings would have cost pocket change. Leadership ignored every slider, and the bank ate billions in fines and a decade of reputation damage.

So park the org-chart goggles. The next insight might come from a receptionist or junior engineer. Remember, a Starbucks store manager dreamed up the Frappuccino; a 3M chemist tinkering after hours created Post-it Notes; an Amazon engineer pitched Prime in an internal memo; a Toyota assembly-line worker pulled the andon cord and birthed modern lean manufacturing. Title is a badge, not an IQ score—qualify the idea, not the résumé.

NOISE FROM THE MARBLE TABLE

One of our board directors opened every meeting with the same gentle hum: "So, what are we doing on Shopify?" He wasn't ordering a pivot—just prodding for an informed stance. We already had a few customers selling on Shopify, we'd been lunch-and-learning with founders in that ecosystem, and the market was humming. His point: Have an opinion because you're already standing near the dance floor. At first, we filed the question under polite curiosity. We parked it and promised to revisit. Six months later Shopify's stock was rocketing, Klaviyo was whisper-valued for an IPO, and the question returned, louder. This time we dove in. The conclusion was the same—too crowded, too margin-dilutive, and our core customer didn't need another dashboard. But now we had data, a memo, and a kill date. "What are we doing on Shopify?" became "Here's why we're *not* doing Shopify."

Your board member doesn't need to be an industry insider to offer industry-changing advice, and they don't need to be a financial engineer to poke holes in your metrics. What most directors *do* have is a hard-won superpower called pattern recognition—after seeing hundreds of business plans rise and fall, they can spot echoes and potholes you haven't lived long enough to recognize. So, when a board member comments, "I'm seeing a lot of success stories around X—what's our stance?," it isn't idle small talk; it's a signal that a pattern is forming outside your daily trench big enough to be brought up.

Consider Borders in 1999–2000.

Several outside directors kept urging management to build an in-house web store while traffic was still cheap and brand recognition was sky high. Management waved it off. *Goal fit?* Selling books online was a direct extension of Borders' mission. *Amplitude?* Online sales across the industry were doubling year over year. *Incentive?* Those directors had no side deal; they simply didn't want to watch a beloved retailer miss the shift they'd seen flatten other categories. *Next step?* A limited pilot could have launched for less than the cost of one flagship remodel. Instead, Borders outsourced its web presence to Amazon, then raced to catch up years later—long after customer relationships (and margins) belonged to someone else. Ignoring their board helped pave the road to bankruptcy in 2011.

Yes, sometimes a board director drops a head-scratcher that earns a private eye roll from the management team—and that's fine. Laugh about it on the ride home if you must. But before labeling a remark "stupid," run it through GAIN. If it clears the sliders, the stupid might be on *you* for shrugging it off. Catch yourself, qualify the opinion, and at a minimum, provide a stance to close the topic.

NOISE FROM ACROSS TOWN

The frequency almost no one budgets for is the one outside your company, competitive landscape, or board. My silent cheat code became a standing Friday call with a Nashville-based founder scaling at the same clip with a completely different business in a completely different industry. No slide decks, no bravado—open-ended therapy sessions on how the week went. From him, I added a cleaner org chart for our small-and-medium business segment. From me, he learned why tiny bolt-on acquisitions stall: mismatched culture, hidden tech debt, and the legal molasses. More important than the tactical swaps, we were allowed to air self-doubt without the boardroom poker face; that alone was worth the hour.

The best signal often comes from people who have nothing to gain by misleading you. Because a stranger's incentives are neutral—and because they haven't marinated in your jargon or politics—their comment already passes half the GAIN test: *incentive* is clean, and their *amplitude* offers a fresh angle, not an echo of the company line. That outsider's lens is why disruptors rarely hire industry lifers at the start; newcomers aren't shackled by "how it's always been done," so they see opportunities incumbents tune out.

Take the birth of the McDonald's drive-through.

In 1975 a franchise in Sierra Vista, Arizona, installed a service window so customers could order and receive food without leaving their cars. The tweak wasn't a grand strategic plan, just a simple response to local demand for faster service. Corporate could have brushed it off as a quirky outpost experiment, but the signals lined up: customers loved the convenience, the owner's incentive was straightforward—sell more burgers—and the test required little more than cutting a window in the wall. Sales jumped, the format spread, and within a few years drive-through lanes became a core part of the chain's playbook. A local workaround, spotted early and amplified quickly, turned into one of fast food's defining features.

So, stay tuned, whether the voice comes from a college buddy, a podcast guest, or your mom during a Sunday call. Ideas born outside your nine-to-five may carry the fresh lens you need to build the next great thing—provided you park the Ego, run the thought through GAIN, and let real insight, not résumé lines, decide what's worth pursuing.

WHEN THE NOISE TURNS TOXIC

Most chatter deserves fair hearing, but some signals come stamped with a skull-and-crossbones. That's when you flip from listening mode to telling a bully to Shut the F*ck Up (STFU), but in corporate. You don't just tune these frequencies out; you speak up and tell everyone why.

At team off-site in 2022 the STFU lights all flashed red. A visibly tipsy product lead, still sore we hadn't resourced *his* roadmap, started trash-talking the big launch slated for Q3—"This is ugly," "Never going to work." The critique was misinformed, but the danger wasn't the inaccuracy; it was the audience. Half the room was the team that built it and had pulled weekend shifts to hit beta. I knew a public beatdown would potentially torch the relationship, yet silence would seed self-doubt in a team already running on espresso and adrenaline. In front of everyone, I said, "Shut the f*ck up." (Let's pretend I said, "Your comments are destructive and you're flat-out wrong.") You could hear a pin drop. The fallout: The bully groveled for forgiveness the next day and the team he made fun of got done with the beta two weeks early because they were motivated to make him look like a dufus.

WHEN TO SPEAK UP

FLAG	TRIGGER	WHY?
S—SOURCE	Is the messenger wrong or malicious?	Letting it stand keeps false information alive

FLAG	TRIGGER	WHY?
T—THREAT	Does it endanger mission or morale?	Trust and culture don't wait for clarification
F—FESTER	Does it have the potential to spread?	Once things go viral, it's game over
U—UGLY FALLOUT	Will silence cost talent or customers?	Cleanup costs dwarf one blunt statement

Here's how to decide when to hit the STFU button:

Source is the first warning sign. If the messenger is flat-out wrong, peddling half-truths, or taking cheap shots to wound a teammate, leaving the statement unchallenged keeps bad information alive in the room. A senior developer blaming a deploy failure on "lazy QA" when the logs show his own commit caused the crash isn't feedback.

Threat comes next. When a comment undercuts the mission or guts morale—"That launch will flop; marketing always screws up"—it erodes trust faster than any missed metric. Team members who just burned weekends to hit a deadline shouldn't have to wonder whether leadership has their back. Calling the shot publicly protects the culture and reminds everyone that attacking is not constructive.

Fester asks how far and fast the poison can spread. A sarcastic line in a private chat may seem harmless, but if it echoes existing frustrations, it can sprint through Slack and become an us-versus-them mantra by Friday. Tackle the rumor before it multiplies; the longer it circulates, the harder it is to disinfect.

Ugly fallout analyzes the cost of silence. If ignoring a jab risks top talent polishing résumés or a flagship customer second-guessing a renewal, the cleanup bill will dwarf one firm "STFU" in the moment. Speak up, set the boundary, and move on—the twenty-second correction today is cheaper than six months of damage control.

Remember, not saying something *is* saying something. STFU moments don't require a soapbox or partisan chant; they demand a human voice that says, "Here's what's true; here's what happens next." People respect that.

CAN YOU HEAR ME NOW?

I didn't always welcome outside noise; in fact, I spent years swatting it away. Growing up, my mom was a walking Hallmark card— every spelling-bee ribbon or half-decent jump shot earned a standing ovation. Those constant words of affirmation hardwired me to treat even gentle critique like a foreign object my body had to reject. When I entered the working world, that reflex came along for the ride: Performance reviews felt like ambushes, peer feedback sounded like betrayal, and I defended every roadmap decision. It took a few painful misses—and a couple of mentors who refused to let me hide behind perfectionism—before I finally recognized that "noise" can be a gift.

But you can't accept external voices until you get a handle on the internal one. Earlier chapters tackled the self-doubt soundtrack that loops inside every founder's head; only after you learn to mute, challenge, or reframe that voice can you make room for opinions that come from beyond your nine-to-five bubble. That's why this discussion lands near the end of the book: Once you've steadied your mental compass, you're ready to let new signals in.

Noise, like doubt, is baked into the founder job description. You can't cling to a single voice—customer, competitor, board member, or Mom—and call that strategy. Your real work isn't to have every answer on Day One; it's to build the reflex that tests every answer offered. Tarot-card reader, pricing guru, or the teacher who drilled you on long division—each messenger is just a signal carrier, and occasionally, as the STFU test reminds us, a carrier that needs to be cut off.

17

BANK THE WIN

ON SEPTEMBER 13, 2019, our first investors wired the Series-A round, and we toasted the long future ahead.

Exactly twenty-one months later—May 31, 2021—a letter of intent landed on our desk to buy half the company we'd just begun to build. I stared at the document and heard Kobe Bryant's voice from the 2009 Finals press conference looping in my head:

"JOB NOT FINISHED. JOB FINISHED? I DIDN'T THINK SO."

Were we ready to cash out on a ten-year dream—one where every brand linked to every channel through a seamless, all-in-one e-commerce suite—when the truth was we still served some brands on some channels, with only some of the features sketched in our roadmap?

Then math elbowed its way in. We were clipping north of 60 percent growth, throwing off real profit, and riding the hottest multiple wave software had ever seen in the hottest category (e-commerce) coming out of COVID-19.

Selling wasn't selling out; it was banking the win—locking in today's value, pricing in tomorrow's upside, and arming ourselves to accelerate. The right buyer would give our early believers generational outcomes *and* hand us the cash to acquire Pacvue, the enterprise engine that would rocket us from scrappy contender to market storm.

Underneath that logic and opportunity lurked the real hang-up: the gnawing fear that the work was still unfinished—that it would *never* feel finished. The same voice that once bargained, "Just one more feature and we'll launch," now whispered, "Just one more quarter of growth and we'll deserve to sell." It's the psychological mirage we've all chased: The next promotion, the next milestone, the next headline will finally grant permission to exhale. Yet the finish line keeps scooting forward, daring us to sprint until the market—or our stamina—gives out.

Founders love to say, "We're not for sale," but every company wears a price tag, whether the motive is Wealth, Ego, Passion, or Control. Wait too long—run out of cash, burn out, squeeze the last drop—and the tag gets smudged or ripped off. Bank the win at the right moment, and you refill the tank for the next race. This chapter is about recognizing that moment and preparing yourself—emotionally, operationally, financially—to grab the pen and sign.

KNOWING WHEN IT'S THE RIGHT TIME

Two forces set the perfect sell window. One is a tide you can't control from Chapter 3—things like market multiples, investor appetite, macro buzz. The other is your position on the company's vision timeline: how much of the vision is already proved versus how much is still a promise? It's a delicate balance, but it's in your control. Sell early and buyers pay for your PowerPoint; wait too long and they'll price on cash flow, assuming the future is spent.

Ideally, you want to lock in a deal at the moment when proof and promise touch: enough evidence that your internal champion won't get fired in two years, but enough upside that the same person looks like a genius—and earns the promotion—five years later. That sweet spot moves as your company moves, which is why it helps to map every exit conversation against a timeline of stages.

THE SELL WINDOW

STAGE	PROOF VS. PROMISE	WHAT HAPPENS
SPARK	Proof is MVP; promise is the PowerPoint	Sell only if you need an acqui-hire exit
EARLY TRACTION	Product–market fit, promise of the market	High multiple if tide high; story sells it
SCALING CORE	Strong core business, promising new levers	Optimal—buyers pay for today and tomorrow
MATURE CORE	Strong core business, limited new levers	Weird zone where anything can happen
DECLINING CORE	Slowing core business, limited new levers	Rational valuation; discount on the future

Spark is when you've shipped an MVP, proved the core concept works, and then realize two jarring facts at once: Solving the rest of the problem will require capital or capabilities you don't have, and the runway clock is almost empty. That's why many Spark exits feel like talent acquisitions. Android's founders sold to Google in 2005 after concluding hardware deals and carrier ties were impossible on their own; they banked a modest return, while Google inherited the roadmap and the team to build it.

Early Traction begins when customers start paying, churn looks sane, and a giant market looms ahead. Selling is triggered when outside multiples are frothy, and inbound interest arrives faster than your ability (or appetite) to raise another round. Waze in 2013 had tens of millions of drivers but no profits; Google bought the promise at a premium because mobile mapping data was exploding. Founders and investors locked in a huge outcome before competition or infrastructure costs could bite.

Scaling Core is the Goldilocks zone: A strong, profitable engine is humming, you're adding new growth levers, and buyers can see—on paper—both today's cash and tomorrow's upside. Founders often sell here to diversify personal risk or because acquirers can pour fuel on the fire faster than they can. WhatsApp's 2014 sale to Facebook fit perfectly: Massive daily usage plus whispers of payments and voice led to a $19 billion payday and rocket-fuel distribution the team could never match alone.

Mature Core arrives when the flagship product is throwing off dependable cash, but fresh levers are scarce or unproven. Trigger points include plateauing growth curves, rising competition, or looming technical debt that would require heavy reinvestment. LinkedIn's 2016 sale to Microsoft is the case study: Recruiting ads were steady, but future leaps (learning, CRM) looked expensive. Microsoft paid for a reliable profit stream and cross-suite synergy; LinkedIn shareholders crystallized value before the curve flattened further.

Declining Core is last call—growth has slowed, new bets haven't landed, and valuation conversations revolve around stabilized cash flow, not blue-sky potential. Companies sell here to salvage value or to let a larger owner wring out operational efficiencies. Yahoo's 2017 sale to Verizon shows the script: Shrinking ad share and aging portals led to a discounted price but still beat letting the business drift lower. Waiting this long isn't fatal, yet the price tag is a fraction of what it would have been two stages earlier.

The stage—where your company sits on the proof-versus-promise timeline—sets the floor and ceiling of what a buyer can justify internally and to their own investors.

Scan "social" businesses over the past two decades and you can trace this. Friendster sold to MOL Global in 2009 for about $26 million[40]—pure *Spark*, little more than proof-of-concept and a user list. Three years later, *Early Traction* appeared when Instagram fetched $1 billion from Facebook[41]—tiny team, explosive growth, zero revenue. The peak hit in 2014: WhatsApp, squarely in the *Scaling Core* sweet spot with 450 million active users and new levers like voice and payments, commanded a jaw-dropping $19 billion. By contrast, *Mature Core* showed up in 2013 when Yahoo bought Tumblr for roughly $1.1 billion[42]—strong brand, flattening growth, and uncertain monetization. Finally, the curve fell off when Myspace changed hands later that year for just $35 million,[43] a classic *Declining Core* fire sale. Same sector, five checkpoints, and a reminder that timing your sell window can swing outcomes from pocket change to generational wealth.

On top of this normal bell curve distribution of stages, the *tide*—the macro heat surrounding an industry—can multiply or muffle the price you fetch even when two businesses sit at the same stage on the proof-versus-promise curve.

Look at four e-mail-marketing platforms that all exited in *Scaling Core*: ExactTarget sold to Salesforce in 2013 for about $2.5 billion during the first cloud-software boom,[44] when public SaaS multiples were inflating fast. Just two years later, the tide had cooled: Constant Contact changed hands for roughly $1.1 billion, even though its revenue base was similar in size.[45] By 2017, investor appetite for mid-tier marketing tech was tepid; Nashville-based Emma was snapped up for only $42 million.[46] Then the pandemic lit a fresh e-commerce fire, and in 2021 Intuit paid a staggering $12 billion for Mailchimp—same stage, same business model, but an industry tide at full moon. Four companies, one maturity level, and a valuation spread that proves timing the market's mood can be as important as timing your own milestones.

Across two decades on the sidelines I've watched brilliant founders miss the clock—selling in low-tide, declining-core conditions after the growth wave had already broken. One team I admired turned down an eight-figure offer during their scaling peak, only to unload the company two years later for pennies once users plateaued and multiples shriveled. Seeing those arcs end in "what-ifs" is heartbreaking, because the loss is rarely about cash alone; it's the squandered chance to reinvest, recharge, and write the next chapter. The lesson is brutal but clear: You can't wait until the finish line to check your positioning.

PAPER VALUATION ISN'T REAL MONEY

The biggest trap in startup land is confusing the sticker price on your last funding round with a guaranteed floor. A term-sheet valuation is a dating price: flattering, provisional, and willing to ghost you the moment the music changes. Only a signed acquisition—or an IPO that actually clears—counts as a marriage contract, backed by lawyers, escrow, and wired cash. I've met founders who strutted like billionaires on paper, then watched those numbers shrivel faster than a postholiday Peloton graph once the tide turned. Paper wealth is intoxicating because it can vanish overnight.

To see how violently that paper can burn, look at four well-known companies whose private-market highs collapsed when reality—demand shifts, rate hikes, execution missteps—finally showed up.

PAPER IS FLAMMABLE

COMPANY	PAPER > REALITY	WHAT HAPPENED
HOPIN (VIRTUAL EVENTS)[47]	$8B > $50M	Post-COVID-19 demand cratered, lost core
KLARNA (BNPL)[48]	$46B > $7B	Rising rates, credit risk, margin squeeze
JAWBONE (WEARABLES)[49]	$3B > $20M	Margin erosion, inventory write-offs
FAB (E-COMMERCE)[50]	$1B > $15M	Pivot fatigue, no path to profitability

Private-round headlines said "unicorn." Closing tables said "clearance rack."

Paper valuations matter for two reasons. First, they define the psychological baseline by which everyone—founders, employees, investors, even the press—measures success. A high headline anchors expectations so firmly that anything less than a "unicorn-plus" exit feels like failure, even if the absolute dollars are life-changing. Second, that number back-calculates the strike price for stock options and the liquidation preference stack for preferred shares; get the headline wrong and you hardwire pain into every future financing, exit negotiation, or secondary sale.

For investors, a lofty paper price can quietly become a hurdle that's nearly impossible to clear. Raise at a $2 billion valuation and you must sell, IPO, or recapitalize north of that mark just to return a single dollar. CB Insights reported that by late 2024 more than 60 percent of the US software companies that raised at $1 billion-plus valuations in 2021 were still underwater, some by 50 to 80 percent.[51] Those rounds felt founder-friendly—less dilution! But every uptick in paper value also raised the bar for investors to break even. Miss that bar and the preferred stack soaks up all proceeds, leaving common shareholders—and often the founders—walking away with absolutely nothing.

Employees feel the squeeze even faster. The higher you set the valuation bar, the higher you set option strike prices, and the thinner the upside looks from the rank-and-file seat. Carta data show that almost 40 percent of private-company option grants issued at 2021 strike prices were "underwater" by 2023, demotivating teams just when execution mattered most.[52] When people can't imagine their shares ever being "in the money," they act like short-timers: Performance slips, recruiting gets harder, and retention costs spike. An inflated cap table might impress at all-hands Day One, but if it kills belief in Day Two upside, the culture—and the valuation that depends on it—follows.

I'll offer an unpopular opinion: Raise your rounds at sober, fair-market valuations—no matter how hot the moment feels. A rational price today won't just spare you cap-table headaches later; it also gives you room to deliver a win for investors without holding out for a binary, moon-or-bust outcome. Even if wealth is your chief motive, keeping the bar realistic now makes it far easier to convince stakeholders to accept a sensible exit later—before the market, or your momentum, decides for you.

WORKING BACKWARD FROM BUYER LIST

Imagine the phone rings tomorrow: "We love what you're doing—who else are you talking to?" If you can't think of five credible buyers, you're already negotiating from your back foot. The smartest founders keep a live shortlist of potential acquirers from Day One. Optionality isn't a vanity exercise; it's leverage. Mentioning other serious suitors—truthfully—sprinkles just enough FOMO into the conversation to turn curiosity into a real offer.

Of course, not every logo on a whiteboard is a real shopper. Private-equity funds (PE) and strategic buyers operate with different scorecards. PE lives in Excel: margin, retention, expansion levers. Strategics (actual companies) care as much about story—tech fit, cultural chemistry, keynote flash—as they do about numbers. Use the BUYER screen to sort wishful thinking from true prospects.

ARE THEY A REAL BUYER?

TEST	QUESTION	VALIDATE BY...
B—BUDGET	Can they actually cut the check?	Cash, fund size, recent deal sizes
U—URGENCY	Do they need you in the next thirty-six months?	Product gaps, competitive pressures
Y—YEAR ONE STORY	Is there a clear Year One story they can pitch?	Draft the press release, do the synergy math

TEST	QUESTION	VALIDATE BY...
E—EXECUTIVE CHAMPION	Is there someone that will fight for you?	Warm intros, past partnerships
R—RECORD OF CLOSING	Do they finish what they start?	Have they acquired similar companies?

Budget is the first gate. You're asking, "Can this outfit actually cut the check we need?" Validate it by following the money: Look at their recent deal sizes, cash on the balance sheet, or—if it's a fund—the committed capital that's still unspent. If the largest acquisition they've ever done is $10 million and you need $150 million, keep the champagne corked or ask them how they'll fund a deal.

Urgency probes how badly the buyer needs your solution in the next eighteen to thirty-six months. Scan their product gaps, looming competitive threats, or strategic deadlines (e.g., a public roadmap milestone). When a public SaaS company snaps up a security startup weeks after a high-profile breach, that's urgency in action. No pressing pain? Expect window-shopping, not wiring instructions.

Year One story asks whether the acquirer can pitch a clear, easy-to-explain win in the first twelve months after closing. Draft their press release yourself and run a back-of-the-envelope synergy model: "We'll cross-sell WidgetCo's five thousand customers at a 20 percent attach rate—boom, $40 million revenue." If you can't script that headline, neither can their CFO.

Executive champion checks for a senior insider willing to fight for the deal through every committee gauntlet. You validate this with warm intros, calendar proof (are they giving you real time?), and their track record of shepherding past partnerships. No champion, no deal—period.

Record of closing looks at whether the buyer finishes what they start. Dig up their last few announced acquisitions: Did term sheets convert into press releases, or did talks quietly dissolve? A company that routinely walks away at the eleventh hour will probably do it to you unless every other BUYER box glows green.

If a prospect ticks most of these BUYER boxes, move them to the shortlist. Almost all of this detective work—cash balances, past deal sizes, product gaps, org charts—can be done from your laptop.

Budget and *record of closing* sit outside your control; a buyer either has dry powder and a track record, or they don't. What *is* in your hands is boosting *urgency* by creating competitive pressure, sharpening the *year One story* with a press-release-ready business case (delivered so it feels like *their* brilliant idea), and cultivating an *executive champion*—sometimes as easy as two extra Zoom coffees or one too many cocktails at the conference bar. Nail those three levers and even a lukewarm suitor can heat up fast.

And for the love of leverage, don't rattle off these questions verbatim; nothing drains negotiating power faster than coming off like you are selling.

GETTING AHEAD
OF PARTNERSHIPS, EARLY

The buyer willing to write the biggest check is almost always a strategic—the company that can inhale you on Friday and start squeezing out cost savings or new revenue by Monday. They'll fight for a premium only if one board-level question lands: "Have we actually worked with these folks before?" If the answer is no, directors default to a punt—"Let's sign a partnership and see how it goes"—and your "bank the win" courtship drifts into a yearlong proof of concept. Worse, by the time that POC wraps, budgets or leadership priorities may have shifted. The fix is simple but often skipped: Plant a lightweight partnership *before* the bankers tap your shoulder, so the eventual deal feels like the next logical step instead of a leap of faith.

That's where the **PARTNER** filter comes in. Think of it as a set of bumpers that keep your trial relationship tight enough to prove fit yet light enough not to derail your roadmap. Run every potential collaboration through these checkpoints before you say yes, and you'll arrive at an M&A table with evidence in hand rather than theory.

ARE THEY A REAL PARTNER?

TEST	GOOD PARTNERSHIP	WHY IT MATTERS
P—PURPOSE	Clear overlap with their main KPIs	Keeps incentives aligned for the project
A—ASYMMETRIC	Low effort, but high potential return	Makes sure you aren't wasting your time
R—REVENUE	Pilot can touch revenue in six months	Board sees hard data, not testimonials
T—TECHNOLOGY	One integration that surfaces in their UI	Familiarizes their PMs with your tech stack
N—NAMED CHAMPION	Sponsor who owns the internal narrative	Prevents deal from getting lost in shuffle
E—EXIT OPTION CLEAR	On the same page about next steps	Keeps the momentum going if successful
R—RICH PARENTS	Partner has cash or investors who do	Hungry wallet plus proof equals fastest path to LOI

Purpose measures whether the pilot lines up with goals that already appear on the partner's dashboard. A good partnership ties your feature—or data, or customer base—directly to something they're graded on, like boosting retention or closing a product gap. When incentives overlap, meetings stay on their calendar and resources show up on time; misaligned goals guarantee drift and ghosting.

Asymmetric means the project is lopsided: low lift for you, outsized upside for them. A successful test bed might be a single-API feed or co-marketing email that takes your team a sprint but could unlock seven-figure revenue for the partner. That asymmetry keeps risk small on your side while making the upside obvious on theirs, so no one feels they're "doing you a favor."

Revenue asks whether the pilot can touch real dollars within six months. Good deals include a measurable billing event—cross-selling licenses, transaction fees, or upsell credits—so the partner's board sees spreadsheets, not anecdotes. Hard revenue turns a nice-to-have experiment into a must-have line item that execs will defend.

Technology (ignore if your company is not in the technology sector) looks for a single integration that surfaces in the partner's user interface. A "click here to activate" tile or embedded widget forces your product managers to learn your stack and expose your brand to end users. Once your code sits in their UI, internal inertia shifts in your favor; ripping you out later becomes painful.

Named champion means a specific exec owns the internal narrative—roadmapping meetings, status updates, and eventual M&A slides. You'll know you have one when that person schedules recurring check-ins without prompting and forwards your wins up the chain. A named advocate prevents your deal from getting lost amid reorgs.

Exit option clear confirms both sides agree on what "good" looks like after a successful pilot—expanded partnership, minority investment, or full acquisition. Stating the range of endgames early keeps momentum going once the pilot metrics hit.

Rich parents checks that the partner—or its backers—has the balance sheet to fund the next step if the pilot sings. Cash, active M&A history, or deep-pocketed investors all qualify. Combine a hungry wallet with proof from the first five tests, and you've built the fastest runway to offer.

Partnerships can feel like a luxury play—a slow-burn side quest when you're sprinting to hit quarterly goals—but the payoff can be massive. A well-structured pilot doesn't just pave a path to acquisition; it can drive real revenue, feature coverage, or customer trust while you wait. Because the work is asymmetric—low lift for you, big upside for them—you gain distribution, data, or brand credibility the moment the integration goes live. That means the partnership pays its way even if an M&A offer never materializes, and if the deal materializes, you arrive with proof points instead of promises.

Plenty of blockbuster acquisitions began with nothing more than a lightweight "Let's-see-what-happens" project. Apple's purchase of Siri started as a simple iOS app that wowed a handful of Cupertino engineers before turning into a $200 million buyout.[53] Microsoft first added a GitHub plug-in to Visual Studio, then wrote a $7.5 billion check once developer usage proved sticky.[54] On the nontech side, Disney distributed Pixar films for a decade before paying $7.4 billion to bring the studio in-house,[55] and Anheuser-Busch began by placing Goose Island taps in select bars before acquiring the craft brewer outright. Each of these giants followed the same arc: low-risk partnership, measurable win, named champion, and—once the tests hit home—an offer too logical to refuse. So yes, the long game takes calendar time, but structured correctly, it stuffs cash in everyone's pocket long before the marriage proposal.

DO A TEST RUN WITH A BANKER

After three separate stints working shoulder to shoulder with bankers—one sell-side, one buy-side, and a recap in between—I've learned a blunt truth: Founders almost never see the full picture of their own company. You're too close to the code, the pitch deck, and the daily fires to spot the hairline cracks in the balance sheet or the hidden gold vein in the customer data. Bankers, for all their fees and clichés, walk in with an X-ray you don't have: fresh comps, buyer whispers, and a radar for risks you've normalized.

Eventually you need a doctor—and in deal land, the banker plays that role. Their job is to live in the conversational slipstream of your industry: who's buying, who's window-shopping, which metrics trigger heart-eyes in a board deck. In the 1990s, intel was harvested over too many old-fashioneds and a corporate-card steak house; today it's Zoom coffees and Slack pings, but the currency hasn't changed. A corporate-dev VP lets slip that the CEO has a soft spot for a niche category, the banker files it away, and at the right moment leaks the tidbit to nudge a term sheet north. You want to be inside that information flow, not deciphering it from press releases after the fact.

Booking a test run—an informal "market check" mandate instead of a full sell-side engagement—lets you tap the network without signaling you're on the auction block. Good bankers will run a half-dozen quiet calls, pressure-test your narrative, and surface the soft spots buyers will probe. You'll come away with comps, current multiple ranges, and a reality check on which logos belong on your active dance card versus your fantasy football roster.

A few ground rules: The banker is a paid fiduciary, not a friend. Their Rolodex is their retirement plan, and they'll protect it by playing both sides. Share just enough for them to sell the vision, but keep existential worries—churn spike, founder feud—inside the trusted-team circle until you decide to go full process. Treat every conversation like a first-round interview: Be candid but never hand over ammunition that makes the advisor look uninformed in front of the buyer. Done right, a test run costs a fraction of a full mandate and arms you with the one commodity even the best founder can't manufacture alone: market truth.

YOU DECIDE YOUR DESTINY

No matter how much equity you still hold or which motive—Wealth, Passion, Ego, Control—sits highest on your stack, one fact never changes: Every stakeholder will look to *you* when it's time to choose the road ahead. You know the product quirks, the market currents, the partnership chessboard, and the culture pulse better than anyone else in the room. Investors can model, bankers can advise, and acquirers can promise the moon, but only the founder sees the whole mosaic and feels the true cost of every move.

That vantage point is a privilege and a responsibility. Use it wisely and you'll convert self-doubt into sharp judgment: You'll sense when to push for another year of compounding, when to line up a quiet market check, when to ignite a partnership pilot, and when to sign the document that adds another comma to your bank account. Misread it and the same board that once applauded your vision will wonder why you missed the pocket.

Remember, timing a sale isn't about surrendering a dream; it's about stewarding it. Bank the win when today's proof and tomorrow's promise peak together, and you'll free up capital—financial and emotional—to chase the next, even bigger vision. The pen ultimately rests in your hand. Write the ending that serves the mission, the team, and yes, the person who started it all.

SMELL THE ROSES

ROUGHLY TWELVE MONTHS after we sold half of Assembly and pocketed the life-changing liquidity founders dream about, I locked onto my next big milestone: proposing to my then-girlfriend.

Step one was misdirection. I spent a month fabricating a John Summit (famous DJ) concert in Chicago—dummy plane tickets, choreographed group texts, even a selfie at LAX departures—to throw her off the scent.

Meanwhile her friends floated a "girls day" cover story on Catalina Island—yes, the same place immortalized as the Catalina Wine Mixer in *Step Brothers*. She pictured boat drinks and a long lunch. Instead, when she climbed the steps to Wrigley Memorial I was waiting with a ring.

She said yes.

A little later our friends burst from hiding just as a band set up against the sunset. They launched into *Con Te Partirò*, the perfect wink to the Catalina *She's Mine* wine mixer pun that framed the whole weekend. I grabbed the mic, adrenaline spiking, and managed only six words:

"THIS IS A MOMENT OF IMPACT."

The phrase summed up everything vibrating inside my rib cage—relief, gratitude, disbelief—and it felt truer than any rehearsed speech. This was more than a milestone; it was a pause-and-inhale instant that deserved to be named and celebrated.

I said it so often that weekend that the joke morphed into early bets on how many times I'd drop it at our wedding (for the record: one, just to keep the gamblers guessing).

Until that point I almost never celebrated moments. I blew past graduating summa cum laude without so much as a dinner. The day I landed my pre-Assembly dream jobs, my only thought was how not to look like an idiot on Day One. Even after selling half of Assembly, my brain shifted to a new anxiety playlist: How do I make sure the acquirer doesn't regret this? The Catalina proposal was the first time I hit pause and smelled the roses—and it made me wonder how many smaller blooms I'd trampled on the sprint to "What's next?"

Founders aren't short on milestones; we're short on permission to honor them. So we deflect (it was a team effort), defer (I'll celebrate when we hit Series B), or, worst of all, pop the champagne for vanity metrics that don't matter. The trick is knowing which moments deserve a spotlight—big enough to feed the soul, small enough to keep us humble—and which should pass without confetti.

It's harder than it sounds. LinkedIn, TechCrunch, and even well-meaning relatives keep broadcasting their own highlight reels, and it's easy to mistake those billboards for your personal scorecard. Society loves $1 billion valuations, "30 Under 30" lists, and Mediterranean honeymoons; your gut might crave an entirely different win: the first customer renewal, the engineer who finally trusted your roadmap, the night you shut the laptop before midnight. Separating their applause from your fulfillment requires a simple test.

THE ROSE TEST

TEST	LITMUS QUESTION	WHY IT COUNTS
R—REAL SIGNIFICANCE	Does this win move the mission forward?	Filters out vanity milestones
O—OWNED OUTCOME	Did we materially cause the result?	Celebrating the things that you control
S—STAKEHOLDER IMPACT	Will the customer feel the benefit of this?	Ensures the toast is shared by everyone
E—ENDURING MEMORY	Will this still matter six months from now?	Invests energy in moments with shelf life

Real significance is the first petal, and it clicks into place the instant a win moves the mission or your life forward in a way spreadsheets can't fully capture. I felt that click over plastic tumblers of margaritas in a nondescript *taquería* the night my co-founder and I finally admitted—out loud—that our little side project was a real company and, like it or not, we were going to be in each other's orbit for the next five years. Nothing had been built yet, but the conversation established a new baseline: This matters now. We didn't pop champagne; we just ordered a second round and let the moment settle.

Owned outcome follows: the satisfaction that comes only when the result is unmistakably yours. That feeling washed over us the Friday before we received our acquisition offer. We'd logged three straight months of one hundred–hour weeks, shoulder to shoulder with the team, and the office smelled like stale coffee and whiteboard ink. No term sheet yet, just a quiet nod across the table that said, *Whatever happens, we showed up fully*. The celebration was nothing more than a shared grin and a walk to the parking lot, but the ownership was absolute.

Stakeholder impact takes the glow and bounces it off the people who benefit. I caught that reflection in an airport lounge when a stranger asked what I did for a living. The moment I mentioned our software, he lit up: his wife used it to quit a dead-end day job and start her own shop. He swore it had changed their family's trajectory. Hearing our code show up in someone else's life story felt bigger than any vanity-metric milestone I'd skimmed past.

Enduring memory is the ultimate test, the measure of whether a moment will still teach or inspire after the quarter ends. The co-founder margaritas, the Friday night nod, the airport testimonial—they're all snapshots I can replay on demand, small but indelible. They remind me why the next push is worth it, and they crowd out the self-doubt voice that loves to rewrite history as luck. When a win hits all four petals—real, owned, resonant, enduring—you owe yourself at least a deep breath and a second to smell the roses before you race off to plant new ones.

Recent research backs up why that pause matters. Employees who feel meaningfully recognized are four times more likely to be highly engaged, and teams with strong recognition cultures see dramatically higher retention. It's not just a morale boost— companies that invest in consistent, earned appreciation report double-digit improvements in performance and turnover, proving that acknowledgement isn't fluff; it's a strategic lever.[56]

Neuroscientists add one more kicker: Emotionally charged wins are encoded more deeply than neutral ones, giving moments that truly pass the ROSE test a longer half-life in our memory banks. Translation? When you reserve the celebration for achievements that are real, owned, felt by stakeholders, and destined to outlast the quarter, you're not just boosting morale—you're compounding engagement, profitability, and institutional memory.

WHAT PASSES THE SNIFF TEST

Before you reach for the champagne—or opt for a simple nod—run each occasion through a quick "sniff test." The two tables (moments to celebrate, moments to downplay) show moments that earn a pause and those that usually deserve only a polite shrug. Count how many ROSE petals each moment lights up: the more petals, the louder the celebration; the fewer petals, the quieter the applause.

MOMENTS TO CELEBRATE

MOMENT	WHY IT PASSES
FIRST PAYING CUSTOMER	Cash in hand proves that the idea works; converts belief into reality and everyone wins
MAJOR PRODUCT SHIPPED	Demonstrates the team's process and reliability; above all, sets a performance baseline
EMPLOYEE ANNIVERSARY	Signals cultural stickiness in a churn-heavy world; boosts loyalty for everyone watching
UNSOLICITED CUSTOMER PRAISE	External validation that the product changes lives; instant morale rocket fuel

Across a career, you'll rack up an endless parade of clink-worthy wins—each meaningful in its own, often personal, way. Yet research shows only a handful of "headline" moments move the cultural needle.

Celebrating your **first paying customer** isn't just nostalgic—it's strategic. Frame the receipt, send a handwritten thank-you, or even take a company holiday; whatever the ritual, ensure every employee remembers that customer's name, the date, and most importantly, why they said yes.

When a **major product ships** on time and on spec, you've demonstrated reliability. One flawless launch becomes the baseline against which every future launch is measured. Without that marker, process tweaks feel academic; with it, they feel essential. A toast, and a short retro memorialize the standard you expect to hit again.

An **employee anniversary** at a high-growth startup is cultural gold. Every year someone stays, they carry institutional memory that money can't buy and recruiters can't poach. Acknowledge the date in team meeting, share one lesson that person taught the organization, and you multiply the loyalty signal far beyond the honoree.

Finally, **unsolicited customer praise** is the purest external validation you'll get; it costs nothing and delivers morale rocket fuel. Forward the note or read it aloud at stand-up. The story reminds everyone that an everyday grind turns a humanization of the problem you're trying to solve.

MOMENT	WHY IT FAILS
EMPLOYEE COUNT	Number of employees at your company has nothing to do with the mission or success
NON-CORE CUSTOMER	Even if it's massive, it's usually off-mission and sends message to team noncore okay
CONFERENCE KEYNOTE	Gets you exposure, but usually paid or self-fulfilling and no benefit to team or stakeholders
SANDBAGGED KPI WIN	Hollow victory that teaches the team that targets are negotiable; participation trophy

Not every milestone deserves a megaphone. Some wins look shiny in the moment but wilt under the ROSE lens, quietly siphoning focus and energy from what really matters. Treat these "near-miss" events as polite tap-ins, not walk-off homers: acknowledge them, harvest any lesson they offer, then move on before they rewrite the company's story in vanity metrics and half-truths.

Growing head count feels like momentum, but a bigger payroll doesn't move the mission on its own. Cheer too loudly and you teach the team that adding bodies equals progress—when in reality each new hire increases coordination cost and burn. A simple "welcome aboard" and a clear role charter keep the spotlight on impact, not the scoreboard of employee IDs.

Landing a **massive noncore customer** can spike revenue, yet it often bends the product roadmap toward one-off requests that leave core users stranded. Celebrate it publicly and you risk signaling that chasing any whale is fair game. Instead, thank the team privately for the hustle, ring-fence the effort, and remind everyone which market you serve.

Headlining a conference keynote may stroke Egos and generate LinkedIn buzz, but most slots are pay-to-play or self-selected echoes of your own marketing. Over-index on stage time and people assume applause equals adoption. Treat it as brand hygiene: debrief learnings, file the leads, and get back to building features that make customers—not commentators—cheer.

And last, **crushing a sandbagged KPI** feels good only until the team realizes the bar was set ankle high. Loud victory laps around soft targets teach that goals are negotiable and effort optional. Swap the confetti for a calibration session: Raise the metric to stretch territory, celebrate the ambition, and reserve ovations for the day the tougher mark is genuinely conquered.

WHAT ABOUT THE MONEY?

We celebrated the day our Series A round cleared, then posed for "candid" founder photos on Abbot Kinney that looked more like a JCPenney catalog than a GQ photo shoot. The wire transfer did wonders for our self-doubt—if serious investors believed, maybe we weren't imposters after all.

On one hand, cash hitting the account felt like a victory lap at the end of a marathon—validation for the nights we worked through dawn, the "no's" that nearly broke us, and the constant hum of self-doubt. But the moment the bank balance refreshed, it was as if a starting gun had fired again: The scoreboard reset to zero, expectations doubled, and every hour of hard-won traction reclassified itself as table stakes for the next climb.

That high five on funding day marked a fork in the road because, in startup land, money shows up wearing two very different jerseys. There's money you raise, which rents runway and trades freedom for expectation, and money you sell for, which converts sweat into realized value and closes a chapter. Confusing the two is perilous: The first buys time under someone else's watch; the second buys options you get to write yourself.

Any money you raise to invest in the company is accountability disguised as champagne. The term sheet comes stapled to liquidation preferences, board seats, and a clock that ticks louder every quarter. Celebrate the close, yet keep the party proportional: You haven't made it; you've merely convinced someone to fund the next mile.

A sale, especially to a strategic buyer who can accelerate the mission, is a different species of milestone. Returning capital and handing the baton to a steward who speeds up the vision checks every ROSE box: real significance, clear ownership, broad resonance, lasting impact. Toast that moment; it's proof the story outlives the original author. Just remember, the size of the check matters less than what the mission does next and how it makes you feel.

VERY MINDFUL, VERY DEMURE

Companies live on a volume dial that ranges from whisper to megaphone. We know the quiet ones because we discover them by accident—an under-the-radar product that just works, or a company name dropped casually by a friend. We know the loud ones because they make sure we do, Blitzing our feeds with splashy launches and headline-grabbing fundraises. Both approaches can win, but the choice of decibel sets the rules of engagement that follow.

We ran at the quiet end of the spectrum. New acquaintances often blinked when they learned we *actually* owned and operated Helium 10 and Pacvue; the low profile suited us just fine. On the opposite pole sat Bolt—one-tenth our revenue, ten times our buzz, splashing fundraising press releases like Oprah at Christmas. Our disparity became a meme: an online article titled "Assembly Is Quiet." The lesson isn't that one style is right and the other wrong; it's that volume is a strategic choice of trade-offs.

Going loud buys speed and surface area. Public wins attract talent, warm up investors, and signal credibility to skittish enterprise buyers. Noise can even create a self-fulfilling prophecy—"If everyone's talking about them, they must be the category leader." But volume also paints a target on your back. When metrics soften, the same headlines that once comped your conference tickets will chart your downfall in real time. Loud founders inherit a second job: managing external expectations.

Staying private shields you from the boom-and-bust gossip cycle. Competitors guess at your numbers, regulators overlook you, and customers judge you on product, not press. The flip side is inertia; silence won't magnetize A-player résumés or tip a sales deal stuck on social proof. Quiet companies must find quieter signals—customer case studies, partner references, internal celebration rituals—to keep the morale and pipeline humming.

So calibrate intentionally. Crank the volume for moments that widen the moat: category launches, trust-building hires, strategic acquisitions. Dial it down when execution speed or margin of error matter more than applause. Apply ROSE to your PR strategy just as you do to milestones: The more real significance and stakeholder resonance a story has, the louder it deserves to play. Otherwise, keep the roses in the garden.

NOT SO FAST, HOT SHOT

Early-stage jitters can be a gift: Each pang of self-doubt forces you to double-check the math, sweat the user story, and stay hungry enough to out-iterate bigger rivals. Over time, that tension should ease—successive wins teach your nervous system you can, in fact, land the plane. A healthy confidence curve slopes upward, replacing "Am I good enough?" with "Let's prove it again."

The danger comes when that curve doesn't plateau but rockets past equilibrium. Shed doubt too much, and yesterday's constructive edge transforms into tomorrow's blind spot. History is packed with otherwise brilliant founders who mistook momentum for invincibility, dialed up the swagger, and blew past the guardrails.

CAUTIONARY TALES

FOUNDER	HOW IT STARTED	HOW IT ENDED
ADAM NEUMANN (WEWORK)	Gritty coworking hustle to shape a category	Hype-soaked S1 exposed gaping losses
ELIZABETH HOLMES (THERANOS)	Quiet vision of affordable blood tests	Fake demos led to fraud conviction
TRAVIS KALANICK (UBER)	"Everyone's private driver" disruptor	Toxic culture and scandals forced out
SAM BANKMAN-FRIED (FTX)	Nerdy quant in cargo shorts	Misused customer funds bankrupted
MARKUS BRAUN (WIRECARD)	Button-down fintech pioneer in Germany	Auditors found cash that never existed
TREVOR MILTON (NIKOLA)	Modest EV car startup founder	Demo exposed vaporware and indictment
RYAN BRESLOW (BOLT)	Bootstrapped e-commerce checkout tool	Revenue lagged hype and high valuation

FOUNDER	HOW IT STARTED	HOW IT ENDED
VISHAL GARG (BETTER.COM)	Mission to democratize mortgages	Leaked Zoom firing wrecked brand
VIJAY SHARMA (PAYTM)	Humble Indian fintech startup	Stock fell 60 percent in Year One after trust eroded

The pattern is plain: Swagger outran substance, scrutiny spiked, and the market wrote the closing chapter. Ego isn't the enemy—unchecked Ego is. Let self-doubt whisper just loud enough to keep you curious. This entire book is worthless if you make it and become an a$$hole.

SECTION 3 RECAP

LATE-STAGE DOUBT DOESN'T question whether the rocket can fly—it wonders whether the crew will mutiny, the dashboard will glitch, or the landing zone will vanish. Section 3 turns those high-altitude anxieties into lasting durability.

→ **Build a Bear.** When you sigh, *I can't juggle culture on top of everything else*, staff the ten Bear Pack personas in sequence, and then promote only when pull demands it.

→ **Beta Blocker.** When the voice hisses, *They'll see right through me*, wire rituals that move you from inner doubt to outer confidence to both your board and your team.

→ **Don't Trust Data.** When panic asks, *Which metric can I even believe?*, run every number through the SIGNAL framework, and treat instinct as a hypothesis generator.

→ **Listen to the Noise.** When pride shrugs, *That outsider doesn't get it*, flip to the GAIN framework, qualifying more helpful opinions but silencing the toxic ones.

→ **Bank the Win.** When ambition insists, *Job's not finished*, map your proof-versus-promise stage, keep a BUYER list warm, and structure asymmetric partnerships.

→ **Smell the Roses.** When hustle whispers, *Next milestone, please*, apply the ROSE test to isolate what to celebrate versus downplay, and avoid success becoming an unchecked Ego.

CONCLUSION

WHEN I FIRST started drafting these pages, I convinced myself a celebrity foreword would buy me permission to speak. The outline wasn't even cold and already I was curating a wish list—Gary Vaynerchuk, Simon Sinek, Brené Brown, that guy on TikTok with perfect backlighting and a $400 microphone—anything to hush the hiss that said, *No one's listening*. Then another voice—the one that usually shows up when I'm cornered—cut through the noise.

F*CK THE FOREWORD

"If this book needs a chaperone, it hasn't earned the right to be published," I said. So, I slammed the door on validation, finished the first draft in two weeks, iterated hundreds of times, and promised myself the only stamp of approval that matters is the reader who makes it to this sentence.

A REMINDER TO MYSELF

I wrote these chapters with one eye on the past and the other fixed on an ultrasound screen: One month from now I would be a first-time dad. That thought lands somewhere between fireworks and freefall, because the minute a tiny hand wraps around my finger, the self-doubt voice will upgrade its arsenal: *Sure, you scaled a company, but can you keep a human alive?*

What I've learned is that self-doubt evolves. When you're young, it feels like a foreign object—something scarier than the closet monsters you swear you saw after lights-out. Enter your career, and it mutates into a life-threatening illness you're desperate to cure. Eventually, if you let it ride shotgun long enough, it becomes a private trainer—still barking but now counting your reps and spotting the bar.

That's the version I'll hand to my son. I'll tell him the doubt never left; it just morphed, learned my new addresses, and crept into boardrooms disguised as "constructive feedback." Every visit came with a bargain: trade paralysis for propulsion or watch someone hit the same milestone. Assembly's billion-dollar headline didn't muzzle the self-doubt; it just turned the volume knob from panic to performance. Launches, layoffs, and résumés that made me feel underqualified—each spike reminded me that comfort is the silent killer of curiosity and progress.

If the day comes when I no longer feel that tightening in my gut —the whisper that says, *"You might drop the wire"*—I'll know the circus lights have switched off. I'm not ready for that, and I don't think I ever will be. Because that's living.

A REMINDER TO YOU

Are you reading this on a red-eye, tray table down, praying your backpack's slide deck survives its first board glare? Or, maybe you're in a dorm room googling "Should I quit college to code my idea?" Perhaps you're fifty years old and think the window closed the moment tuition invoices arrived. Here's the punch line:

None of that math matters as much as what you do when the self-doubt elbow lands.

They always say most startups fail. We repeat the statistic like it's weather—inevitable, impersonal. But why do they fail? Does a black-swan event swoop in and wipe these companies from the map? Ask the founders, and you'll rarely hear meteor stories. You'll hear a quieter verdict: It just didn't work. Dig deeper and the autopsy reads the same—someone stopped pushing forward, let the self-doubt win, tossed in the towel, and called the fight early.

So when that shadow murmurs, "*You're unqualified,*" translate it: Unqualified means unprepared; unprepared means prepare. When it sneers, "*Someone smarter already tried,*" nod respectfully—then check whether they tried with your timing, your tools, and your mindset. Odds are they didn't. Doubt's favorite trick is convincing you that yesterday's obituary predicts tomorrow's headline.

It doesn't.

Most important, remember that it always looks scarier from the outside. I once watched high-wire artists in Peru, Indiana, convinced gravity would claim them. It didn't. What I missed at five years old, popcorn jammed in my throat, was the net stretched just out of sight. Their secret wasn't fearlessness; it was engineered survival. Build your net: mentors who answer at midnight, metrics that expose drift before it's fatal, guardrails around the parts of life that make triumph worth having. Then climb.

In the meantime, I'll be somewhere in the rafters, fixing typos for the next edition, and listening for the gratifying sound of an audience gasping as you refuse to fall.

NOTES CITATIONS

1 Peru became the "Circus Capital of the World" by hosting the Ringling Brothers winter quarters; its legacy endures via the Circus Hall of Fame and an annual amateur show.

2 Joe Perella is the Wall Street rainmaker who co-founded Perella Weinberg Partners after leading M&A at First Boston and Morgan Stanley; I worked there 2012–2014.

3 David Bonderman is the billionaire co-founder of private-equity giant TPG Capital, famed for early bets on Continental Airlines and Uber; I worked at Wildcat Capital from 2014 to 2016.

4 Michael Moritz, famed Sequoia partner behind Google, Yahoo, PayPal, and YouTube, now oversees Sequoia Heritage; I was on the Sequoia Heritage team from 2016 to 2018.

5 Sandeep Kella bootstrapped Metric Collective, a franchisor software-and-services conglomerate, scaling it debt-free before selling the portfolio to Wpromote in 2021.

6 Assembly sold a majority stake to private-equity giant Advent International in the summer of 2021, closing a $1.4 billion deal that fueled its global e-commerce expansion.

7 A J-curve is when progress—or returns—first dip into the red before rising above the start point, tracing a letter "J" shape: early pain, later payoff once momentum kicks in.

8 Multiple surveys peg 2024 US startup founder pay under $150K: Kruze Consulting finds a $132K average, while Deel's 2024 data shows ~$148K. Kruze Consulting, LinkedIn, 2024, https://www.linkedin.com/posts/kruze -consulting_2024-ceo-salary-report-activity-7184212352156798979-oYn6; Deel, *The State of Global Compensation Report 2024*, https://www.deel.com /resources/state-of-global-compensation-report/.

9 "How Long Does It Take for a Startup to Exit or Go Public?," Bezinga, accessed November 12, 2025, https://www.benzinga.com/money/how-long -does-it-take-for-a-startup-to-exit-or-go-public; Elizabeth Pollman, "Startup Failure," Harvard Law School Forum on Corporate Governance, September 29, 2023, https://corpgov.law.harvard.edu/2023/09/29/startup-failure/.

10 Carta, "Founder Ownership Report 2025," January 2025, https://assets
.ctfassets.net/y88td1zx1ufe/5zYTlz3gdNzuFU7fQS5gjh/fbe271b0fbb5947e
0223757d73254bb5/Founder_Ownership_Report.pdf.

11 CB Insights, *483 Startup Failure Post-Mortems*; Christopher To et al.,
"Going for it on Fourth Down: Rivalry Increases Risk Taking, Physiological
Arousal, and Promotion Focus," *Academy of Journal Management* 51,
no. 4 (September 2016), https://doi.org/10.5465/amj.2016.0850.

12 Bumble's February 11, 2021, IPO priced at forty-three dollars per share,
valuing the dating app at $8 billion and crowning Whitney Wolfe Herd the
youngest female founder to take a US company public.

13 Pew Research Center reports US adult smartphone ownership jumped from
35 percent in May 2011 to 46 percent by February 2012—just when Uber
expanded nationally. Pew Research Center, *Mobile Fact Sheet*, November 13,
2024, https://www.pewresearch.org/internet/fact-sheet/mobile/.

14 Joan S. Lublin and Dana Mattioli, "J.C. Penney CEO Ron Johnson to Leave,"
Wall Street Journal, April 8, 2013, https://www.wsj.com/articles/SB1000142
4127887324504704578411031708241800.

15 Pete Evans, "Target Closes All 133 Stores in Canada, Gets Creditor
Protection," CBC News, January 15, 2015, https://www.cbc.ca/news/business
/target-closes-all-133-stores-in-canada-gets-creditor-protection-1.2901618.

16 This happened in 2021. One SaaS founder under $2 million ARR had not
one, but two EAs join while "working remotely" from Joshua Tree—
safe to say this lifestyle didn't last long.

17 Webvan raised over $1 billion, scaled too fast, and sought Chapter 11 in
2001; two decades later, the same model thrived—Instacart rode smartphone
adoption to a ~$10 billion IPO valuation in 2023.

18 Pitchbook, *2023 Annual US VC Valuations Report* (February 7, 2024),
https://pitchbook.com/news/reports/2023-annual-us-vc-valuations-report.

19 Median EV/ARR sank 61 percent within two quarters after March 2020
market shock; similar 59 percent dive recorded post-Q2 2022 pullback.
See: PitchBook, *2020 Annual US VC Valuations Report* (March 1, 2021),
https://pitchbook.com/news/reports/2020-annual-us-vc-valuations-report;
PitchbBook, *2022 Annual US VC Valuations Report* (February 8, 2023),
https://pitchbook.com/news/reports/2022-annual-us-vc-valuations-report.

20 McKinsey Global Institute Corporate Resilience study (2023): 40 percent+
of S&P 500 firms suffer more than 70 percent one-year profit crash each
decade; 15 percent enjoy comparable surge gains.

21 Hans K. Hvide and Paul Oyer, "Dinner Table Human Capital and
Entrepreneurship," National Bureau of Economic Research, working paper
24198 (January 2018), https://doi.org/10.3386/w24198.

22 Theodore Roosevelt, "Citizenship in a Republic," delivered at the Sorbonne, Paris, France, April 23, 1910, full text available at https://www.worldfuture fund.org/Documents/maninarena.htm.

23 Losing two hours sleep/night for five nights drops cognitive scores 30 percent, matching twenty-four hours awake; creativity and impulse control slump in EEG labs. Federico Salfi et al., "Effects of Total and Partial Sleep Deprivation on Reflection Impulsivity and Risk-Taking in Deliberative Decision-Making," *Nature and Science of Sleep* 2020, no. 12 (May 2020): 309–324, https://doi.org/10.2147/NSS.S250586.

24 Xiao Ma et al., "The Effect of Diaphragmatic Breathing on Attention, Negative Affect and Stress in Healthy Adults," *Frontiers in Psychology* 8 (June 2017), https://doi.org/10.3389/fpsyg.2017.00874.

25 Humorous nod only—neither author nor book is sponsored, endorsed, or paid by Rice Krispies, Kellogg's, or any affiliate; no trademark claim or commercial tie intended.

26 "Goosfraba" is the calming mantra Jack Nicholson leads in *Anger Management* (2003), said to be an Inuit lullaby; fans recite it like "breathe" to melt flare-ups fast.

27 Matthew T. Schmolesky et al., "The Effects of Aerobic Exercise Intensity and Duration on Levels of Brain-Derived Neurotrophic Factor in Healthy Men," *Journal of Sports Science and Medicine* 12, no. 3 (September 2013): 502–511, https://pmc.ncbi.nlm.nih.gov/articles/PMC3772595/; Maureen Salamon, "Want a Calmer Brain? Try This," Harvard Health Publishing, October 29, 2024, https://www.health.harvard.edu/blog/want-a-calmer-brain-try-this -202410293078.

28 Alex Sherman, "What Doomed CNN+? How Rival Strategies and Executive Intrigue Fueled the Streaming Service's Rapid Demise," CNBC, April 24, 2022, https://www.cnbc.com/2022/04/24/cnn-plus-what-went-wrong-why-it -was-canceled.html; Sara Fischer and Erin Doherty, "Warner Bros. Discovery is Shutting Down CNN+," *Axios*, April 21, 2022, https://www.axios.com /2022/04/21/warner-bros-discovery-shutting-down-cnn-plus.

29 Slush, "Slush Startup Struggle Survey 2025," accessed November 13, 2025, https://slush.org/newsroom/slush-startup-struggle-survey-2025.

30 Data Driven VC, "Data-Driven VC Landscape 2024," accessed November 13, 2025, https://landscape2024.datadrivenvc.io/.

31 Colin Bryar and Bill Carr, *Working Backwards: Insights, Stories, and Secrets from Inside Amazon* (St. Martin's Press, 2021).

32 BLS data show only about 30 percent of US startups last ten years—meaning more than 70 percent fail; see US Bureau of Lavor Statistics, "34.7 Percent of Business Establishments Born in 2013 Were Still Operating in 2023," TED: The Economics Daily, January 12, 2024, https://www.bls.gov/opub/ted/2024

/34-7-percent-of-business-establishments-born-in-2013-were-still-operating
-in-2023.htm. CB Insights' 2024 review of 483 postmortems puts "ran out of
cash/failed to raise" number one at 38 percent; see CB Insights, *483 Startup
Failure Post-Mortems* (May 29, 2024), https://www.cbinsights.com/research
/startup-failure-post-mortem/.

33 A 2023 TikTok trend turned "How often do you think about the Roman
Empire?" into a gag; hashtag #RomanEmpire topped 1.3 billion views as
men confessed they ponder it daily.

34 USPTO TESS shows no active registration for "Stoic Adam"—the ™ here
is tongue-in-cheek, though imagine the swagger boost if the mark were
someday formally filed.

35 Isabelle Simonette, "Shopify Is Laying Off 10 Percent of Staff," *New York
Times*, July 26, 2022, https://www.nytimes.com/2022/07/26/business
/shopify-layoffs.html.

36 Alexei Alexis, "SaaS License Waste Tops IT Spend Challenges," CFO Dive,
February 27, 2024, https://www.cfodive.com/news/saas-license-wastage
-ranked-as-top-it-spend-challenge/708580/.

37 LinkedIn, *Global Talent Trends* (October 2024), https://business.linkedin.
com/talent-solutions/global-talent-trends?trk=bl-po_employees-stay-41
-percent-longer-at-companies-that-do-this.

38 Federal Bureau of Investigations, "Fyre Festival Founder Sentences," news
release, November 5, 2018, https://www.fbi.gov/news/stories/fyre-festival
-founder-sentenced-110518.

39 These rule-of-thumb bands reflect broad SaaS averages; real "good" versus
"bad" can swing dramatically by industry vertical, deal size, and growth
stage—benchmark against peers.

40 Malaysia's MOL Global bought Friendster for about $26.4 million, valuing
the once-hot social site mainly for its patents and 115 million users.
"Malaysia's MOL Global Buys Friendster," Reuters, December 10, 2009,
https://www.reuters.com/article/idUSTRE5B90RV/.

41 Facebook snapped up two-year-old Instagram for $1 billion (cash plus stock)
in Apr 2012—thirteen staff, zero revenue, but 30 million iOS users and
surging daily growth. Alexei Oreskovic and Gerry Shih, "Facebook to Buy
Instagram for $1 Billion," Reuters, April 10, 2012, https://www.reuters.com/
article/technology/facebook-to-buy-instagram-for-1-billion-idUSBRE8380M9/.

42 ABC notes about three hundred million monthly visitors yet scant ad
revenue—highlighting mature-core reach with hazy monetization. "Internet
Giant Yahoo to Buy Blogging Website Tumblr for $1.1 Billion," Australian
Broadcasting Corporation, May 20, 2013, https://www.abc.net.au/news/2013
-05-20/internet-giant-yahoo-to-buy-blogging-website-tumblr-for-1-1bn/4701
862?future=true&.

43 News Corp. unloaded Myspace to Specific Media and Justin Timberlake for about $35 million in June 2011—plummeting from its $580 million 2005 price, a declining-core yard sale. Dominic Rushe, "Myspace Sold for $35M in Spectacular Fall from $12bn Heyday," *The Guardian*, June 30, 2011, https://www.theguardian.com/technology/2011/jun/30/myspace-sold-35-million-news.

44 Salesforce, "Salesforce.com Signs Definitive Agreement to Acquire ExactTarget," news release, June 4, 2013, https://www.salesforce.com/news/press-releases/2013/06/04/salesforce-com-signs-definitive-agreement-to-acquire-exacttarget/.

45 Endurance International's thirty-two dollars-per-share, all-cash deal valued email-marketing stalwart Constant Contact at roughly $1.1 billion as SaaS multiples peaked. Constant Contact, "Endurance International Group Announce Definitive Agreement to Acquire Constant Contact," news release, November 1, 2015, https://news.constantcontact.com/press-release-endurance-international-group-announces-definitive-agreement-acquire-constant-contact.

46 *Nashville Business Journal* coverage notes Insight Venture Partners' Oct 2017 buy-out of Emma; VC sources pegged the undisclosed price near $42 million for the email-SaaS firm. See: Joel Stinnet, "Nashville Tech Darling Emma Sold, CEO Stepping Down," *Nashville Business Journal*, October 10, 2017, https://www.bizjournals.com/nashville/news/2017/10/10/nashville-tech-darling-emma-sold-ceo-stepping-down.html.

47 Miguel Neves, "Hopin Events and Session Products Sold for $15 Million," Skift Meetings, August 9, 2023, https://meetings.skift.com/2023/08/09/hopin-events-and-session-products-sold-for-15-million/.

48 Marion Dakers, "Klarna's Valuation Slashed by $39 Billion Amid Fintech Rout," Bloomberg, July 11, 2022, https://www.bloomberg.com/news/articles/2022-07-11/klarna-funding-round-cuts-value-to-6-7-billion-from-46-billion?embedded-checkout=true.

49 Steve Kovach, "Fitness-tracking Company Jawbone, Once Worth $3 Billion, Is Shutting Down and Liquidating Its Assets," *Business Insider*, July 6, 2017, https://www.businessinsider.com/jawbone-shutting-down-liquidating-assets-2017-7.

50 Sarah Buhr and Ingrid Lunden, "PCH Buys Design Portal Fab in Stock and Cash Fire Sale," TechCrunch, March 3, 2015, https://techcrunch.com/2015/03/03/pch-fab/.

51 CB Insights, *State of Venture 2024 Report* (January 7, 2025), https://www.cbinsights.com/research/report/venture-trends-2024/.

52 Peter Walker, "Trends in 409A Valuations," Carta, June 27, 2023, https://carta.com/data/trends-409a-valuations-2023/.

53 Leena Rao, "Confirmed: Apple Buys Virtual Personal Assistant Startup Siri," TechCrunch, April 28, 2010, https://techcrunch.com/2010/04/28/apple-buys -virtual-personal-assistant-startup-siri/.

54 Microsoft, "Microsoft to Acquire GitHub for $7.5 Billion," news release, June 4, 2018, https://news.microsoft.com/source/2018/06/04/microsoft-to- acquire-github-for-7-5-billion/.

55 The Walt Disney Company, "Disney to Acquire Pixar," news release, January 24, 2006, https://thewaltdisneycompany.com/disney-to-acquire-pixar/.

56 Gallup and Workhuman, "Empowering Workplace Culture Through Recognition," 2023, https://www.workhuman.com/resources/reports-guides /empowering-workplace-culture-through-recognition-gallup-report/.